Pompeii, Naples and Southern Italy

Anthony Pereira

Pompeii, Naples and Southern Italy

B. T. Batsford Ltd, *London*

For Robin and Maureen

First published 1977

© Anthony Pereira 1977

ISBN 0 7134 0815 4

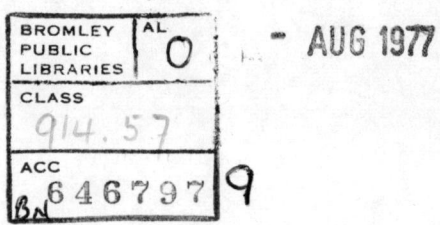
Filmset by Elliott Bros. and Yeoman Ltd., Liverpool
and printed in Great Britain by
Butler & Tanner Ltd., Frome, Somerset
for the publishers B. T. Batsford Ltd,
4 Fitzhardinge Street, London W1H 0AH

CONTENTS

List of Illustrations

vi

Acknowledgements

I would like to thank Count Sigmund F. Golfarelli, Head of the Press and Publicity Departments of E.N.I.T., Rome, for his assistance in the preparation of material for this book. And my special thanks are due to the Heads and Staff of the Provincial Tourist Boards at Naples, Salerno, Cosenza, Reggio di Calabria, Catanzaro, Taranto, Brindisi and Bari for their many helpful suggestions, and for their friendly and valuable assistance at all times.

I am greatly indebted to Mr. John Greenwood, Head of the Press and Publicity Department of the Italian State Tourist Office in London, for the encouragement and help he has given me in the early stages of planning this book. It has made possible the scope of the present volume, for which I am very grateful.

I would like to thank A. F. Kersting for illustrations 3, 6, 18, 21 and 22; Italian State Tourist Office, 2, 11, 14; Featurepix, 9. The remainder are from my own collection.

Foreword

The choice of routes open to the prospective traveller to the resorts on the shores of the Bay of Naples, and to the Regions covered in this book—Campania, Calabria and Apulia—is wider than existed only a few years ago. Firstly, the Autostrada A2 linking Rome to Naples now continues, as the A3, all the way to Reggio di Calabria, opening a fast route for travellers by car; and secondly, a new international airport at S. Eufémia Lamezia is due to begin operations at about the same time as the publication of this book.

For some, the idea of flying to Southern Italy and hiring a local car as part of an inclusive holiday package is attractive, and both main airlines flying from Britain to Italy offer such schemes. Such a plan should become increasingly popular when it is realised how greatly the roads and, equally important, the hotel and motel accommodation have improved and multiplied in the last five years—(in the chapters concerned I have given details of many of the latest additions).

For others a more traditional holiday plan by air or rail will have its own appeal. For me the most convenient way was to fly by ALITALIA to Naples, and so start my Italian journey in the heart of the old southern kingdom, thereby adding to the obvious advantages of flying a taste of Italian cuisine, even before leaving British airspace . . . a small thing in itself, but enough to stimulate pleasing thoughts in anticipation.

Peschici
M.Gargano
Vieste
A14
Manfredonia
Siponto
G.of Manfredonia
Foggia
Barletta
Trani
Molfetta
A17
Canosa
Andria
BARI
Benevento
Bitonto
Conversano
C
A
M
P
A
N
I
A
Caserta
MURGE
Monopoli
A2
Avellino
Altamura
APULIA
NAPLES
Prócida
VESUVIUS
Pompeii
Ostuni
Alberobello
Brindisi
Ischia
Salerno
POTENZA
TARANTO
Gulf of Naples
Amalfi
LECCE
Capri
PAESTUM
BASILICATA
(LUCANIA)
G. of Salerno
Metaponto
Otranto
Gallipoli
Punta Licosa
A3
GULF
OF
TARANTO
Sapri
C. S. Maria
de Leuca
Cape Palinuro
Camerota
POLLINO
MTS
Sibaris
G.of Policastro
Maratea
Castrovillari
Rossano
Tyrrhenian
Cetraro
A3
SILA GRECA
Punta Alice
Sea
Paola
Cosenza
SILA GRANDE
Amantea
CALABRIA
Crotone
NICASTRO
S.Eufémia
Catanzaro
C. Rizzuto
Lamezia
Soverato
Tropea
GULF OF
SQUILLACE
Vibo
Nicótera
Valentia
Ionian
Gulf of Gioia
A3
Serra
S.Bruno
Punta Stilo
Palmi
Sea
Gerace
Siderno
Messina
Montalto
Reggio
Locri
Calabria
C. Spartivento
Str. of Messina
N
SICILY
0   50   100 mls.
Autostrade
0   80   160 km.

Adriatic
Sea

Part I

CAMPANIA

1. Naples: the city

The wide expanse of the gulf with its dancing reflections; the distant Monti Lattari rising above a blue haze; the dramatic outline of Capri etched against a bright sky; the incomparable majesty of Vesuvius across the bay—these are the memories that linger when one thinks of Naples. One puts out of mind those days when the south wind blows, or when smog threatens to envelop Naples' glorious panorama in its clammy embrace. So too, in the pages of this chapter, we will walk the promenades and streets with the sun on our faces and a cooling breeze from the bay to lower the temperature—the rule rather than the exception for all but a fraction of the year in Naples.

Not every hotel in Naples has a view of the sea, but it is not difficult to find one that does, and to do without is to deprive oneself of one of the major pleasures of visiting the city. During my last stay I enjoyed from the balcony of my hotel on the Via Partenope, if not the 'classical' view as seen in so many paintings and reproductions, at least a view that would satisfy the most demanding of tourists. I could see only part of Vesuvius, but it was a tantalizing part promising the whole; in front, over a wide arc of the horizon, was the famous prospect of mountains, sea and sky, the latter during the first few days competing in grandeur with the solid mountains with an ever changing pattern of towering cumulus clouds. To my left I could see the ships anchored in the waters outside the harbour proper, including the bulky outline of an American aircraft-carrier with its aircraft parked on deck—while ferry boats to Capri and Ischia, and pleasure boats of all kinds constantly passed by or circled around.

On my right hand side, beyond the curving line of the Via Caracciolo, and beyond the little port of Mergellina rose the heights of Posíllipo, its luxurious apartments reflecting in fiery red window panes the early morning sun as it crept above the lower slopes of Vesuvius, and at night alive with myriad lights. In front of me rose the severe, though not grim lines of the Castel dell' Ovo, a strangely shaped building with rich historical associations, built on an island and attached to the headland of Pizzofalcone by a causeway. Immediately below the castle

3

throughout most of the day and through half the night hummed the machinery designed for the happiness and well-being of visitors—a well-oiled and well-maintained mechanism known as the QUARTER OF SANTA LUCIA. From here, into the small hours the bright green and white lights of 'La Bersagliera' and 'Zi Teresa' reflected against the ceiling of my room, bringing pleasurable and sleep-inducing thoughts of carefree indulgence.

Before describing the Quartiere di S. Lucia as it is today, I would like to make a short digression. There have not been a large number of books written about Southern Italy in the past 200 years—compared with the output on Rome say, or Florence, a mere drop in the ocean— but what has been lacking in output has been amply compensated for in quality. One thinks of Lear, and Ramage, writing in distant times, and more recently of George Gissing and Norman Douglas. It is pleasing to read these earlier writers, not only because of their erudition and style, but for the light they throw on the scene as it was then, which explains so much that has happened since. For this reason I will make room to quote them at times in this book.

For instance it is interesting to read what the Victorian novelist Gissing has to say about Naples at the time he was preparing to leave on his journey to the Ionian Sea. It was in 1897 that he left Naples for his beloved Ionian shores. About to leave the city he wrote:

> Sirocco, of course, dusks everything to cheerless grey, but under any sky it is dispiriting to note the changes in Naples. '*Lo sventramento*' (the disembowelling) goes on, and regions are transformed . . . I pass the Santa Lucia with downcast eyes, my memories of ten years ago striving against the dullness of today. The harbour, whence one used to start for Capri, is filled up . . . They are going to make a long straight embankment from the Castel dell' Ovo to the Great Port, and before long the Santa Lucia will be an ordinary street, shut in among huge houses, with no view at all. Ah, the nights that one lingered here, watching the crimson glow upon Vesuvius, tracing the dark line of the Sorrento promontory, or waiting for moonlight to cast its magic on floating Capri.

Well, here Gissing was over-pessimistic. Much has been done since those words were written to capture the spirit of Santa Lucia of old, even if the intimacy (together with the squalor) has gone for ever. The small port of Santa Lucia has been resited since his day. True, there is no longer much of a view from where one dines, but the little harbour is very much alive. One eats overlooking streamlined yachts and luxury motor cruisers from many nations, while small fishing boats, with oars or outboard motors are normally (but not always) moored round the corner away from the smart yacht clubs. Which is not to say that there is any evidence of deliberate class distinction here, either of boats or owners. Yard hands mix with owners, and diners rub shoulders with fishermen. Waiters scamper with practised step over coiled ropes or fishing nets under repair, and small boys dive off the harbour after coins. There is animation and a loud buzz of conversation as the guests enjoy the food and the company. I can speak for 'La Bersagliera' where the food, especially the fish, is good and the prices moderate.

The only disadvantage of having a room overlooking Santa Lucia is the incessant traffic noise which even double glazing does not shut out. Outside, five lanes of traffic take the flow all one way towards the centre of the city. To escape the commotion I would sometimes rise before sunrise and cross over to the small cluster of buildings forming the Borgo Marinaro behind the yacht basin where the boatyards and fishermen's quays are to be found. Here, the peace disturbed only by the occasional splashing oar and the voices of fishermen hailing one another in their rough dialect, one could watch the sun rising above Vesuvius across the bay, and refresh oneself with the best coffee I have tasted in Naples—(there can be no higher recommendation).

For me it is the maritime flavour of Naples that has the greatest appeal. On one occasion, passing the time on deck as the ship I was in prepared to leave for Sicily, I spent an absorbing couple of hours as dusk changed to night, the lights came on in the town piled before me, the old monastic buildings of S. Martino glowed, it seemed, high in the sky—and to the right the string of lights sparkled in a graceful easy curve up the side of Vesuvius before coming to an abrupt halt. The activity of the port of Naples at night is little reduced from that during the day, and is fascinating to watch. I have spent many happy hours wandering around the port whilst awaiting transit at various times. Great liners, as well as all manner of ships leave from these moles, and it is common to find a British or American warship in harbour.

Yet for those who arrive at Naples for the first time by sea, it must be a bit of a shock to take one's first step into the city through the gates of the dockyard. Here one is suddenly confronted with the ugly face of Naples, pock-marked, sallow and bleary-eyed. From the dignity, even gentility of the floating hotel, one is suddenly accosted by strident hawkers of every conceivable trashy object, lurking touts and pimps, commission men, con-men, aged men trying to sell 'filthy pictures', persuasive but implausible middle-aged men trying to sell gold watches or Parker pens made in Japan—in fact the whole con-glomerate of the seedy underworld that comprises Naples' highly unof-ficial tourist industry.

Once you have shaken yourself free of these parasites you are free to make your first move in exploring the town. The PIAZZA MUNICIPIO which faces the ocean berths of the port is in fact very near to the heart of the city. The fashionable Via Roma, the San Carlo Opera House, the Galleria Umberto I, the Piazza Plebiscito and the Palazzo Reale are all within easy walking distance.

The Piazza Municipio is enormous, as are many of Naples' squares, and has not been improved in recent years by the uprooting of the holm oaks and the redesign of the central gardens, though it is shady enough in the heat of the summer. Nor is it a restful place, for it is on a considerable slope, of which advantage is taken by the traffic that turns the corner from the Via Vittorio Emanuele and hurtles down the hill. On the other hand it has many useful buildings: money changers who do business over long hours (the banks in Italy now open only during the morning for five days a week), tourist agencies, including c.i.t. the official Italian agency and the old fashioned Hotel Londra; (a short distance away in Via Medina is the high-rising modern Hotel Ambassador's Palace). But grand though the square and some of its buildings are, the monument which completely dominates the square is the CASTEL NUOVO, built by Charles I of Anjou in 1279. This Angevin fortress is as grim and foreboding as any castle I can recollect. Its five great round buttressed towers thrust up alongside massive walls that drop down to foundations many metres below ground level, where the moat is now used for parking official cars.

Unlike the Castel dell' Ovo, the Castel Nuovo has a dampening effect on my spirits. Perhaps it is because the former is constructed of limestone and the latter of granite, the one weathered into a rich honey colour, the other to a grey-black; but the grimness of the Castel Nuovo stems less from its colour than from its shape and associations. It is uncompromisingly and brutally a fortress. By day this is obvious and by night, its dominating presence seems even more tangible and oppressive.

The event best known in a long catalogue of tortures, deaths and imprisonments connected with the castle, is the bloody deed involving the suppression of the Barons' Revolt in 1486. The barons in question came from Apulia, led by the powerful Sanseverino family, and they conspired to rid themselves of Ferdinand I of Aragon (Ferrante) and support the Angevins who had been ousted in 1442. The cunning Ferrante hearing of the plot, invited the feudal princes to celebrate the marriage of his own niece with one of the disaffected barons, and here, in what is now called the Baron's Hall, at the height of much feasting and conviviality, the ringleaders were arrested and later put to death by sword and by strangling. Only one of the conspirators escaped; the elderly Duke of Salerno on receiving the invitation hurriedly left for

1 The Galleria Umberto, Naples

2 Amalfi –
overlooking the gulf of
Salerno

3 Norman &
Saracenic styles blend
in the 13th century
cathedral of S. Andrea,
Amalfi

Rome, but not before leaving a note pinned to the door of his palace which read, 'An old sparrow does not enter the cage.'

It is all the more extraordinary given the overall grimness of the Castel Nuovo to find an astonishing piece of architectural light relief in the shape of the Triumphal Arch that forms the entrance to the castle. The arch is a fine example of Renaissance work, possibly designed by Luciano Laurana. Certainly much of the carving was done by Francesco Laurana. The work was commissioned by Alfonso il Magnanimo in 1454 to commemorate the capture of Naples from the French, and the major relief depicts the entry of Alfonso. Both Alfonso and his illegitimate son Ferrante surrounded themselves with artists and humanists and were typical Renaissance princes, though the cruelty of the latter seems to mix oddly with his humanistic inclinations. It is known that Ferrante liked to have his enemies in sight whether dead or alive. Alive, they were imprisoned in the castle (then used as a royal palace) and dead, they were mumified and dressed in the clothes they wore when living.

The chapel of Santa Barbara standing off the courtyard is basically part of the original Angevin castle structure: it has a fine Renaissance doorway, with a beautiful Catalan rose-window above, replacing the Angevin original. A considerable proportion of the original castle was rebuilt by the Aragonese, though the towers are original.

From the Castel Nuovo it is only a short distance to the Piazza Trieste e Trento and to reach it one passes the Theatre of San Carlo on the left side of the narrow street, and the Galleria Umberto I on the right—both buildings quite unmistakable. Before describing either, a word or two about the Piazza. Unlike many in Naples it is small and intimate, yet very Neapolitan in character. Exceptionally busy, one takes one's life in one's hand crossing the road here—yet there is really no need to do so since there is an underpass although nobody seems to use it. When there is opera or music at the theatre the entire corner becomes an impossible traffic-jam-cum-car-park and the noise is surprising, even to those adjusted to the normal level of decibels in the city.

Retracing our steps for a moment we come almost at once to the Galleria Umberto I, comprising a vast area of mosaic-covered floor and a neo-classical inner architectural arrangement which rises at a great height to a barrel-vaulted roof of glass and iron trellises. The late nineteenth-century Italians had a weakness for this type of gallery (a similar one can be seen in Milan), but whatever we might think today of its style and taste, it is certainly impressive. In fact it is one of the places where I like to linger in Naples; it is very pleasant to sit outside one of the bars, letting the Neapolitan world flow by. Nowhere I feel, can one get a better idea of the Neapolitan temperament, for it is a favourite place for men to gather, standing in groups large and small under the great central dome, where animated, not to say heated discussions take place and histrionics are much in evidence.

It has been said before that Naples is not unlike a vast popular theatre—and certainly the comparison is apt. There is drama on all sides, obvious to anyone who takes a walk in the streets, or to anyone who tries to do the smallest transaction with a Neapolitan. To the Northerner much of this seems artificial, but it is in fact a true reflection of the Neapolitan temperament. In no other European city can I recall the tension or excitement that one senses here. Not everyone likes it, but certainly it is stimulating.

On the other side of the street from the Gallery is the THEATRE OF SAN CARLO which is open to the public during the morning. I had avoided these visits, fearing to find a vast empty auditorium too much of an anti-climax and I was especially pleased when I was offered a seat in a private box during a recent stay in the city. Unfortunately it was not the season for opera, but a well-known ensemble was performing and the theatre was well filled for the concert. The interior of the opera-house, all lit up before the curtain rises, is a wonderful spectacle: a candelabra of five lights is positioned between each box, and six tiers of boxes sweep in a great horse-shoe around the centre seats. Stendhal is reported to have said in 1816, 'the first impression is that of being in the palace of an oriental emperor. There is nothing in all Europe that I can say approaches this theatre ...'. The colour scheme is predominantly red and gold—red velvet soft furnishings and gold and white stucco decoration most artistically handled. The great central royal box is overhung by a huge red canopy with a golden crown above. The splendid painted curtain by Mancinelli and the very fine painted ceiling by Cammarono add greatly to the warmth and splendour of the setting.

The theatre owes its origin to Charles III of Bourbon who desired to add to the many splendid buildings that adorned his kingdom. The commission for the design was given to Giovanni Medrano, a Sicilian, who also designed the royal palaces at Capodimonte and Portici, and the building was completed in 1737 in the astonishingly short space of eight months under the eye of the Neapolitan architect, Angelo Carasale, In 1816 the theatre was gutted by fire, but was rebuilt in the space of seven months by Niccolini on an even more abitious scale. It is said that Niccolini, in order to amplify the acoustics of the auditorium and to make the great walls lighter and more sonorous, inserted hundreds of clay pitchers in the walls, similar to those in which the Neapolitan water-seller of today offers the spring waters of Chiatomone. Six years before this reconstruction Niccolini had added the handsome portico and loggia which survived the fire.

A great Neapolitan operatic tradition, already well-founded by Alessandro Scarlatti, was given room to expand and develop by the opening of San Carlo. Operas were written especially for the company by Rossini, and Donizetti's *Lucia di Lammermoor* was first performed there in 1835. All the great singers have performed in Naples' Royal Opera house. Today it may rank behind La Scala in the opinion of some, but for all Neapolitans it can be squarely rated 'second to none'.

Returning to Piazza Trieste e Trento, this opens out into the vast PIAZZA PLEBISCITO. This square has been carefully planned with the Palazzo Reale facing the church of S. Francesco di Paola, and the Palazzo Salerno opposite the Prefettura—forming the four sides—but whatever merit it might have had has been ruined by its use as an enormous bus and car-park. Granted the usefulness of the easy access to the buses, nevertheless the square has been desecrated.

It is not in any case my favourite piazza in Naples. The huge Palazzo Reale is certainly an impressive sight with its grey and deep-red washed walls, its enormous arcade, and its statues in niches depicting the heads of the eight dynasties which have reigned in Naples—from Roger the Norman to Victor Emmanuel II of Savoy. But opposite, the church of S. Francesco, in spite of its ambitious scale and perfection in execution, has no warmth. The church was built by the order of Ferdinand I and IV of the Two Sicilies in 1817 in thanksgiving for the recovery of his kingdom, and is clearly modelled on the Pantheon. Inside—marble everywhere—it is coldly neo-classical.

The PALAZZO REALE may be visited by the public between 9.30 and 4.00 p.m. daily and the main places of interest are the sumptuous apartments on the first floor, rich in fine carpets, Neapolitan furniture in baroque and imperial styles, and porcelain and paintings of the various schools, (though the best paintings have been removed to the other royal palace at Capodimonte). The palace was created between 1600 and 1602 by Domenico Fontana by order of the Spanish Viceroy Ferrante di Castro, and the interior partly renovated in 1734–8. The Staircase of Honour was designed by F. Picchiatti in 1651, and at the top of the stairs one can visit the delightful Court Theatre designed by Fuga, built in 1768 and now restored after bomb damage during the war. The Court Chapel was built in 1660 by Cosimo Fanzago and has a fine painting on the ceiling by Domenico Morelli.

The BIBLIOTECA NAZIONALE is housed in part of the Royal Palace, and can be reached through a gate in the gardens on the far side of the Theatre of S. Carlo. This famous library has developed from the Farnese collection brought to Naples by Charles III. It has many precious manuscripts and *incunabula*, and among its finest possessions is the Herculaneum Papyrus found in a villa at the excavations in 1752. At the time of writing viewing is restricted to the mornings only.

On the western side of the church of S. Ferdinando and running northwards directly from the piazza, the VIA ROMA begins its long steady ascent to Piazza Dante, after which it changes its name. It is the favourite shopping street of the Neapolitans (though the area around the Piazza dei Martiri is more fashionable) and after about six or seven p.m. is packed with evening strollers. The inhabitants prefer to call it Via Toledo after the Spanish viceroy of that name, who, while rebuilding this part of Naples in 1536, constructed quarters for his soldiers, lying immediately off this street. These can be seen to the left, steeply rising, and now densely populated. It is interesting to walk through these narrow dark-stepped streets and see life as it is lived in these cramped and seemingly unhealthy conditions. The usual display of washing strung between windows of opposing houses is here no problem at all.

Only a short distance up Via Roma, on the left, is the station for the funicular that takes passengers to the heights of VOMERO. Another funicular leaves from S. Teresa a Chiaia and from Corso Vittorio Emanuele, itself on a hill—and a third from Stazione Cumana, off Via Montesanto. Vomero has really reached the stage of being an independent town, and is fast developing in the district beyond Arenella. It is cooler up here and very much in favour with wealthier Neapolitans.

A spur off the Vomero heights was fortified by Robert of Anjou in 1329, and this, now the castle of S. Elmo, was rebuilt on the orders of Viceroy Toledo in 1537. It is an enormous structure and utterly dominates this part of the city. Its surrender in 1799 to the Sanfedisti Cardinal Ruffo marked the end of the brief Parthenopean Republic.

The former Carthusian monastery of S. Martino, briefly mentioned earlier, lies immediately beside and just below the castle, and from the terrace nearby one has a really splendid view over the old city spread out like a monotone patchwork, and sliced through by the dark thin gash of the *Spaccanapoli*. (This famous thoroughfare will be described later when we have returned to that level of the town.)

S. MARTINO is now a museum, and should be put high on the list of places to see in Naples, apart from most interesting sections devoted to the life and arts and costumes of the people of Naples, the museum possesses some notable paintings in a large and varied collection. Plenty of time should be allowed for a visit since there are 90 rooms in the museum proper, and seven chapels in the church where works of art can be seen. From some of the rooms overlooking the city and the sea there is a marvellous view, and as a break from studying the wealth of material in S. Martino one can stroll round the superb Great Cloister, a happy blend of Renaissance and Baroque architecture. Before leaving S. Martino I must not fail to mention the Christmas cribs. An authority on Naples, Max Vajro writes:

> The eighteenth century saw the triumph of the Baroque and gave the Neapolitan crib rich decorative elements . . . Sammartino (the creator of 'Christ Veiled' in the chapel of Sansevero) Vassallo, Govi, Celbrano left their great marble statues to model, one by one, the little terracotta figures with glass eyes, which represent the countrymen, washerwomen, drovers, hawkers and animals of the courtyard . . . their models were chosen from the people, the vivacious Neapolitans of that day . . . an anachronism that has given beauty to the Neapolitan crib . . .

No great distance away from the National Museum of San Martino, on Via Cimarosa, is the park and villa (now the Museo Nazionale della Ceramica) that comprises the Villa Floridiana. The park grounds are spacious and contain some magnificent trees, especially stone pines of great age and enormous girth. The ceramic collection of the Duca di Martina housed in the splendid neo-classical building designed by Niccolini in 1817, includes some fine specimens of Italian and foreign porcelain. All in all the Villa Floridiana is a refreshing antidote to the ugliness of Vomero's cubic buildings.

Returning to Via Roma and heading northwards we will soon reach Piazza Carita, and forking right, come to the small Piazza Monteoliveto. It is here, up some steps, that there is one of the most interesting churches in Naples—S. ANNA DEI LOMBARDI. The church, created in 1411, owes much to the patronage of the Aragonese, and is probably the richest repository of Renaissance sculpture in the city. Among many beautiful monuments, tombs and reliefs in the numerous chapels, note especially the monument to Maria d'Aragona by Rossellino in the Piccolomini chapel (first on the left), the beautiful sculpture by the Florentine Benedetto da Maiano in the Mastrogiudice chapel (first on the right) and the marble relief by Giovanni da Nola in the apse, the latter depicting Alphonso II and Gurrello Orilia . . . the major benefactors. However, the most remarkable works in the church to my mind, are the extraordinary life-like terracotta figures in the group of eight forming the 'Pieta' by Giudo Mazzoni of Modena. These can be found at the end of the long side-chapel on the right, in line with the altar. These figures, in various attitudes of shock, revulsion, despair and sorrow are gathered round the prostrate figure of the dead Christ on the ground. Approached in a half-light they are almost startingly realistic. They were made in 1492 and were originally polychrome and are considered to be lifesize portraits of various members of the court of Ferrante—King Alfonso II, the poet Sannazzaro, etc. A remarkable tour de force. Vasari painted the frescoes that can be seen in the old sacristy, which also contains beautiful inlaid stalls with views of Rome and Naples executed by Fra Giovanni da Verona in 1506.

On the other side of the street (Via Monteoliveto) from S. Anna lies the elegant Palazzo Gravina, which is considered by many to be the finest Renaissance building in Naples, now housing the Faculty of Architecture of the University of Naples. It was built for Ferdinand Orsini, Duke of Gravina, in 1539–41. At one corner of the piazza is a rather charming small baroque fountain surmounted by the bronze statue of the boy-king Charles II of Spain.

A short distance away from this point along Calle Trinità Maggiore we reach a piazza dominated by two great churches—the Gesù Nuovo, after which the piazza is named, and the church and monastery buildings of Santa Chiara. It also contains an architectural set-piece in the baroque style topped by a gilded statue of the Virgin, the 'Guglia dell' Immacolata'—a popular object of devotion which, by an agreeable custom, is decked with flowers annually on the appropriate feast-day. I have seen it described in one Neapolitan guide-book as 'unforgett-able', but I'm afraid that this adjective is hardly the one I would select—though it is in one sense very typical of Naples and has several competitors in awfulness in the city.

Lying slightly back from the Piazza Gesù, the church of S. CHIARA is reached through an original fourteenth century gateway. It is, I think, my favourite church in Naples—a church that has a character so strong that it has survived the appalling damage that was caused when it was hit by allied fire-bombs on the night of 4th August 1943 and burned for 48 hours. Some of the finest Gothic and Renaissance sculpture in the south of Italy was lost, including works by Giovanni Bertini and Tino da Camaino. Fortunately other fine works were saved or partially salvaged, such as Tino di Camaino's Tomb of Mary of Valois (1333–8), and Giovanni and Pacio Bertini's Sepulchre of King Robert I (1343) behind the high altar. Although the latter work is badly damaged, its impressive quality has not been lost.

The church of S. Chiara has of course long been repaired, and is happily now free of the baroque accretions of 1742–7, which were consumed by the fire—some would say a fitting end. Baroque decoration handled in this manner—added to the simple dignity of these early churches—is nearly always disastrous, as can be seen in countless instances in Southern Italy. Fortunately with aid from the funds of Cassa di Mezzogiorno many of the great churches and cathedrals have been restored to their former pristine beauty.

The damage at S. Chiara was so great that it was not possible to execute an exact restoration of the original—built between 1310 and 1328 in the Provençal-Gothic style—though what we see now has great dignity. It is a large basilican church retaining the original dimensions, with about 20 side-chapels, nearly all containing interesting works of art. At the back of the church, behind the choir, is the large CLOISTER OF THE CLARISSE, a place of beauty and peace which should on no account be missed. The structure of the cloister itself is contemporary with the church, but the design for the refacing of it was by Domenico Vaccaro in 1742, and the attractive and colourful majolica tiles of the same period are by the Neapolitans Guiseppe and Donato Massa. It is an extraordinary experience to leave the noisy and bustling streets of Naples and find oneself in these cloisters. Very few people seem to visit them, yet there can be no more tranquil or refreshing spot in the city. Paths with low walls and evenly spaced octagonal pillars cross the semi-wild central garden of flowers, flowering shrubs and trees (a typical Neapolitan rustic garden)—and all the structural parts are covered with blue and yellow majolica tiles with lively scenes mainly of country life, where men are seen fishing, carnivals are in full swing and people sit in groups picnicking. Appropriately, bunches of grapes and vine leaves form a substantial part of the overall decoration, for these walks across the garden are roofed with vines, trained from ancient stock beside the pillars to spread their leaves across wooden beams for shade.

The church of the GESÙ NUOVO on the opposite side of the square to S. Chiara is very large and very sumptuous—a feast for the eye if one's tastes extend to acres of coloured marble marquetry. It is interesting to compare this Jesuit church with that in Palermo, which is even more extravagant. All the same I noticed that even in the Gesù Nuovo a degree of economy is effected since the inside of the pillars (facing away from the nave) are in fact cleverly painted to simulate marble. The high altar is a masterly creation in polychrome marble, and indeed most parish churches in Italy would be proud to possess almost any of the side altars of the Gesù. Incidentally the church is called 'Nuovo' to distinguish it from the old church of the same name (Gesù Vecchio) which is incorporated in the University buildings. The 'Nuovo' was built by P. Guiseppe Valeriano from 1584–1601, making use of the foundations and some of the structure of the quattrocento palace of the Sanseverino family—Princes of Salerno. This explains the *piperino* or pointed-diamond decorative surface of the facade, which formed the original front of the palace. The church contains a large and varied collection of paintings, some by well-known artists.

Leaving the church and the square we find ourselves about a third of the way along the famous street known as *Spaccanapoli*—literally 'cut' or 'cleft' Naples—since it cuts the city in half from east to west. Since the street changes its names six times in the course of about 1500 metres the popular name is convenient. The street is very ancient in origin, forming, with the Via dei Tribunali (the next street to the north) the lower and middle *decumani* of Graeco-Roman Naples, and now running through the heart of Naples as it did in old Neapolis.

Lying either between or just off these two streets are several important churches, though due to limitations of space it will not be possible to describe them here in any detail. S. DOMENICO MAGGIORE was founded in 1289 by Charles II of Anjou incorporating an earlier church. The church and the monastery are closely associated with St. Thomas Aquinas, who studied here in his youth and later returned to teach theology. His cell may be visited by applying to the Dominican fathers. The church has suffered greatly at the hands of restorers, but in compensation there are many fine works of art to be seen here.

The church of S. LORENZO MAGGIORE was built for the Franciscans at the end of the thirteenth century on the spot where a much older church of the time of Bishop Giovanni II (533–55) had stood. Excavations have revealed part of the older church and also, at various levels, a paved Roman road, a basilica, and massive tufa blocks from the original Greek city. S. Lorenzo is one of the great Gothic churches of Italy and a thorough restoration is in progress to rid the church of 'embellishments' of previous centuries. We can now see the soaring pointed arches of the apse and ambulatory—a masterpiece of French architecture of the thirteenth century—and admire the many fine tombs in the church undistracted. The high altar by Giovanni da Nola is especially fine, a mass of decorative detail carved with masterly control, while in the apse nearby is Tino di Camaino's beautiful tomb of Catherine of Austria who died in 1323.

The church of the GEROLOMINI has an attractive baroque façade designed by Ferdinando Fuga in 1740 but this disguises the true period of the church which dates from 1592. It is the church of the Oratorians and the repository of many riches, including an enormous collection of paintings. It is a tragedy however that the Congregation in Naples fell on such hard times after the war that they felt obliged to sell a veritable treasury of *objets de vertu* in gold and silver, thought to have been worth more than half a million pounds sterling. These were melted down and sold as ingots. Not surprisingly the sale caused a scandal and it is astonishing that it was allowed to take place. Here at the Oratory, as in Rome, there is a magnificent library, which may be visited during weekday mornings. It is in the House of the Fathers of the Oratory which is attached to the church, and here one can browse among precious bindings and early manuscripts that once belonged to G. Vico and others. One can also visit two beautiful baroque cloisters. The entrance to the Oratory is exactly opposite the cathedral in Via Duomo, and during a visit one can take the opportunity of seeing the oldest collection of paintings in Naples.

It is difficult to raise much enthusiasm for the vast spaces and ornate interior of the Duomo, and for the usual reason—that the original building, begun in 1294 and completed in 1323, has been changed out of all recognition by a long series of 'improvements' over the centuries. Now it has become internally a huge baroque basilica. Externally, the pseudo-gothic façade of 1877–1905 is a disaster, shown up only too painfully by Baboccio's Gothic main portal (1407) which by the greatest good fortune has survived. And yet it would be absurd to 'write-off' the Duomo of Naples since it does incorporate some places of great interest and beauty, namely the church of S. Restituta, the Baptistery, the crypt of S. Gennaro, the chapel of the Minutolo family, and last but certainly not least in the minds of Neapolitans, the Cappella di Tesoro (the chapel of S. Gennaro). The last named was not begun until 1608 almost 90 years after a terrible plague subsided, for which relief the building of this chapel is a form of thanksgiving. However the citizens of Naples have made up for the dilatoriness of execution by the lavishness of their decoration, and they have done St. Januarius (Gennaro) proud. The great gilded bronze doors are by Fanzago (1668), the *Paradise* in the cupola by Lanfranco (1643). All the other frescoes are by Domenichino, who had to fight off intense competition from the 'Cabal of Naples' (Corenzio, Ribera and Caracciolo) who did not hesitate to use foul means to try and break the commission offered to the man from Bologna, even to the extent of attempting to murder his servant.

It is in this chapel that the head of S. Gennaro is preserved, encased in a silver bust, together with two phials of his blood. It is the ceremony in connection with the miraculous liquefaction of this blood in May and September that has the greatest hold on the imagination of Neapolitans. On these occasions the chapel is packed, stormy scenes ensue and much basic Neapolitan abuse is heaped upon the saint in the case of a non-event, but should the miracle occur and the celebrant turn and face the people with a loud cry of 'It liquefies! It liquefies!', then there is pandemonium and much rejoicing and the happy congregation spills out into Via Duomo to follow the procession behind the holy saint's blood. The point here is that should the blood remain congealed in the course of the ceremony it is felt by the people that some great disaster will befall the city, and should the liquefaction be delayed the outlook is sombre. Fortunately the saint seldom fails to satisfy their wishes.

The tradition of St. Januarius is very ancient. He was Bishop of Benevento when he suffered martyrdom at Pozzuoli under Diocletian's persecution, and it was Bishop Severus who arranged for the body to be transferred to the catacombs of Naples at the time of Constantine, at which time it is said, the blood first liquefied in the hands of the holy bishop.

A doorway off the left aisle of the cathedral leads down to the church of S. Restituta—originally built in the fourth century, and the first ever Neapolitan basilica. However it was not until the eighth century that the church was dedicated to S. Restituta, for it was only then that the saint's remains were brought over from Ischia.

There are three chapels in the church of particular interest, and these can be found to the left of the altar. The middle of the three contains a fine mosaic of the Virgin and Child between S. Restituta and S. Gennaro, executed in 1332 by Lello da Roma—and in the chapels on either side there are beautiful examples of early thirteenth century low-reliefs. At the right of the altar a door leads through to the Baptistery which can be dated to the second half of the fifth century, and is interesting architecturally by reason of the early use of squinches in support of the dome. There are traces too of early Christian mosaics.

The Crypt of S. Gennaro (sometimes called the Cappella Carafa or the Succorpo) lies beneath the choir and can be reached by stairways. The beautiful Carafa Chapel designed by Tommaso Malvito of Como between 1497 and 1508 is considered to be one of the most elegant Renaissance creations in Naples.

The Via dei Tribunali near the Duomo leads directly to the large building called Castel Capuano, which now functions as the Law Courts, and lying behind it across a wide piazza is the PORTA CAPUANA, a magnificent Renaissance fortified gateway designed by Giuliano da Maiano in 1484. Behind the gateway is one of Naples' several street-markets (there is another near Porta Nolana), and needless to say these are lively places. Yet I have found the street markets in Naples a little disappointing. There is generally a wide selection of articles but the goods I saw were very inferior in quality, and the traders strangely subdued. The main noise really comes from the eternal pop-music which blares out through makeshift equipment either on disc or tape—little of it of true Neapolitan pedigree. Naples has the reputation of being the city of spontaneous song, but where does one hear it today? There seems to be no spontaneous gaiety left in the streets. A local guide-book which I have acquired speaks of Naples as 'the land of songs and spaghetti, of mandolins and urchins'; not so, as regards the musical reference anyway. The writer goes on to declare that the tourist will take away with him 'not only a memory of the bluest skies, the sea that eternally mirrors the sun' (fair enough) 'but also an historic and human thread, trembling with joy and sorrow, greatness and misery, ancient glories and recent sufferings. Of that in fact, which makes the eyes of children unforgettable, that lights the faces of women, that gives men that dreamy resigned sense of apparent lightheartedness in every Neapolitan street.' Well really . . . ! how far can parochial romanticism go? I must say I have never had the good fortune to meet a Neapolitan male who was remotely dreamy. Lighthearted perhaps, sharp certainly, a sharpness that is stimulated perhaps by the thought of having to provide for a family or five or six or more; it would be interesting to know how many Neapolitan family men have regular jobs. A little over a decade ago the figure for the whole population was 200,000 out of a total of about one million. As for the urchins, they must, in general terms, surely be among the naughtiest kids to be found anywhere, and again the reason is not hard to fathom. They grow up quickly these *scugnizzi*—the world has few secrets for them by the time they are 10 or 12.

The above-mentioned guide-book is obviously written with care and much research by a Neapolitan who wishes to give a fair picture of the city he loves, but for the outsider many of his observations are ludicrous, and it makes one wonder how many more Neapolitans are similarly imaginative. For accuracy foreigners are far more reliable. Gissing wrote in 1897:

> When I first knew Naples one was never, literally never, out of hearing of a hand-organ; and these organs, which in general had a peculiarly dulcet note, played the brightest of melodies; trivial, vulgar if you will, but none the less melodious, and dear to Naples. Now the street music is rare . . . I miss them; for in the matter of music it is with me as with Sir Thomas Browne. For Italy the change is significant enough; in a few more years spontaneous melody will be as rare at Naples or Venice as on the banks of the Thames.

From the Porta Capuana the Via A. Poeria leads into the Piazza Garibaldi, a vast square filled with tourist buses, cars, trams, and corporation buses that lies before the central railway station—(Stazione Centrale F.S.). The latter is modern and efficient but incredibly draughty due to its construction in stressed concrete on huge stilts; it must be one of the coldest places in Italy when the *tramontana* is blowing in winter. There are many hotels either on or in the neighbourhood of Piazza Garibaldi, and these are convenient if a little noisy.

From the south-west corner of the Piazza, the Corso Umberto I slices through the packed districts of old Naples, and must rate as the ugliest street in the city. It is an experience to be trapped in this dreary thoroughfare during the rush-hour and to hear the comments of one's taxi-driver and to watch the antics of the frustrated Neapolitans. The state of the traffic in Naples has long since passed from being the subject of light humour to that of a very sick joke indeed. There is now a bus and taxi lane down the right side of the Corso but after a certain pressure point in frustration has been reached, all traffic codes and rules and regulations are cast to the winds, and the Neapolitan motorist grabs whichever bit of the road he can, risking a heavy on-the-spot fine.

The Corso Umberto I, known by Neapolitans as the *Rettifilo* was driven through the overcrowded Porto and Mercato districts after the serious outbreak of cholera in 1884, in an effort to ease the congestion—but is quite inadequate today.

Let us return to *Spaccanapoli* for the sake of visiting an interesting small chapel—the Cappella Sansevero, which is very close to S. Domenico Maggiore. Walking along *Spaccanapoli* it is sad to see the state of the buildings in many of the roads lying to the north, which have degenerated into slums. Former fine palaces are now crammed with poor families, and have badly deteriorated. And yet it is undeniable that slum-clearance would destroy the character and colour of the old city; as in Palermo. But what of the people themselves? One needs no special powers of observation to see that Neapolitans appear to revel in close human contact and might not appreciate a transfer to high-rise blocks, no matter how hygienic.

The CAPPELLA SANSEVERO, built in 1590 as the sepulchral chapel of the Sangro family, is really remarkable for the extraordinary assortment of monuments collected in the eighteenth century by the alchemist, magician and eccentric Prince Raimondo di Sangro of Sansevero. Here we see among many oddities; Cecco di Sangro depicted with sword raised, about to leave his tomb; a group labelled 'undeceived' which shows a man disentangling himself from a net with the encouragement of a seated angel; and 'Chastity' a beautiful and voluptuous woman covered with a thin clinging veil. Both the net and the veil are carved in the block of marble itself with astonishing skill. There is also on view in the nave the remarkable 'Veiled Christ' by Sammartino, which shows the prostrate figure of Christ after the crucifixion.

In order to reach the Museo Archeologico Nazionale from this point one can take the street called S.M. di Constantinopoli which, from just opposite Porta Alba, leads directly northward until it reaches the museum. The Via Porta Alba leads, in the shape of a semi-circle, into the wide Piazza Dante which was designed by Vanvitelli in 1757.

The NATIONAL MUSEUM OF NAPLES is without doubt one of the most important museums in Europe, and as a specialist archaeological museum ranks with any in the world. It houses not only an exceedingly rich collection of classical sculptures, but also an unforgettable display of frescoes and mosaic pictures from Pompeii and Herculaneum, as well as a wonderfully varied range of bronzes from both cities. It is really not possible to do justice to the Museo Nazionale in a single visit and much enjoyment would be lost in so doing. I would recommend two separate morning visits—reserving one for the mosaics, murals and bronzes from Pompeii, Herculaneum and Stabia (including perhaps also the magnificent collection of Roman glass and the domestic, surgical, dental and personal objects on the same floor)—and keeping the other for the extensive galleries and rooms that contain statues and decorative sculpture from all corners of the classical world.

It is strongly advisable to purchase a copy of the official guide to the museum on sale at the entrance. Here it is only possible to single out a few of the masterpieces: the group 'Orpheus and Euridice'—a Roman copy of a fifth-century Greek work, the superb 'Doryphoros' (Javelin Thrower) of Polycletus—a wonderful copy of one of the most famous statues of the ancient world, the 'Farnese Bull', a huge group dominating the gallery which came from the Baths of Caracalla in Rome, it was carved from a single block of marble but has been heavily restored. The 'Venus Callipyge' (Venus of the Beautiful Bottom) is a most graceful work and represents probably not Aphrodite, but a *hetaira* who turns her back while removing her dress in preparation for a bath. The right leg (below the knee) has been rather clumsily restored, but not so as to spoil this justly famous piece of sculpture.

To my mind the most interesting of all the exhibits at the National Museum, are the mural paintings from Herculaneum, Pompeii and Stabia, and above all, the mosaic pictures from Pompeii. The quality of the mosaics is extraordinary and cannot be captured by the written word; they must be seen. The colour, the execution, the expressiveness of these pictures combine to produce a perfect match of technical accomplishment and artistic resource. My own favourites include the really remarkable 'Portrait of a Woman', with lovely colour shades in tiny *tesserae*, the brilliant picture of marine fauna and the two small signed pictures by Dioscurides of Samos—also in minute *tesserae*—'The Wandering Musicians', and 'The Love-philtre'—in which three hags sit around a bow-legged table while the ugliest of them holds up the concoction in a cup and beckons the recipient to approach, with a hideous grimace; the colouring here is very subtle. Finally I must mention the most famous picture of all, the astonishing 'Battle of Issus with Alexander and Darius', from the House of the Faun. This is a great work on a huge scale, and takes up a large part of the end wall of Room

LXI. It is astonishing that the mosaic artist could have captured so faithfully the turmoil at the height of a great battle; the apprehension on the faces of the defeated, the perspectives as the horses twist away in fright or fall wounded to the ground, the shock-waves of the onslaught and the tumult of the whole, are recorded in amazing fidelity with these little coloured cubes of marble.

The mural paintings on display are far more numerous than the mosaics and much more varied in quality—in fact some of them are not of a high technical standard. In the main they are the work of ordinary craftsmen and not accomplished artists, yet all are of the greatest interest. Among the finest paintings here are the 'Portrait of Paquio Proculo and his Wife'—a work impossible to overpraise—from Pompeii, 'Theseus and the Minotaur' from Herculaneum, the fine 'Hercules watching the young Telephus', and the extraordinary life-like 'Delivery of Briseis to Achilles'. In addition there are some delightful scenes from nature and a brilliant selection of still lifes: a plucked chicken and a hare hanging from hooks, a row of pomegranates beside a jug of water. Even the paintings of less technical merit are full of interest, for we see a series of landscapes, in one view of the port of Puteoli, in another a rustic shrine such as might have been found in a large private villa and in a third, the colonnade of a great villa on the seashore with a boat under sail passing by.

Wandering around these galleries we can begin to form an idea of the tastes of the Roman wealthier classes in the fateful year A.D. 79. Most of the works were painted directly on wet plaster—the al fresco technique, though some are in tempera, and in two of the rooms, LXXI and LXXII, we can see the only known examples from antiquity, of coloured line-drawings on marble. We are indeed lucky to see these paintings for it has required an enormous amount of skill, dedication and patience to enable them to be exhibited at all.

To what extent, one wonders, are these paintings—especially the mythological and allegorical ones—derived from Greek originals? Since much of Greek painting is lost to us the answer is of particular interest, but unfortunately cannot be given with any certainty by scholars at present. However, the Campanian painter (possibly an immigrant Greek) who worked on the great frieze from the Villa of Boscoreale (also in the Museum), certainly had a Greek composition as a model—and this is probably true of the great mosaic of Alexander and Darius, the battle itself being fought in the year 333 B.C.

For those who have the time, a visit to the ROYAL PALACE OF CAPODIMONTE should not be missed. Charles III employed a Sicilian, Medrano, to design the palace in 1738, but it was not completed for another hundred years, when it became one of the main residences of the Bourbon King Ferdinand II. Charles set up a porcelain factory in the park of his palace, hoping to rival the products of his father-in-law at Meissen; a display of Capodimonte porcelain can be seen here today, and the original kilns still exist.

It would be an exaggeration to say that the palace building is handsome, but it is undoubtedly splendid, surrounded by its agreeable park, while from the terrace there is a marvellous view with the full advantage of its position on the hill. On the first floor several of the apartments have been maintained in their original state, but the second floor has been transformed to house a varied, and in parts important collection of paintings from various sources including the National Gallery, the Accademia di Belle Arti (Neapolitan paintings) and the gallery of the Banco di Napoli; these constitute a large number, and among the more important works are paintings by Mantegna, Giovanni Bellini, Titian, Pieter Brueghel the Elder, Claude Lorrain, Van Dyck, Ribera, Goya, the Neapolitan Salvator Rosa, and the important Calabrian painter Mattia Preti. Several of these pictures are masterpieces, and include 'The Transfiguration' by G. Bellini, and 'Danaë' by Titian.

2. West of Naples

No visit to Naples is complete without seeing that area which stretches west beyond Posillipo to the volcanic regions of the Campi Flegrei, the ancient places of strong classical associations such as Pozzuoli, Baia, and Cumae.

It was at Cumae (in Greek, Kyme) that the first civilization in this mainland area began with colonists arriving from Kyme in Euboea, probably not long after the first Greek settlement in the neighbourhood, at Pithecusa (Ischia), at around 750 B.C. (there is no support for the year 1050 B.C., which is the traditional date of the founding of Cumae). The colony soon expanded and was obliged to found a new city to which they gave the name Parthenope, after the legendary siren of that name. On the arrival of new colonists from Athens and Chalcis, the Greeks built themselves another town which they called Neapolis—or 'new city',—and Parthenope was given the name Palaeopolis or 'old city', but the use of the last two names gradually declined and only Neapolis—Naples, survived. It is thought that Palaeopolis was situated on the site of the present district of Pizzofalcone, while Neapolis as we have seen, lies under the very heart of old Naples today. The exact relationship between the two cities remains obscure, and much hard fact is awaiting the spades of the archaeologists, though because of overbuilding they may never have a chance to excavate in vital areas.

Breaking out of the mists of legend is the fact that the Greeks of Palaeopolis incurred the wrath of the Romans in the year 328 B.C. by attacking Rome's allies in Campania, and the city fell after a long siege to the consul Pubilius Philo. The sister city Neapolis surrendered at the same time (having received favourable terms) and became a loyal allied city of Rome.

Because of its history we find that the greater part of this area is dominated by Roman associations rather than Greek, and indeed the Greek remains are very scanty. Present-day Pozzuoli, still a substantial town, was Puteoli, one of the most important ports in the Roman Empire and Baia was once covered with magnificent Roman villas,

4　Bronze faun at Pompeii at the entrance to the house named after it,
once decorating an *impluvium* tank

5　Looking down the Via degli Augustali, Pompeii

6　A gate in the Forum at Pompeii

among them villas belonging to Pompey and Julius Caesar, in what was then the luxurious residential district of Baiae.

It will not be possible within the limitations of this short chapter to do more than touch on the many fascinating places in the Campi Flegrei (the Phlegraean Fields), or to investigate fully the delightful shore between Capo Miseno and the islands of Nisida. Ideally a whole day should be spent exploring this area by car and on foot, but as many may not have either the time or the opportunity, I will follow here roughly the tour organized by c.i.t. (which though limited, is convenient) adding my own experiences from an earlier visit.

The c.i.t. bus leaves the Via Partenope having collected from the hotels the last of the passengers for the tour and proceeds along the Riviera di Chiaia, with its fine palaces, bordering the public park known as the Villa Comunale. (It is in the middle of this park that one finds the Aquarium, one of the finest in the world, and a fascinating place to visit). After passing the Church of St. Maria di Piedigrotta, and Porto Sannazaro at Mergellina—where fast Aliscafi boats leave for Capri and Ischia—the long climb up the hillside of Posillipo begins. Snaking up the steep Via Oronzio in low gear the slow speed of the bus gives the traveller an opportunity to admire the fine luxury flats and villas in this most select residential area, and to enjoy a truly spectacular view over the Bay of Naples, with the metropolis laid out behind the long curving line of the waterfront Via Caracciolo and the busy port area beyond, sprawled at the foot of Vesuvius.

The first stop is the extinct crater of Solfatara, over which one can walk (with a guide) and inspect the hot volcanic mud that bubbles up from the ground, at a temperature of around 350°F, accompanied by noxious sulphurous vapours which, despite their unpleasant smell, are said to be beneficial to health. In many places at this arid spot jets of steam (fumarole) break out, and the ground beneath one's feet is both hot and uncomfortably thin and resonant. The dangerous areas are carefully roped off, but caution is called for and it is advisable to keep up with the guided party.

From here the bus takes the main road that leads past the beautiful dark still Lake Avernus, a crater-lake (which the ancients believed was the entrance to the underworld), and under the impressive Arco Felice. All along this road there are wonderful views to seaward, with Capo Miseno and the islands of Procida and Ischia outlined against the sky—while inland the view towards Monte Bárbaro and the Phlegraean Fields is more mysterious and, for those not afraid of a touch of romanticism, more Greek, for the spirit of the ancients lingers here. The Arco Felice, in an excellent state of preservation, was built by the Emperor Diocletian when he constructed a coast road to give better access to Puteoli and Misenum, and the *pavé* beneath is original.

A short distance from here to the north-east are the remains of the ACROPOLIS OF CUMAE which is approached by a path flanked by olean-ders. Half-way up on the right are the remains of the Temple of Apollo, and at the summit in a magnificent position is the Temple of Jupiter (possibly fifth century B.C. in origin). Both these temples were rebuilt or transformed in later times, and both converted into Christian churches in the fifth or sixth century A.D. Little other than the floor and the foundations remain.

Across the Acropolis hill, a tunnel is hewn in the rock leading to the cave of the Cumaean Sibyl which was excavated only in 1932 and is almost certainly the actual cave of the famous prophetess. A long cor-ridor cut in the form of a perfect trapezium and lighted by side vents, is cut into the living tufa. Here, shut off in her gloomy surroundings in the *oikos endótatos* (the holy of holies), she uttered the prophecies that were to have such far-reaching consequences. Virgil tells us that it was here that Aeneas came to receive the inspiration to found Rome.

It is hard to tear oneself away from this beautiful spot, but this is no picture-postcard prettiness rather, a wild and hard beauty that takes in the severity of the basically volcanic terrain, the marsh shore by Lake Fusaro and the immense arc of the coastline that stretches all the way to Gaeta—a distance of 55 kilometres. Behind the great plain rise the mountains of Campania—smoky blue in the haze. This is the coun-try of Virgil, who so often described the region in his poems—

Mantua me genuit, Calabria rapuere, tenet nunc
Parthenope; cecini pascua, rura, duces.*
*('Mantua bore me, Calabria carried me off,
now Parthenope holds me; I sang of flocks, fields, and heroes.')

Pozzuoli was originally a Greek foundation (refugees from Samos arrived in 529 B.C.) but it grew much in importance, when as Puteoli, it was greatly developed as a harbour, becoming the chief port in the Roman dominions for trade with Greece and countries in the eastern Mediterranean and Asia Minor. The Roman harbour works were mar-vels of their day, and it was at Puteoli that the Roman engineers fully developed their skills with concrete (*opus caementicium*) which was made with the local volcanic sand (*pulvis puteolanus*). It was a par-ticularly valuable property of this concrete that it hardened on contact with water, and vast quantities of it were shipped to Rome for the building of bridges, aqueducts etc. until it was discovered that the local red volcanic sand (*pozzolana*) when mixed with lime had exactly the same properties and a phenomenal strength.

The size and importance of Puteoli may be judged by paying a visit to the ruins of the Flavian amphitheatre. This is a vast structure; after the Colosseum, and that of Capua, it was the largest amphitheatre in Italy. The remains of the building are substantial, and for those interested in Roman building techniques an independent visit would be worthwhile, (it is not on the tour itinerary).

The so-called Temple of Serapis, is really a fine example of a market building or *macellum*, types of which can be found at Pompeii. The name was given to this building after the discovery of a statue of Serapis during excavations in 1750. The paved courtyard, 125 feet square with a central pavilion, was surrounded on all sides by a two-storeyed portico, off which 32 small shops or stalls open alternately inwards and outwards. According to J. B. Ward-Perkins it is possible that the market was placed under the protection of Serapis. The whole of the pavement area is now under water.

Pozzuoli today is a busy port, and the town, with its tightly packed picturesque houses is lively. The quickest way to return to Naples is to take the long straight main road that passes the huge Italsider steel works at Bagnoli. However for those with time, by far the pleasantest route is the coast road that passes the causeway leading to the island of Nisida, and then winds up over the heights of Posillipo. A turning off this road leads down to the delightful fishing village of Marechiaro where one can dine off fresh sea-food at one of the pleasant restaurants overlooking the lido.

3. Ischia, Prócida and Capri

There are many ways of getting to Ischia from the mainland: one can go by the car-ferry from Pozzuoli or the hydrofoil (Aliscafi) from Mergellina, or one can fly direct by helicopter from Capodichino airport to Casamicciola. Alternatively one can take the ferry boat from Calata Beverello in Naples harbour, and this route was in fact my choice when I went to the island on a recent visit. The comparative slowness of the voyage in the steamer gives one ample time to appreciate the beauty of the scenery which is spectacular at times and subtle at others. On a fine day the colouring and brilliance of the scene is breathtaking, the pollution of Naples harbour soon forgotten as the boat passes Cape Posillipo and heads out into the deep, dark blue waters of the gulf.

ISCHIA is easily the largest of the islands that partially enclose the gulf of Naples, and is extremely important to the economy of the region, not only because of the number of tourists it attracts, but because its volcanic soil is super-fertile and produces an abundant harvest for wine-making. The best-known wine is 'Epomeo' and is popular in the whole of the Neapolitan region (to what extent the ordinary labelled Epomeo is adulterated is a matter of opinion, but it is considered by the locals rare to find a bottle of pristine quality). The vineyards stretch over countless acres of the slopes of Monte Epomeo and give in summer, the overall effect of greenness which is characteristic of the island, and in autumn, a welcome contrast in colour. The mountain itself is 788 metres, or just over 2,600 feet high.

Perhaps the first thing that should be said about Ischia is that it is a very beautiful island. Some would say in fact that it is more beautiful than Capri but I think comparisons between the two are rather pointless; each is entirely different. For example, Ischia has miles of sandy beaches where bathing is safe for children and indifferent swimmers, whereas Capri has no beaches worthy of the name at all.

The people of Ischia these days, in the summer months devote all their energies to ensuring that the tourists who arrive in the season do not leave disappointed after their holiday, and in this they are so successful that the island may be considered by some to be overcrowded in the peak months of July, August and September.

During my visit to Ischia I stayed for a while at a typical new hotel almost on the beach of the town of Ischia, full of Germans on packaged holidays, where the standard of cleanliness was faultless and the food adequate if uninspiring. I soon changed to a 'bed-and-continental-breakfast' arrangement. Thereafter in the evenings I often wandered along to the harbour to inspect and admire the great variety of private boats and yachts in port and perhaps dine at one of the *trattorie* over-looking the harbour. The port of Ischia, roughly elliptical in shape, was originally formed by a volcanic crater and it was not until 1854 that the Bourbon Ferdinand II's engineers cut a canal through from the sea and developed the harbour facilities. The new town, which developed rapidly after the opening of the port, lies to the south-east, and here the shops and boutiques of the Via Roma form a magnet to the footloose during the casual hours before dinner. The Via Roma leads directly into the Corso Vittoria Colonna, which in turn eventually links with the causeway—(Ponte Aragonese) which leads to the great rock on which the Castello d'Ischia is built, which is interesting and can be visited. The castle is inevitably connected with the memory of one of its most distinguished occupants, the poetess Vittoria Colonna who was married here in 1509, and who lived in Ischia for many years. The castle is certainly older than 1438, the year when Alfonso il Magnanimo built the causeway. Not least among the pleasures of visiting this fortress are the glorious views that can be had of Ischia and the whole sweep of the Bay of Naples.

The small town here at the foot of the causeway is called Ischia Ponte and is still inhabited mainly by fishermen's families and a poorer class of people. Between Ponte and the main tourist centre of Ischia, there is the area known as the 'pineta' studded with hotels and villas and justly celebrated for the beauty of its stone pines that flourish in the weathered lava from the last eruption in 1302.

The thermal waters and the therapeutic mud and sand of Ischia are part and parcel of the facilities that are offered to the visitor to the island, but I wonder what proportion of the thousands that flock to Ischia each summer go for medicinal purposes. The answer is of no great consequence, but my guess is that the number is small and that they are probably rather rich. Two luxurious hotels at Lacco Ameno on the north coast tend to their needs, and there are other thermal establishments at Casamicciola Terme. Also there are special facilities at two of the major beaches—the Spiagga di Citara and the Spiaggia dei Maronti—both superb stretches of sandy shore. At the latter the volcanic activity is particularly marked: 'fumarole' issue jets of steam alongside the path leading to the beach, and once there, at the western end, it is not uncommon to see the heavily perspiring faces of people wallowing up to their necks in hot volcanic mud. Since the ordinary sand during the summer is too hot to walk on with bare feet, the endurance of these people must reach heroic proportions. Unfortunately this marked volcanic activity has had its tragic side. The last and most devastating disaster was the earthquake at Casamicciola in 1883, when a total of 7,000 people perished, nearly half of them in the space of a few seconds.

For the second half of my stay in Ischia I selected a comfortable hotel between Lacco Ameno and Forío. Forío has great character, more than any other town in Ischia to my mind, (though S. Angelo, only a village, comes close to it). It is the centre of the wine-growing district of Epomeo, and once must have been a fairly important fishing harbour. The port is guarded by a tremendous tower (Torrione) that manages at the same time to be both formidable and attractive. It was built in 1480 as a defence against the corsairs by King Ferrante. Unfortunately it was anything but efficacious. The island suffered terribly at the hands of Dragut and Barbarossa.

Forío possesses some interesting and colourful buildings, and deserves a leisurely exploration. There are two distinctive churches in the town—S. Maria di Loreto with its twin towers crowned with majolica tiles—and the delightfully simple whitewashed church of the Soccorso which stands on the extreme western point. This must have been the church for fishermen and mariners as one can see from ex-votos inside. Set into the walls of this church are some beautiful majolica tiles.

One of the most pleasing aspects of Ischia is that it is large enough to enable one to escape from the crowds if that should be one's inclination. One must expect the Marina dei Maronti (the beach can be reached by fishermen's boats from S. Angelo for those unwilling to take the path) and the Spiaggia di Citara to be packed with sun-worshippers in the season—but with a little ingenuity it is no great trouble to find much more secluded beaches, though admittedly private transport is a great advantage in this respect. In addition many of the villages in the hills and on the slopes of Monte Epomeo are quite unspoilt. The summit of M. Epomeo can be reached from the village of Fontana—which is on a bus-route—and the view from the top on a clear day is wonderful, scanning a radius of 60 miles at least.

And yet for the majority of people Ischia is not remembered for its small, peaceful villages devoted to viniculture, but as a holiday island—gay, exuberant and geared for the most exacting demands of its multi-national visitors. There is never any difficulty in getting anywhere on the island. There is an adequate bus net-work, and if this should fail a constant stream of three-wheeler scooter 'mini-cabs' ply between the main places on the island: from Ischia—Casamicciola—Lacco Ameno—Forío—Serrara—Barano—and completing the circle, back to Ischia town. These scooters have largely replaced the colourful pony-traps of old, but they are very useful, being far cheaper than taxis and moreover, a little bargaining is quite acceptable, bringing to mind similar if more capacious arrangements in Tel Aviv, Istanbul or Manila.

As for the climate, this is really splendid; the air is fresh and laced with the fragrance of pine. Quite apart from the therapeutic qualities of the mineral waters for which Ischia has been for many centuries famous, the produce of the island, the vegetables, the fruit, the wines all draw extra health-giving properties from the fertile volcanic soil—so that Ischia deserves its envious reputation.

The island of Prócida is a rare place in the Mediterranean area these days—a beautiful spot that is practically unaffected by the ravages of tourism—and it seems, incredible to say, that the inhabitants have no real interest in that direction. The island is in consequence a most satisfying place to visit, for one is seeing here island life that has hardly changed over the centuries. There is in fact only one hotel, plus a scattering of *locande* or inns where one can find a bed. During my short visit to the island I found myself wishing that I had allowed myself time to stay for a few days, but I had planned it otherwise and the boat time-tables allowed me only a few hours, during which time I covered as much of the island as I could on foot. It is not large about 2¼ miles from north to south and about ½ mile across the waist—but I found I was short of time.

Prócida lies only about two miles to the north-east of Ischia and must once have been connected. The island is composed, like Ischia, of pumiceous tufa, separated by beds of pumice and fragments of cellular lava, while the volcanic top-soil allows for an exceedingly rich growth of vegetation. An enormous quantity of high quality citrus fruit and desert grapes are produced and promptly shipped to Naples. There is also a lively fishing industry.

The Marina Grande at Prócida lies on the north coast and from here a road winds up to the castle (since many decades a prison) and to the centre of the town that straddles the north-east corner of the island, with glorious views over the Gulf of Gaeta and the Bay of Naples. However what makes the greatest impression in Prócida is the architecture, which is quite distinctive. There is a strong hint of the orient about the style of the buildings, especially those on the water-front at the Marina Grande, opposite the port. They are massive and

colourful, the arches are very deep and the contours of all outside surfaces moulded rather than rigidly formed.

The island is named after Giovanni da Prócida, one of the principal
conspirators in the revolt against the Angevins sparked off by the incident of the Sicilian Vespers, and who held the island in fief. Many
legends have grown up around this celebrated man who lived in the
thirteenth century. Historically the island has been closely tied to the
fortunes of Naples. There are several churches on the island and the
most interesting of these is S. Michele. There is good bathing at the
Lido di Prócida, or at the southern extremity of the island at the
Marina di Chiaiolella, a small bay which is partially enclosed by the
islet of Vivara.

To write about CAPRI in the space of only a few hundred words is to
risk a failure to do any kind of justice to it, for the subject is much more
complex than might be thought from a casual glance. The number of
people through the ages who have been able to claim comprehensive
knowledge of the island—its history, its people, its flora, its geology
etc., must be extremely small; but one who undoubtedly could make
the claim was the British expatriate Norman Douglas. He lived on the
island for many years and was able to combine the precision of a
trained scientific mind with his unusual talent as a novelist and writer.
Some years before his novel 'South Wind' appeared (the characters
were drawn from the life he knew on the island) Douglas wrote eight
monographs on Capri wide-ranging in subject: *The Blue Grotto and its
Literature, The Forestal Conditions of Capri, Tiberius,* and *Saracens
and Corsairs in Capri* among them. These are scholarly, well-
researched works that were written unhurriedly over a long period
(between 1904 and 1907) and they are extraordinarily interesting to
anyone visiting the island today, providing the vital element of perspective.

Moreover in the Preface to G. Orioli's limited edition of these
monographs, published in Florence in 1903, Norman Douglas is
enlightening about the social side of life in his time:

Capri has changed since I first landed there on 26 March 1888. In
those days it still possessed some of the dreaminess and remoteness
for which it had been famed. It was a restful place, full of lovable
freaks of various nationalities who lived contentedly on next to
nothing, gave each other unpretentious dinner parties, and took no
heed of the annual invasion of Teutonics . . . The island has been
subject to invasions from hoariest antiquity . . . There was the Rus-
sian invasion, the American one, and now the Italian. Yes, after all

these centuries, Capri was discovered by Neapolitans . . . the gentlemanly freaks, meantime, had been gathered to their fathers; a new class of foreign residents, having more money than was good for them and nothing whatever to do, broke into cantankerous little cliques (amusingly described in two of Compton Mackenzie's books) and made the place almost uninhabitable . . .

For one who has not been a permanent resident in the island it is not possible to give an account of life as it is lived day by day in Capri, and here I am perforce restricted to giving my impressions as a visitor, which indeed is the rôle of most. When Douglas writes 'Capri has changed since I first landed there . . .' it sounds a chord that must have been familiar throughout the ages. In exactly similar terms could Tiberius have written, or, leaping a good few centuries, could Gracie Fields write now. But it does not appear to have changed much in the short span of years that I have known the island.

About five years ago when I first planned to visit Capri I found myself hesitating. I had been rather put off by a less than flattering reference by a well-known travel-writer whom I respect and admire, and I began to wonder whether the delights of the island's obvious natural beauty would be outbalanced by the crushing weight of massed tourism. Moreover the Ischiots to whom I confided my plan were aghast at the idea. 'What in heaven's name can you expect to find in Capri that you can't find here in Ischia?' one of them said to me in obvious puzzlement. This age-old rivalry (or jealousy) was of course only to be expected; I am glad I decided to make the journey.

As one approaches Capri from the sea from the direction of Naples, and while still a few kilometres off, one begins to appreciate the tremendous drop of the sheer cliffs, that form both ends of the great mass of limestone that rises out of the sea in such a dramatic fashion. Actually the extraordinary shape of Capri is perhaps more dramatic seen from Naples, 32 kilometres away, for then the peak of Monte Solaro, the steady then abrupt descent to the plateau where the town of Capri nestles, and the steep rise again to the eastern point at Il Capo form a vigorous outline. Yet the beauty of the island's rock formation cannot be appreciated until one closes in to within half a kilometre or so, for it is the colouring of the limestone as well as its infinite variety in shape and form, etched over the centuries by rain and wind, that together provide such an aesthetically-satisfying sight. Clinging to the rock are lichens, mosses and wild herbs, and also, wherever a cleft can trap a drop or two of water, the vigorous dark green of the maritime pine that sprouts in the most unlikely places. Together with the blue of the sea and sky, it makes a wonderful combination of colour and form. The island is quite small—just over six kilometres in length and just under three kilometres at its widest point.

The ferry boat from Naples harbour passes close to the Sorrentine peninsular towards the end of its passage (in fact some of the boats call in at Sorrento en route) and the short time that elapses between passing Massa Lubrense high up on the cliff, and arriving at the Marina Grande brings home to one how close Capri is to the peninsular's termination at Punta Campanella—a distance of only five kilometres. Geologically Capri is, of course, a continuation of the Sorrentine peninsular.

The Marina Grande, the main harbour of Capri, is one of the three main centres of population—the other two being the small towns of Capri and Anacapri. To say that the Marina Grande, on the arrival of the ferry-boats, is a lively and bustling place is really something of an understatement. One must be prepared for an assault on the ears, rather than a greeting. Boatmen bombard the visitor with offers to whisk him off straight away to the Blue Grotto . . . 'Grotta Azzura! Grotta Azzura!' they shout at one and all as the mass of visitors struggle forward along the quay towards the town. Mingling and pushing their way through the crowds are touts from the innumerable hotels and pensions, not to be out-shouted by the boatmen, porters and lads from the various hotels, tour operators, and, almost insignificant in the *melée*, people meeting friends. It is important to detach oneself as fast as one can from this hotch-potch collection, and having made arrangements for porterage, make for the funicular that will take one up to the town of Capri and away from the worst aspects of commercialization.

One has splendid views climbing up to the town in the funicular. The Piazza Umberto I which is just round the corner from the exit of the funicular station is justly famous, not because of its architecture, though it is a delightful place, but because since time immemorial it has been the main meeting place in the town. Here at one of the cafés with their many rows of chairs spreading out into the piazza, the famous, the notorious, aspiring 'stars' of film, theatre and opera, intellectuals, writers, artists, 'red' revolutionaries, Douglas's lovable gentlemanly freaks, a variety of beautiful women, and a vast number of unknowns have met and talked. Of course missing from the above list are the ordinary working people of Capri, and the omission is deliberate for although they mix in a quite unselfconscious way with the visitors, they do not as a rule sit and idle the hours away as the foreigners are inclined to do, but stand around in groups in the age-old manner. Perhaps Sunday morning just after midday when Mass is over, is the best time to see the *piazzetta* at its liveliest. A large number of locals will have spilled out of the charming and beautifully kept parochial church of S. Stefano, descended the steps and having reached the piazza formed up into groups of friends and relations, while their children play boisterous games, suck ices, or try and find room to kick a football. There is a pleasant little baroque clock-tower in the *piazzetta*, though nobody bothers much about the time . . . and railings, guarding a sheer drop, on which one can lean and admire a superb view across the bay towards Naples, or below to the Marina Grande, or westward towards the magnificent sheer limestone rocks that form the northern part of the island.

One of the joys of staying in Capri is that many of the streets in the heart of the town are for pedestrians only and it is a delight to walk through these streets in the warmth of a late summer or autumn evening. It is then that the island is at its most relaxed—though to be fair, the great crowds of tourists who arrive by boat or hydrofoil every day from Naples, Ischia, Sorrento, Positano, Amalfi (the majority on a day's visit) do not greatly spoil the characteristic atmosphere of Capri. The island is one of the most relaxing places I have ever come across. It is part of Capri's charm, and for this reason there is little point in trying to define it. It has something to do with the air, the colours, the flowers, the terraced gardens, the happiness of everyone, the contentment, the joy of just being alive in Capri on a sunny day—even though one might know that in a few hours one will have to take the last boat back. In spite of the rather sour remarks made by some *cognoscenti* who knew Capri in the 'good old days', I would hazard a guess that the charm, the magic of Capri forms as powerful an attraction now as it has ever done.

The longest I have ever spent in Capri at one time is five days, and that is just long enough to appreciate the subtlety of its beauty, and to compare the various parts of the island. There is no space regrettably, to do more than give here my impressions and the briefest historical sketch, and to indicate which are the most interesting places to see.

I stayed at a pleasant hotel just off the Via Vittorio Emanuele, and so was well placed to take advantage of the delightful walks that are a feature of Capri, for it is a place where walking is easily the best as well as the most enjoyable way of getting around (nevertheless for those who cannot or who do not wish to walk any distance the bus service is efficient). A favourite walk of mine was down traffic-free Via Vitt. Emanuele, past the luxurious and famous Hotel Quisisana, past the fashionable shops in the Via Camerelle and then into Via Tragara—a lovely walk that eventually leads down to the small port of Tragara, with splendid views en route of the unusual and strangely beautiful Faraglioni Rocks that lie just off the coast near Tragara. Here I would spend the morning with friends, swimming off the rocks quite near the port at a makeshift bathing place. The water at this spot is splendid and

a strong swimmer can swim through the narrows of the Faraglioni and
find some deserted and inaccessible (from the land) caves and rock-
ledges. The Faraglioni rocks are a feature of Capri; the three beautifully coloured huge bare limestone rocks soar up almost vertically from
the sea, becoming every day more weathered and sharp. They originally formed a long serrated spur joined to the main island, but the
softer rock between the limestone was washed away. It is on the Faraglioni that one can find the celebrated blue lizard, a species extinct on
the main island—and it is reasonable to suppose (though not con-
firmed by expert opinion) that this small creature was present when the
separation of the island took place and has been protected by its iso-
lation since. There are also rare seagulls nesting on the Faraglioni.

In general terms the flora of Capri is of enormous interest to the
botanist, since there are about 850 species and some 133 varieties of
plants here—some of which can be traced to Roman times. The de-
afforestation which was the scourge of the second half of the
nineteenth century has long been reversed and planned reforestation
schemes are reaching maturity. All the emphasis now is on con-
servation, though in parts of the island irreparable damage was done
by past excesses.

A place which should be visited if at all possible is the site at Lo Capo
of the Emperor Tiberius's VILLA JOVIS now in a state of ruin, but excavated and patched up comparatively recently. It is true that the present
sprawling ruins give no more than a hint of the splendour and luxury of
Tiberius's most important villa on the island, (more accurately, a
palace), but they are interesting none-the-less, and the view alone is
worth the fairly long walk from the centre of the town. It was to the
Villa Jovis that Tiberius retired from the cares of government at the
age of 68, spending ten years on the island and interfering as little as
possible in the machinery of the State, yet reserving for himself any
decisions of fundamental constitutional importance. As for the legendary stories of the terrors and depravities (originating from the pens of
Suetonius and Tacitus) that were said to have been perpetrated by the
ageing emperor . . . these can be safely consigned to the limbo of
rhetorical invention. Certainly they have not been accepted by the
great modern historians of the past hundred years. Norman Douglas in
his mocking manner makes fun of the islanders' skill at profiting from
the emperor's reputation: 'Tiberius—the Tiberius of Suetonius—has
made Capri, and it is really time that the inhabitants, who owe to him
more than to all the saints in the calendar, put up a memorial to their
benefactor.'

It is almost certainly true that Augustus did more for the island than
Tiberius. Augustus is reported to have visited Capri in 29 B.C. on his

return to Italy after his victory over Antony and Cleopatra. He was greeted by a most fortunate augury when a withered holm-oak burst into leaf on his arrival and, being much taken with the place, during the next 40 years spent larges sums on building aqueducts, baths and palaces, and eventually acquired it from the Neapolitans, to whom it then belonged, in exchange for the much more productive island of Ischia. There are scanty ruins of Augustus' Palazzo a Mare near the Marina Grande and some remains of the Greek steps leading to Anacapri, (mis-named Scala Fenicia) that he rebuilt. Originally they numbered 800.

Although the Greeks certainly settled in Capri there are no clear historical details concerning their arrival. Indeed the very origin of the word 'Capri' is in doubt. Some think it might have derived from the Greek *kapros* (wild boar) others that the Latin *capra* (goat) is the more likely. It is however certain that the island was called *Capreae* by the Romans.

Mention has already been made of the villas of Tiberius, and on the site of one of these another famous villa has been built—that of the Swedish writer Axel Munthe—called the Villa San Michele. From here there is a very fine view over the bay.

The oldest church on the island is that dedicated to the patron saint S. Costanzo, and it was built in the eleventh century in the shape of a Greek Cross. The saint was once Patriarch of Constantinople and his remains were brought here at the time of the iconoclastic controversy. Four antique columns from a Roman villa support the unusual Byzantine dome. It is believed by the faithful that the saint, acting as intermediary, was responsible for warding off the massive Saracen attack of A.D. 881. These Saracen and Corsair attacks were a menace, though of course the influence of the Saracens was not by any means wholly destructive, as can be seen in the history of Sicily and other regions of the south. Yet Saracenic culture at Naples and its environs was nowhere near so permanent or prominent as at Palermo, (one of their good deeds however was to introduce the Capri date-palm). As for the corsairs and sea-pirates nothing good can be said of them. They terrorized this whole area, and at Capri forced the inhabitants to flee from the coastal town behind the Marina to the comparative security of the present site of Capri town—with the added protection of the megalithic wall, which is the earliest human monument on the island.

There are few who will visit Capri for any length of time and not succumb to the lure of the BLUE GROTTO. The most usual method of reaching it is by motor-boat from the Marina Grande, and on arriving at the entrance one is transferred to a rowing-boat, since only by crouching in this can one enter the very low entrance to the grotto. For this reason visits can only be made on a calm day. The extraordinary and very beautiful colour of the water—a silvery mercury-blue—is caused by a refraction of the light as it enters from an opening below the sea. It is fairly dark inside but some of the colour is reflected against the rocky ceiling, and when the boatman splashes the water with his oars there is a brilliant cascade of silvery-blue. Having been over-exposed to the glories of the 'Grotta Azzura', I was prepared to be disappointed—and delighted that I was not. The grotto is purported to have been discovered by the German painter Kopisch in 1826, but in fact it was then well-known to all the fishermen of the island and indeed had been shown on a map published in 1696 as the Grotto Gradola. There is little doubt that the 'discovery' was a clever piece of sales promotion by the hotelier Don Guiseppe Pagano, after an earlier attraction, the Grotta Oscura had been blocked up by a landslide, and the effect must have been beyond his dreams for the Blue Grotto achieved almost instant fame.

The Blue Grotto is in fact only one of dozens of grottoes and caves that have been carved by the sea into the softer rock around the coast. Two of unusual beauty are the Green Grotto and the White Grotto. Visits to these and to wind-sculptured rocks such as the Arco Naturale, may be made by taking a motor-boat trip round the island, enabling one to see to the best advantage the astonishing cliff formations and to enjoy the beauties of these coastal waters. For obvious reasons boatmen only go out in fine weather, and it is advisable to strike a bargain before setting out. (The Grotta de Matromania, used by the Romans as a sanctuary in honour of Cybela, the Mater Magna, is best reached by land.)

One interesting landmark that can be clearly seen off the southern shores of the island, is the ruin of the Carthusian monastery—the Certosa di S. Giacomo—which was suppressed under French influence in 1807. Building of the Charterhouse began in 1371 on the site of one of the villas of Tiberius.

A visit to ANACAPRI is highly recommended for those with the time to spare. The small town stands at a height of 980 feet (compared with Capri at 450 feet), and the two places were connected by a carriageway in 1874. The mini-buses are regular and frequent, and leave from a small bus-park quite close to the *piazzetta*.

The rivalry and feuds between the citizens of Capri and Anacapri were notorious, but fortunately time has mellowed their antagonisms to the point where they no longer exist. The charm of Anacapri comes partly from its position—high on a flattish plateau with wide horizons and superb views—and partly from the distinctive style of its architecture—its buildings, flat-roofed, cubic, generally white or pink in colour and so rather Moorish in style.

The village lies at the north-western foot of Monte Solaro and is set among olive groves, gardens and vineyards. One can take a chair-lift to the summit of Monte Solaro (1920 feet) and this is a relaxing and enjoyable experience. The view from the top on a fine day is really marvellous.

There are two churches of note in the village—the small parochial church of S. Sofia, which is now baroque in style though originally medieval—and the eighteenth century church of San Michele, remarkable for the majolica pavement showing the Garden of Eden, and the Expulsion of Adam and Eve. It is the work of Leonardo Chiaiese, based on the designs of D. A. Vaccaro.

4. Around Vesuvius:
Pompeii and Herculaneum

It is a fact of course, that the entire Bay of Naples from Cape Posíllipo to the Sorrentine peninsular, is dominated by Vesuvius, but the dominance is nowhere more marked than the stretch of the coast that runs from Pórtici to Castellammari di Stábia. On one occasion I stayed at a modern hotel near S. Maria la Bruna to be conveniently placed between Herculaneum and Pompeii, and I came to know this Vesuvian coast fairly well.

Pórtici is no longer the charming coastal resort that made it famous in the eighteenth century as a retreat for the Neapolitan aristocracy, for the industrial slums spreading from S. Giovanni a Teduccio have threatened to swamp it. After 1738 however it could boast of being a royal resort, for it was in that year that Charles of Boùrbon visiting the villa of the Prince of Elboeuf was so delighted with the place that he commissioned Medrano to design him a royal palace—known simply as Palazzo Reale—which became the second royal residence. It is now the home of the Faculty of Agriculture of the University of Naples.

The stretch of coast between Pórtici and Resina has become so built-up that it is hard to isolate the few *settecento* Vesuvian villas that still remain—the Villa Elboeuf, the Villa Meola, the Villa Caravita, and on the 'Golden Mile' between Resina and Torre del Greco, the royal residence of La Favorita. Torre del Greco is now an extremely populous and congested town.

The most convenient way of making the ascent of Vesuvius is to take the narrow-gauge Circumvesuviana railway that travels between Naples and Sorrento (a few trains, as the name implies, travel round the base circumference of the volcano) and to alight at the station of Pugliano-Resina. From here special buses leave at regular intervals for the Stazione Seggiovia (but it is advisable to consult a timetable first) from where a chair-lift will take you to the summit.

The height of Vesuvius is now approximately 4,200 feet, though it varies year by year due to erosion. The volcano consists of two distinct portions. On the northern side a great cliff, reaching a height of about 3,700 feet half encircles the present cone and descends in long slopes to the plains below. This precipice known as Monte Somma, forms the wall of an ancient crater of far greater size than the present one, indicating that the volcano was once probably twice its present size until a vast explosion, in pre-historic times, blew the top half of the cone away. The present crater is about 600 feet deep and rather more than 600 yards across, and quite impressive enough—though the few little 'fumarole' issuing steam are indeed tame in comparison with the wrath of Etna. There has been no real activity since 1944—and yet this very fact probably makes it dangerous, for there is little doubt that the forces below are far from spent.

The early part of the ascent of Vesuvius is especially interesting. The lower slopes of the mountain are richly cultivated, for as at Etna, the soil is incredibly fertile. Among the luxurious vegetation, one can see the acres of vineyards that produce the well-known *Lacrima Christi*—a wine that is popular throughout the region. At the summit on a fine day there is a magnificent view, but since clear weather in these parts is often accompanied by a cool wind it is advisable, outside the hot season, to take some warm clothing.

The town of Castellamare di Stábia, lying at the point where the coast turns south-west, is especially interesting since it is near here that excavations have revealed two large Roman villas overwhelmed, as indeed was the ancient town of Stabiae, by the eruption of Vesuvius in A.D. 79. The story of the excavations is a fascinating one for it was largely through the perseverence of a local antiquarian, a retired schoolmaster, that the villas were brought to light. Discoveries at the site are in fact being made almost daily, and now that officialdom has added its seal of approval and recognition, excavations are proceeding at a greater rate. An assessment has now been made of the extent of the pre-Roman town, and much knowledge has been gained of the detailed lay-out of the Roman town.

Few will visit the area of the Bay of Naples and not find time to visit POMPEII. As to the amount of time that should be spent there—this is of course a matter of personal inclination, but anyone hoping to see the extent of the ruins in less than a whole morning is liable to be disappointed. It is just possible I suppose to get around Pompeii in a couple of hours, but really this should be attempted only by the very fit and the very rushed. But to those who have decided to visit this uniquely memorable place my advice is, take your time, do not be hustled by guides or anyone else, and if necessary pay more than one visit. Try and time your visit as early as possible in the morning (the opening time is 9 a.m.) and avoid the hours of early afternoon in the hot season, for there is very little shade among the ruins. There is however a very welcome little rest-house with refreshments.

To attempt a comprehensive description of Pompeii within the limitations of this chapter is not possible. The excavations have revealed an enormous number of private dwellings belonging to both the wealthy and the artisan classes as well as public buildings and only a very select number can be described here, so the following pages will be more of a general description than a detailed account. (Those who wish for something more exacting cannot do better than buy Amedeo Maiuri's *Pompeii* available on bookstalls.)

Entering the Porta Marina one's first impression is of the elevation of the town, its wide panorama and fine view of Vesuvius. The volcano appears to be remarkably close, which indeed it is, for the summit is only eight kilometres away. Pompeii itself was built on the ridge of a prehistoric lava flow which explains its elevation.

The origins of Pompeii go back into antiquity. It was an Oscan town, probably founded as early as the eighth century B.C. and later came under the influence of the Etruscans, the Greeks, the Samnites and finally the Romans. In all likelihood it had a very mixed population as a result. But in fact we know very little of its history before the outbreak of the Social War (91–89 B.C.) when it withstood a long siege by Sulla and was one of the last cities of Campania to surrender to the Romans. Pompeii then made her peace with Rome and was admitted to the rank of a *municipium*, but Sulla planted a colony of Roman veterans there to keep the citizens in order, and the town was increasingly romanized. Under Nero in A.D. 55 Pompeii became a Roman colony, but long before that it had become one of the favourite resorts of the Roman nobility, several of whom bought or built villas in or near the town. Among them was Cicero, whose letters abound with references to his Pompeian villa.

Two events are recorded at about this time—one of comparatively minor consequence and the other of catastrophic proportions. In A.D. 59 a riot took place in the amphitheatre between the locals and some visitors from the neighbouring town of Nuceria which ended in a bloody fight and the loss of many lives. On appeal to Nero the Pompeians were held to blame and all exhibitions and public spectacles were banned for ten years. Only four years later however, a far worse punishment was inflicted on the city when an earthquake struck Pompeii with great severity, destroying or irreparably damaging a large part of it, including most of the public buildings. Public confidence was so badly shaken that for a time the city was evacuated, but eventually the people returned and began the long task of rebuilding and repairing.

The process of reconstruction was still far from complete when, 16 years later, a second and final catastrophe overwhelmed the town. The eruption of Vesuvius in the year A.D. 79 is vividly described by Pliny the Younger in his letter to Tacitus, in which he explains how his uncle, in command of the Roman fleet stationed at Misenum, organized a rescue mission to the coastal towns below Vesuvius and in consequence suffered the loss of his life at Stabiae by asphyxiation from the poisonous fumes. The morning of 24 August was calm and very hot and the skies quite clear, but suddenly in the early afternoon a booming roar, not unlike a heavy crash of thunder made everyone turn towards Vesuvius . . . it seemed as if the top of the volcano had burst open, while fiery lava spewed forth and a tremendous jet of steam and black smoke shot up into the sky. (Pliny describes this as not unlike the shape of a pine tree, so the mushroom shape must have been similar to that of an atomic explosion.) Very soon intermittent explosions occurred, hurling great boulders into the sky together with a vast quantity of pumice stone, rocks, cinders and ash, the density of the smoke and steam increased, and in an incredibly short time the sun was blackened out as on the darkest night, with only the lurid flashes of the detonations lighting the sky. The tremendous quantity of water vapour that had been released condensed into storm clouds, lightning flashed across the black vault of space and it began to rain. The rain mixed with the debris, the ash and the dust, and it was the weight of pumice-stones (*lapilli*) followed by the ash-mud, that almost completely submerged Pompeii.

It would indeed be remarkable if panic had not set in within minutes of this terifying phenomenon. It has been estimated by scholars that Pompeii had a population of around 20,000 at the time of the eruption, and it is thought from the number of skeletons found that about 2,000 lost their lives. Many of these might have saved themselves had they fled from the city, for a great number were found huddled in cellars and were as likely as not buried alive. Others must have perished from the lethal fumes for in one of the remarkable plaster casts obtained from the impressions of bodies trapped in the volcanic mud, it appears that the victim had wrapped a towel or scarf around his face in a desperate attempt to keep out the noxious fumes.

The disaster made a tremendous impression on people living at the time and besides Pliny, it is mentioned by Martial, Tacitus and Suetonius. The Emperor Titus sent a commission to look at the possibility of restoring both Pompeii and Herculaneum, but nothing came of it. A few poor people tried to build homes over the ruins, but the whole site was abandoned after the eruption of 472, and by the Middle Ages Pompeii was entirely forgotten.

The story behind the modern excavation can be taken up in the year 1748, when a careful inspection of an underground aqueduct built in

1594–1600 showed that it covered the site of entombed ruins. Proper excavations began in 1763 but of a haphazard nature, and it was not until the mid-nineteenth century that scientific work was put in hand under the direction of G. Fiorelli. In 1911 the main excavations were begun in the eastern half of the Strada dell' Abbondanza, opening up a large new area, a process that has continued, so that at the present time about three-fifths of the ruins of the ancient city have been revealed.

On entering at the Porta Marina, which is the best point to enter (though there is another entrance at Porta di Nocera which is nearer the main railway station) one comes almost at once to the small museum on the right-hand side which contains some interesting exhibits showing the development of the city. Immediately after the museum one sees the remains of the large temple of Venus Pompeiana; beyond this is the Basilica and opposite, on the other side of the Via della Marina, is the Temple of Apollo. The large open area adjacent to the last-named, lying on a North-west–South-east axis, is the Forum, which will be described in more detail later.

Religious life in Pompeii centred around the nine temples. Of these, the Temple of Apollo and the Doric temple in the Triangular Forum date from the earliest times; three others, the temple of Jupiter at the head of the Forum, the temple of Jupiter Meilichus and that of Venus Pompeiana are certainly of pre-Imperial date, and the other four were post-Republican foundations. One of these was dedicated to Isis, and it is thought that there must have been many adherents of this favoured Oriental mystery-religion, since this temple was one of the very few public buildings that had been completely rebuilt and redecorated before the eruption. The tufa porticoes and pavements of the Forum area itself were in the process of being replaced by travertine at the time of the earthquake of A.D. 63 and work was still in progress in A.D. 79. The Temple of Apollo and the amphitheatre suffered comparatively little and only needed patching-up and buttressing—but in the main the public buildings of Pompeii, had there been no eruption in 79, would have taken on the appearance of new buildings.

The FORUM was always at the heart of any Roman town whether one of the great metropoleis, or a second-rate provincial town. At Pompeii, which falls into the latter category, this can be seen very clearly. Adjoining the Forum at the southern end and forming an L-shape, is the Basilica, where legal matters were hammered out, judgements pronounced, and commercial transactions made. It was also a public meeting-place where citizens could bargain or just gossip. The Temple of Apollo on the western side is, as we have seen, one of the oldest of the temples and therefore must have been an uniquely sacred piece of ground. In the most priviledged position facing straight down the length of the Forum, is the Temple of Jupiter, or more accurately perhaps, the Temple of Jupiter, Juno and Minerva with three separate *cella* side by side for the worship of the three gods.

The next important building, to the north-east of the Forum, is the *macellum*, the meat, fish and livestock market. It consisted of a rectangular courtyard surrounded by a deep colonnade with a central pavilion composed of 12 columns in a circular plan carrying a roof. This probably served as a fish-stall. In addition, there were three rows of *tabernae* (single-storey shops)—one row facing inwards and two outwards—one onto the Via degli Augustali, and the other on to the public area beside the temple of Jupiter.

The next large building to the south is known as the BUILDING OF EUMACHIA and some idea of its importance can be gained from its size. It was in fact the headquarters of the Guild of Fullers—the most important of the town's commercial corporations. It was erected for the guild during the reign of Tiberius by their patroness, the priestess Eumachia. After the Basilica, this is the most impressive building on the Forum, and reflects the importance of the clothing trade in the economic life of the city. The building was two storeys high with a large court surrounded by a colonnade. Its main purpose was to provide a splendid and up-to-date Exchange for the use of the trade. As all Roman citizens were obliged to wear the heavy and voluminous white toga, it is not really surprising that fullers were more numerous in Pompeii than any other kind of workers, with the possible exception of bakers. Five fulleries have been discovered in the course of excavations.

Pompeii, like all Roman towns and cities, was not lacking in well-organized public bathing facilities; or rather, that would have been the case had it not been for the earthquake. Easily the most ambitious of the bathing establishments was the complex now known as the Terme Centrali; this was still being built at the time of the eruption, and this fact gives a clue as to the devastating effect of the 63 earthquake on the economic prosperity of Pompeii, for not only were repairs on the Terme di Stábia incomplete but the splendid new baths had yet to be finished. Roman citizens regarded well-run baths as a way of life rather than a luxury, and this failure to provide baths for the public over such a long period of time is a sure indication of the depressed state of the economy. However, towards the year 79 a revival was gathering momentum and the Terme Centrali, when finished would have been the most up-to-date building in Pompeii, with numerous and spacious rooms, a large exercise yard (*palaestra*) and admirable bathing facilities. Externally the walls were brick-faced, and the decoration of half-columns and wide windows also in brick. However, the core of the building is made of concrete, and in spite of the gauntness of its present condition it is worth going in to look at the vaulted construction which anticipates in a simple manner, the great imperial baths at Rome.

For the majority of people the most interesting buildings in Pompeii are the houses, especially the ones more recently excavated, where the wall paintings have been allowed to remain *in situ*, and the contents in general disturbed as little as possible. One reaches these houses through narrow streets paved with large polygonal blocks of lava shiny with use, sometimes deeply rutted by single line traffic and overlooked more often than not by the high bare walls of the backs of houses, many with hardly more than slits for ventilation. In this way the noise of the streets could be shut out to a large extent.

Pompeii was enlarged to its present size in the fifth century B.C. when the area was enclosed by new town walls and divided into large plots by a network of streets. In the early decades of the new town the amount of room between the houses was spacious. But in the course of time with the increasing commercialization of town life and the development of industry, the demand for building-land overrode considerations of environment, houses were crammed into any available plot and the result was what we can see today with our own eyes—a somewhat confused mass lacking any regularity.

The houses which sprang up on the original building plots were of two types: those of the well-to-do, generally detached and occupied mainly by farmers who owned land near the town—and those rented or owned by humble artisans and shopkeepers, crowded together in the terraced town-house manner and of very simple construction.

One of the earliest of the larger houses fourth-third centuries B.C.) is the HOUSE OF THE SURGEON (*Casa del Chirurgo*) near the Porta di Ercolano. The building materials are of the simplest kind, rough rubble and clay walls supported by massive limestone blocks. Only the façade is embellished with ashlar masonry. The floors are of beaten earth and the interior walls covered with plaster and decorated with a simple colour wash. It was in this house that there was found a remarkably varied selection of surgical instruments, which now form a fascinating exhibit in the Naples Museum. In plan the house is basically very simple with rooms grouped around an open *atrium* and consists of a vestibule, living rooms, two *alae*, a postern, a *tablinum* and a garden. Yet it is an interesting building since it probably derives directly from the Etruscan plan of a house. The Etruscans had borrowed and developed the idea from a primitive type of farm-house which they had found among the Italic tribes.

It is a far cry, indeed a jump of about two centuries, from the last described to the great town houses of Pompeii—such as the House of

Pansa, the House of the Vettii, the House of the Faun, or the House of Menander.

The House of Pansa was one of the most magnificent of all the houses of Pompeii, occupying, with its garden, an entire *insula* (building plot, or block). Built in the Samnite period for a single family, regrettably nothing remains of its decoration. It consisted of a vestibule, an atrium, and *impluvium* (to catch rain-water) two *alae*, a postern, *tablinum*, and a spacious peristyle—with the main living rooms overlooking it. The most notable addition here is the peristyle which became a feature of houses at Pompeii in the second and first centuries B.C. and well into imperial times. The idea of the peristyle (a courtyard surrounded by a colonnade) might have come from Sicily or the Middle East, but it is quite likely that the Etruscans had already adopted the idea (if we are to believe Diodorus). It certainly provided a measure of privacy and quiet after the more excitable meetings and gatherings in the atrium which formed the traditional main reception hall for the *pater familias*. Often a *triclinium* (dining room) led directly off the peristyle area and this was so in the Casa di Pansa. It is very interesting too that the outer shell of this house, on two sides consisted of shops.

The HOUSE OF THE VETTII with its splendid murals and beautifully laid out gardens, well illustrates the luxury in which the commerical classes lived during the last decades of the city's life. The Vettii brothers were dealers in agricultural produce, and a series of paintings in a room in the Casa shows Cupids gathering grapes and pressing them and buying and selling wine. Another painting shows olives being crushed to make oil. The house is a rich museum of 'Fourth-style' wall paintings. The rooms which offer the finest examples of this style are the sumptuous *triclinium* and the rooms which open onto the peristyle on either side of the atrium entrance; these belong to the luxurious type of reception room, known as *oeci*.

In general the colouring of these Pompeian paintings, whether on site or in the Museum of Naples, is wonderfully fresh and vivid. I am thinking in particular of the marvellous 'Courtship of Venus and Mars' (now detached and moved to Naples) from the House of Marcus Lucretius Fronto, and two delightful scenes from nature 'Heron in a Garden' and in the same house 'Birds' showing a raven and a magpie, the one perched on an elegant vase, the other on a balustrade.

The HOUSE OF THE FAUN is named after the delightful little bronze of the dancing faun that decorated one of the *impluvium* tanks (original in Naples, copy on site). The splendour and size of this house leaves little doubt that it is one of the finest examples of a private dwelling to have survived from antiquity. There are good reasons to believe that it was once the residence of P. Sulla, L. Sulla's nephew, who had responsibility for the reorganization of the first Roman colony. It was in this house that the great mosaic 'The Battle of Issus, with Alexander and Darius' was found, (see Chapter 1 under Naples Museum) and other most valuable mosaics. The house covers the area of an entire *insula*. Not content with one atrium and one peristyle the owner decided on two of each, and the plan of the house is very ambitious.

The HOUSE OF MENANDER is a magnificent residence, named after a portrait of the poet Menander which was found here. In addition a great hoard of silver was discovered and now is exhibited in the Naples Museum. Actually to use the word 'hoard' is not really accurate, since at the time of the 79 disaster the house was being renovated and the wealthy owner had deposited his splendid silver dinner service in a chest in the cellar. The superbly carved and embossed plates, jugs, *canthari*, bowls, dishes and trays, numbering in all 115 pieces, are now in the Naples Museum. There are some very colourful murals *in situ*; for instance the beautiful *atrium* is richly decorated in the Second Pompeian style, a splendid geometrical combination of deep Pompeian red with old-gold borders, with 'pilaster strips' of hard pure white or deep black sandwiched between, and only a feather-light touch of additional decoration.

It is not possible to conclude this short account of some of the major houses at Pompeii without mentioning the really remarkable VILLA OF THE MYSTERIES (*Villa dei Misteri*) excavated in 1909. The villa was built solely as a suburban residence, but it lies only a few hundred yards from the Porta Ercolano. Its present ruins show how large the villa had become at the time of its devastation, but in fact what we see now is the culmination of many additions and improvements from the third century B.C. Between A.D. 14 and 63, a large rustic wing was added to house domestics and agricultural slaves, but the work could only just have been completed before the earthquake. The patrician family who owned it then sold up, and it passed into the hands of a freedman named L. Istacidius Zosimus who proceeded to make plans to convert it into an agricultural factory, making drastic alterations with complete disregard for existing decoration. In the circumstances, we are very fortunate to find in an excellent state of preservation the famous series of wall-paintings which were discovered in a room off the original portico.

There has been a great deal of comment about these paintings, but it is now generally accepted that the existence of them did not mean that secret and mysterious rites were actually performed in the villa. Probably the room concerned and the adjoining one, formed the private apartments of the master and mistress of the house, and the paintings suited their personal taste—or more likely that of the *domina*. She appears to have been a lady of enlightened artistic tastes, for the whole villa was decorated with great elegance. Whether or not she was also an initiate and priestess of Dionysius, as insisted by Maiuri, cannot be proved, but it is certain that the paintings on the walls of her salon show a sequence in the initiation of brides in the Dionysiac mysteries. These mysteries were imported into Rome from Etruria and Campania and in spite of the grave sanctions of the Senate, they were widely practised. The paintings themselves are strikingly colourful and the work of an artist of genius.

There are an enormous number of scratched inscriptions (*graffiti*) on the walls of Pompeii which bring to life the doomed city in a very remarkable way. For the most part the inscriptions were scratched with a sharp instrument, but sometimes scrawled in charcoal or red chalk. In many cases they had to do with the election of officials to the city council, supporting the candidate of the particular guild or individual concerned, and they are of extraordinary interest since they allow us a lively reconstruction of day-to-day existence in Pompeii. We hear from farmers, mule drivers, carpenters, fishermen, bakers, barbers, fullers, shoemakers, jewellers and many more. The *graffiti* also help us to see Pompeii as not unlike a typical holiday resort today, with a limited population of its own which increased enormously during the season. Sometimes the inscriptions are accompanied by rough and ready pictures—or there are pictures on their own, and these too are of the greatest interest. A fresco on the walls of the *Macellum* shows cupids as millers celebrating the festival of Vesta, their patron. There is a mill in the background (a somewhat primitive affair) and the workers have decked out the donkeys with wreaths. Baking was almost certainly the most extensive industry in the city, although many private houses had ovens where bread or cakes could be baked; the commercial product invariably had the name of the baker stamped on every loaf, (carbonised loaves were found in the ovens by the excavators and are now in the Naples Museum). We know from the excavations that inns (*hospitia*) were common and that eating houses and hot-drink shops (roughly equivalent to our snack-bars) were very popular. The latter were called *Thermopolia* and probably served mainly stews kept in hot jars. The people who used these establishments were mainly commercial travellers, and other itinerants such as gladiators. Some of the *graffiti* on the walls of these places are far from complimentary: One client wrote 'Talia te fallant utinam mendacia copo, tu vendes acquam et bibes ipse merum'—'curses on you landlord; you sell water [for wine] and drink unmixed wine yourself'.

In addition to the above examples of *graffiti* in Pompeii, there are many other instances of the mainly amateurish work of porters, coppersmiths, surveyors, shoe-pedlars, tenant farmers, professional ball-players, and of course, lovers. An example of the lofty sentiments of one of these last reads, 'Whoever loves, long may he live; but perish who knows not how to love; whoever forbids loving, let him die twice.' But in the main the *graffiti* are light-hearted, apparently written by young people of the poorer classes who only occasionally let melancholy interrupt their natural gaiety. Typical of the general attitude are the words written by a *scriptor* (professional wall-writer) 'It is a wonder, O Wall, that thou hast not yet crumbled into ruin under the weight of so much written nonsense!'

Pompeii, like all Roman and Italian towns, was not deficient in brothels and the most notable of these is the two-storeyed Brothel of Africanus and Victor with interesting pictures and *graffiti*. It seems in one case that a gambling den and a brothel were combined in one establishment.

The open-air theatre which lies east of the triangular Forum is of great historical interest. It was built during the second century B.C. and thus shows that while Roman literature was still in its infancy, the culture and literary appreciation shown by the Samnites of Campania had reached a high level. (It is one of the extraordinary facts about the Pompeians that the standard of literacy was so high. Everybody could read and almost everybody seemed to write.) No manuscripts were found in Pompeii, but they were all probably destroyed by hot ashes. At Pompeii there is also a small covered theatre, dating from the beginning of the Roman colony, which specialized in musical recitals and mime shows.

The gladiatorial spectacles had just as fanatical a following in Pompeii as in other Roman cities and towns. Notices of the games were brought to the attention of the people by official proclamation, and there are more than 50 inscriptions at Pompeii, concerning the shows. More often than not the spectacle would be a free public show sponsored by a magistrate. Apart from the main attraction—the gladiatorial combats (fighting was on horseback as well as on foot), there were a number of supporting events such as fights against wild beasts, boxing-matches or gymnastics. However, the gory spectacle of the *bestiarii* in action was the most popular of the 'appetizer' events. Bulls, wild boars, stags and lions were slain. The amphitheatre where these spectacles occurred is of great historical interest, since it is the oldest stone amphitheatre known from either literary or archaelogical sources. It was built in 80 B.C. of very simple construction. A great hollow was excavated near the south-easterly corner of the town walls, the earth piled around the whole and retained by a wall buttressed by sturdy arches. It had a seating capacity of about 20,000, but it was more than a century before the seats were completed. The significance of this building is shown by the fact that it was not until 29 B.C. that the first stone amphitheatre was built in Rome.

In one sense a visit to HERCULANEUM is more satisfying than a visit to Pompeii, since one can get a far better idea of the original state of the houses. The reason for this is that whereas Pompeii was buried under a hail of pumice-stone and volcanic ash, Herculaneum was over-whelmed by a gigantic flow of volcanic mud that poured through every building and street and eventually filled and covered the entire site to a depth of 40 feet. Rather different in composition to the mud that formed the top-layer at Pompeii, this effluent finally set rock hard—into tufa in fact—and sealed and preserved almost everything that it contained. Thus we find at Herculaneum, in addition to the main stone-work and brick-work, important, load-bearing wood-work still intact, such as the frame-work of upper floors. Also, a great number of ordinary household goods are preserved: loaves, cakes, bowls of beans, a large amount of furniture such as beds, divans, etc., some even with their covers; and in one house sliding wooden doors blackened but almost intact. The mosaics too are in a better state of preservation than at Pompeii. It is pleasing to realise that practically the entire popu-lation escaped, since the town was spared the hail of pumice and hot ash, and the lava flow took time to arrive.

Naturally the very fact of the entombment of Herculaneum has made excavation difficult and lengthy. It has often been necessary to use power drills, and when one sees with what incredible care the houses have been opened up, it is easy to appreciate how slow the pro-cess must have been. Excavations which began in earnest in 1738 under Charles of Bourbon (the 'new' excavations began in 1927) are still being carried out, and indeed only a small part of the town has been uncovered, so that exciting discoveries are almost certain in the years ahead. In addition to the physical difficulties already explained, a large part of Herculaneum lies under the modern town of Resina, and so apart from the expense, there are obvious physical obstructions to rapid progress.

The name Herculaneum (in Greek Herakleion) is derived from its legendary foundation by Hercules—but in all likelihood the history of the town followed the same pattern as its neighbour Pompeii, 13 kilometres to the south-east; that is, it was originally an Oscan town which came under Etruscan and Greek influence, was conquered by the Samnites and finally fell to the Romans to become a *municipium*. But there are important differences between the two cities. Firstly, Herculaneum had no trade to speak of whereas Pompeii exported wine and a well-known fish sauce called *garum*. There is little sign of any commerical activity at Herculaneum except that an enormous quantity of fishing nets and other tackle were found; the town walls were at that time overlooking the sea, and there must have been an active local fishing industry. Secondly, it was a much smaller town than Pompeii, with only about 5,000 inhabitants. However to judge from the quality of many of the houses excavated and the style of living that is clearly indicated, the owners of these homes were properous gentlemen, probably many of them retired. There are other tell-tale signs, the streets do not have the deep wheel-ruts we see at Pompeii, nor the high stepping-stones to enable pedestrians to step clear of the mud and refuse. This could mean that commercial street traffic was completely banned in the town (as we know it was in at least one street, the Decumanus Maximus) or more likely, that trade was so slight that there was no need for intensive cartage as at Pompeii. This is borne out by the few workshops that have been discovered, which were for the manufacture of luxury goods, presumably for local consumption.

Not all the houses at Herculaneum are in the luxury class, of course, the homes of the artisans and shopkeepers clustered near the *Palaestra* are of the apartment block or tenement type, but undoubtedly it is the houses of the rich which are of the greatest interest to us as we explore the ruins.

Easily the most desirable area for these luxury homes was the edge of the promontory overlooking the ocean, where the terraces have been designed and the gardens landscaped to make the most of the sea-view. It is in this corner that we find the House of the Relief of Telephus, the House of the Gem and the Houses of the Mosaic Atrium and of the Deer, all planned to take full advantage of their high position on the walls. Today we can get little idea of the setting since the sea has retreated, and our imagination has to supply the deficiency.

The House of the Wooden Partition is wonderfully well preserved, and here we can see one of the most complete examples of a private residence in either Herculaneum or Pompeii. The Partition itself is a screen of three double-leaved doors which closed off the *tablinum* and turned it into a separate room. The excavators have done a marvellous job at this house. On the upper floor a marble table-top is supported by a figure of the Phrygian god Attis, and other furniture can be seen including two beds.

In the House of the Bicentenary a very interesting discovery was made. In an upstairs room there is what appears to be a wooden cupboard, but closer inspection made the archaeologists think again for there are certain aspects of the piece which indicate that it is a primitive shrine, or even, it has been suggested, a *prie-dieu*. Lending support to this theory is the fact that above the spot in which it was found, a cross appears to have been inserted in the stucco, possibly a wooden one. If so, it is the earliest evidence of the form of the cross used in Christian worship that has yet been found. There is no reason to doubt the possibility of Christians in the locality at such an early date, for it is known that St. Paul made converts when he landed at Puteoli (Pozzuoli) on his way to Rome in the year 61.

Two bathing-complexes can be seen at Herculaneum: the Town Baths, with some very fine floor mosaics in the better preserved Women's section and the Suburban Baths outside the town walls. The latter are situated below the House of the Gem and the House of the Deer, and have recently been excavated, allowing us to see one of the best preserved bathing-establishments of the Flavian period. Light floods in from a skylight above four sturdy columns in the atrium-type hall, illuminating a fine bronze *herm* of Apollo from which water flowed into a marble bowl and then into the *impluvium*, with the effect of a fountain.

5.   Sorrento and the Costiera Amalfitana

About six kilometres along the coast from Castellammare one comes to the delightful small town of Vico Equense—an upper town and a sea-side resort at the base of the cliffs, where there is some shelter for small boats at the Marina di Equa. The views along the coast on either side from Vico Equense are very beautiful—in one direction the rising slopes of Monte Faito and the lovely sweep of the Bay, and in the other fine cliffs, abruptly cutting off the gentle slopes covered with thick green vegetation and foliage. At the water's edge Le Axidie Hotel is highly regarded, though unfortunately I cannot speak from personal experience.

Just a few kilometres further along the peninsular from Vico the town of SORRENTO stand high on a plateau about 300 feet above the sea surrounded by the plain of Sorrento, rich in orange and lemon groves and famous for its walnuts and fruits. The resort itself has acquired its fame mainly because of the mild climate especially in winter, and its beautiful situation. It was a favourite place—with Baiae and Capri—for wealthy Romans to build their seaside villas and its popularity is in no way diminished today. Among a very wide range of hotels and pensions there are a number that have retained a comfortable nineteenth century atmosphere. Certainly during the second half of that century it was extremely popular with visitors from northern Europe—and among well-known names there is a strong literary flavour. Ibsen came here from Ischia to finish *Peer Gynt*, and Nietzsche is known to have been a visitor. In the present century Maxim Gorky lived in a villa near Sorrento on the road to Massalubrense between 1924 and 1933.

In a building, the remains of which are now incorporated in the Albergo Imperiale Tramontano, the great poet Torquato Tasso was born in 1544, and today the main piazza in the town is named after him.

The name Sorrento (Surrentum of the Romans) is probably derived from an ancient reference to the sirens, who were believed to have lured sailors to their deaths from many points in the Bay of Naples. The town has a museum, a cathedral and one or two interesting churches, in particular S. Antonio and S. Francesco. The Museo Correale di Terranova is housed in an eighteenth-century palace and set among gardens with a very fine view. It has a varied collection of sculptures, porcelain and period furniture and several examples of inlaid woodwork, called *tarsia*, for which the district has long been famous.

The much rebuilt cathedral was originally constructed on the site of an ancient temple. The present building is mainly of the fifteenth century though the façade is modern Gothic.

One of the most interesting buildings in the town is the Sedile Dominova, one of two *sedili* where the nobility of Sorrento met to discuss official matters. Originally a fifteenth-century open loggia, its aspect has been changed by a majolica-tiled cupola added a couple of centuries later. It can be found where the Via S. Cesareo meets the Via Reginaldo Giuliani.

Sorrento is deservedly popular with visitors today; it has a marvellous climate, exceptional views and is very well placed for excursions. Naples, Capri, Castellammare, Vesuvius, Pompeii and Herculaneum can be reached comfortably in a day's outing, and there is no difficulty in arranging tours either at one's hotel or directly through a travel agent.

The shortest way of reaching the southern coast of the Sorrentine peninsular from Sorrento is via the small town of Meta, but the longer route (ss No. 145) leading out from the west end of the town takes in some glorious scenery as one climbs to a height of over 1500 feet near S. Agata a due Golfi. From here, spread out on either side, one has magnificent views over the Gulf of Naples and the Gulf of Salerno. The road then descends, links up with the road from Meta and with many a hair-pin bend hugs the coast as it approaches Positano from the west. This coastal road commands a view of mountains and sea that has been described as perhaps the most spectacular in the world. For the car-driver in the past this was a mixed blessing, for the twisting, precariously suspended road required the most concentrated attention. Now the road has been widened and improved in parts as far as Amalfi—though great care is still needed.

POSITANO is a small town of great charm and individuality. One is tempted to call it picturesque, which of course it is, but the epithet has lost its power to convey much more than picture-postcard prettiness, and Positano merits more than that. Apart from its splendid situation commanding wonderful views, the little town has character in abundance. For instance, the very way it has been built is extraordinary. Clustered tightly together, the colourful cubic buildings cling to the steep hill-sides in a dramatic manner, with many delightful terraced gardens standing in between. One only appreciates how steep these hills are when one has stayed for a while in the town and has exercised one's leg muscles on the many flights of *scalinatelle* (steps) that link the various levels.

The mood of Positano changes according to the season. Between the beginning of July and the end of September it is bulging with visitors many of whom have come to find a complete break among fishermen's families and to soak up the sun on tiny beaches littered with small boats. But of course the simple life is elusive during these months for all Positanese are then engaged in keeping their many visitors contented. A range of hotels from first category downwards, guarantee a wide slection. The small street that leads down to the beach from the municipal car-park is crammed with boutiques selling rather expensive casual wear, and overlooking the main beach the celebrated bar and restaurant, the Buca di Bacco meets the requirements of the more sophisticated visitor, as do some of the hotel restaurants. If one's ambition in life is to rub shoulders with the international jet-set, Positano in August is as good a place as any to make for. Moreover for the Italians themselves, it has become one of the smarter holiday resorts. Prices in the main season are high—though surprisingly good value can be had by taking a 'packaged' holiday such as offered by c.i.t.

Positano of course did not escape the ravages of pirates and Saracens. The forts so noticeable along this coast, were created more as a deterrent than an actual defence, and as watch-towers. One famous defeat of a Saracen attack is still celebrated annually by a mock battle—which takes place on the second Sunday in August. This spectacular affair is known as *Sbarco dei Saraceni*. The lights in the town are all extinguished and the attack is launched from the sea in a highly realistic manner with the aid of flares and maroons. Once the 'infidels' are seen to have been repulsed, hundreds of candles are lit on the flat roof-tops and terraces, the church bells peal triumphantly and the celebrations stretch far into the night.

John Steinbeck visited Positano not long after World War II, and he described his experiences in a lively article in *Harper's Bazaar* in 1953. Steinbeck appears to have got his historical facts from the owner of the hotel he visited, the celebrated *Sirenuse,* who was then the mayor. After describing the prosperous trade of Positano in the sixteenth and seventeenth centuries he wrote:

Then the large and beautiful baroque houses that stand against the mountain were still built and decorated with the loot of the world. About a hundred years ago a tragedy came to the town. Steamships began to ply the ocean. Positano could not compete; year by year it grew poorer and more desperate. At that time there were about

7   A street in the ancient hill-town of Caserta Vecchia, Campania

8 The castle of Ischia, with the town behind and Monte Epomeo in the background

9 A view of Positano on the lovely Amalfitan coast

eight thousand citizens. Between 1860 and 1870 about six thousand of the townsmen emigrated to America and the great houses stood vacant and their walls crumbled and the painted designs paled out and the roofs fell in. The population has never got much above two thousand since.

A few years ago I was fortunate enough to spend some time with friends who had rented a villa for the autumn in Positano, and I was doubly lucky in that it was just one of those baroque villas mentioned above by Steinbeck. Needless to say it was in good condition, for with the great increase in popularity of Positano during the last decade or so, many fine villas have been bought by foreigners as well as Italians and now command high prices both for sale and for letting. We were well over on the western part of the town at Fornillo and we had magnificent views across the Bay of Salerno, along the coast, and inland where the Monte S. Angelo a Tre Pizzi soars up in seemingly close proximity.

The suddenness with which the season ends in Positano is remarkable. The first two weeks of September still finds the beaches full, but by the end of the month the numbers have dwindled and by October they are almost empty. By then the boutiques have closed their shutters and the town reverts to a slower pace—as if going into winter hibernation to store energy for the onslaught that awaits it in the following season. It is then that one can best appreciate the real character of this delightful small town.

About four kilometres along the coast to the east from Positano, the headland of Capo Sottile juts far out into the ocean. There is an hotel at this point and it is a fine spot from which to see a Sorrentine sunset with land, sea and sky reflecting all too briefly the marvellous colouring. Round the corner from here is the village of Praiano, and a few kilometres further on, after passing the entrance to the Grotta di Smeraldo (at the Ristorante La Conca Azzurra), the coastal road continues with wonderful views until at last AMALFI is sighted, piled high up the sides of seemingly sheer cliffs. It is not until one has passed through the approach tunnel and reached the central parking area by the sea, that one can see how the town spreads itself in the valley formed by two steep hills and that much of it is on comparatively level ground.

The fame of Amalfi was at its height during the three centuries before its conquest by the Norman King Roger in 1131, when, as an independent republic, it was the strongest maritime power in the Mediterranean. Independence became possible after the defeat of the Lombard prince of Benevento in 786. The republic rapidly gained a reputation for trade and was fully capable of defending its merchant ships. Colonies of Amalfitan merchants became established in the ninth century at all important cities in the Levant, Constantinople, and Arab-occupied Palermo. At the height of its power Amalfi could boast the largest arsenal in the world, and cne can see today substantial remains of the ancient Arsenal of the Republic. The buildings make a very interesting comparison with the Seljuk shipyards in Alanya in Southern Turkey, and were constructed at about the same time—the beginning of the twelfth century.

The early Middle Ages saw the growth of rivalry amongst the cities of Pisa, Genoa, Venice, Amalfi and Gaeta. It is probably accurate to say that Amalfi came out on top. Her rules of fair trading set out in the *Tavole Amalfitane* became the recognised maritime laws of the Mediterranean, and remained so until 1570. Whether or not the town was the birth-place of Flavia Gioia, as is claimed, is a matter of dispute—and indeed it is not at all certain that this famous navigator ever existed. It is said that he invented the mariner's compass, but whatever the truth it is indisputable that sailors from this district were the first Europeans to use the lodestone at sea, early in the fourteenth century.

The trading successes of Amalfi ensured her enormous wealth. At the peak of her power the republic contained a population of some 70,000 but soon after the conquest by the Normans, the town and neighbouring territories were subjected to a savage attack by the Pisans. The town was sacked and its importance declined rapidly thereafter. In 1343 a large part of the town was destroyed by an inundation, and the harbour is now quite unimportant. Today it is a small town of between 5–6,000 inhabitants.

Unquestionably the most important monument in Amalfi is the CATHEDRAL CHURCH dedicated to ST. ANDREW. It dominates the Piazza del Duomo, containing the baroque fountain of S. Andrea, and towers above the surrounding buildings. The atrium is approached by a long flight of steps which accentuate the height of the façade and the splendid lofty central arch of Saracenic inspiration. Indeed the entire cathedral was rebuilt in the Norman-Saracenic style in 1203 and has been restored many times since. The whole façade was reconstructed at the end of the last century but fortunately the architect has remained faithful to the original. It is a very fine composition. The remains of the apostle St. Andrew lie in the crypt beneath the high altar—minus only the head, removed by Pope Pius II in the fifteenth century. A feature of the cathedral are the magnificent bronze doors donated by Pantaleone di Mauro Comite, a wealthy Amalfitan merchant in Constantinople and made in that city in the year 1066. Above, in the tympanum, there is a mosaic after the design of Domenico Morelli (1826–1901) showing 'Christ in Glory'.

The campanile that stands separate from the Duomo and slightly out of true is very handsome. It is older than the present church and dates from the eleventh century; it was the bell-tower to the original cathedral. The tower is crowned with a drum with four small turrets seated at the corners, and this unusual arrangment is accentuated by the colourful use of green and yellow tiles and interlacing blind arches. This might be though somewhat bizarre, but the overall effect is very pleasing.

The entrance to the CLOISTER OF PARADISE is at the left-hand side of the atrium. The light is rather poor in the cloister but it is immediately apparent that here is an architectural arrangement of unusual beauty. It is of purely Saracenic inspiration. Inter-laced arches rise steeply from slender columns and the result is both daring and very striking. Ancient and medieval sculptures have been disposed around the cloister, which was built in 1266, and was once used as a burial place.

The town possesses a small museum at the Municipio and here can be seen a copy of the famous *Tavole Amalfitane*. It is a late copy, probably of the fifteenth century, and was found in Austria, though there is little doubt that the laws and practices set out in this copy were current in the eleventh century.

Two of Amalfi's hotels, the Hotel Cappuccini and the Hotel Luna are of special interest since they are conversions of old monasteries. Each has a delightful cloister, cleverly incorporated in the hotel area, and visitors are welcomed. Both are hotels of the first category, and command superb views.

Proceeding eastward along the coast road, and having passed Atrani (an attractive little town with an interesting church—S. Salvatore de Bireto) a junction at the village of Castiglione leads up to the little town of RAVELLO perched high up on the hill. I suppose this hill-resort can claim to have one of the most beautiful panoramas in the world, taking in a generous range of the green clad Lattari mountains and a long stretch of the rugged coastline that dips steeply to the flat ocean and is dotted with villages, villas, watch-towers and terraced orchards and vineyards.

An explanation is required for the existence of a splendid cathedral and two fine villas that adorn this small resort. In the ninth century the town was subject to Amalfi and its prosperity grew with that of its protector. It was not saved from destruction by the Pisan attack in 1137, it had recovered its fortunes by the following century and is then thought to have had a population of 36,000 inhabitants. Wealthy merchants built themselves magnificent villas—the best known of which is the

Palazzo Rufolo. Parts of this building go back to the eleventh century, though mainly it is of the thirteenth. There is a strong Moorish flavour in the design of parts of the villa, no doubt influenced by contemporary fashion in Sicily. The gardens of the villa are beautifully kept and there is a very fine view eastwards along the coast from the terrace below the house.

Another villa which may be visited is the Villa Cimbrone, and in this case the gardens are more interesting than the house which has been reconstructed. The villa and grounds stand in a commanding position on the spur of the hill, and the views from the belvedere are exceptional.

The cathedral church of S. PANTALEONE is one of the most interesting in southern Italy. It possesses superb bronze doors by Barisanus of Trani (1179) and a very fine pulpit of coloured marble mosaic in the style made popular by the Cosmati marble workers. It was commissioned by Nicola Rufolo in 1272, and executed by Nicolo di Bartolomeo da Foggia. There are several notable pieces of carving and sculpture in the cathedral but it is rather alarming to see that the removal of some stucco has revealed great cracks in the masonry at the rear of the nave. A major and expensive piece of maintenance will be required.

To mention briefly the remaining resorts on the road to Salerno—Minori is quite small, but Maiori is becoming increasingly and deservedly popular; here the River Reginna, its banks walled in, flows through the centre of the town from the valley of the Tramonti, and a road with splendid views leads up through the mountains to the village of Corbara. Maiori has a good beach and is well placed for excursions.

Between Capo d'Orso and Vietri the road passes through the attractive little town of Cetara with its harbour in the evening crowded with fishing vessels. It is indeed fortunate that tourism has passed this village by, for here one can find the authentic flavour of an Amalfitan fishing village quite without sophistication, which not so long ago was the rule rather than the exception along this coast.

6. Salerno and La Cava: Paestum

SALERNO, the capital of the province named after it, is a city of contrasting styles and varying ages. The commercial district of the town remains as it was in the late nineteenth century; the area comprises the wide Via Roma just north of the Lungomare merging into the Corso G. Garibaldi—and the part to the east of Via Velia. Typically, here we see the grandiose ornate façades with their heavy balconies and oversize neo-classical columns, and here in the streets is all the congestion that one finds in an Italian town today. The modern quarter is built mainly on the hills lying to the north, and is undistinguished.

Fortunately Salerno also has an old quarter which is of great interest, for it reflects to a large degree the long, and at times hectic record of its past. There was probably an important settlement here in the eighth century B.C., though whether the town then, and later in Etruscan times, was at its present location is debatable. The city was called Salernum by the Romans, and praised by the poets for the beauty of its situation, but it was not until the Middle Ages that it became important, since then, for a long period it was the only port that the princes of Benevento possessed. After the break-up of the Duchy of Benevento in the ninth century, Salerno established itself as a separate state under its own Lombard princes. This state of independence lasted until the town was captured by Robert Guiscard, Duke of Apulia, in 1077, at a time when Gisulf, Prince of Salerno was the only ally remaining to Pope Gregory VII in South Italy.

Apart from its port, which was far more important relative to the town in the Middle Ages than it is today, Salerno gained stature from the fact that it possessed the most celebrated medical school known in the western world. St. Thomas Aquinas wrote that it was as pre-eminent in medicine as Bologna was in law, or Paris in theology and science. Even during the early Middle Ages the School was described as ancient, but it probably reached the height of its fame in the eleventh century when Constantine the African lectured there, using Latin translations of Arabic theories of medical science. The School's reputation was enhanced by the absence of racial discrimination, remark-

59

able for the times: so we hear of Jews and Arabs lecturing with the Western professors. Neither was there sex discrimination among pupils or staff, giving the School a secular flavour which must have been rare indeed in Italy in those times.

The old town is best reached from the centre of Salerno by way of the Via dei Mercanti which is an extension of the Corso Vittorio Emanuele, leading into the old quarter from the Piazza Portanova. Immediately, one enters another world with the strong light shut out from the narrow streets. One's attention is easily held by the interesting details of architecture in spite of the many distractions. Life is lived more intensely and colourfully in these old streets.

The first major intersection is the Via Duomo, and turning right here we soon reach, further up the hill, the most important monument in the town—the cathedral church of St. Matthew; it was founded in 845 and rebuilt by Robert Guiscard between 1076 and 1085, and consecrated in 1085 by Pope Gregory VII.

The best approach to the cathedral is up the balustraded steps and past the two crouching lions that flank this fine Romanesque doorway known as the Porta dei Leoni, (there is also a side entrance along the Via Roberto Guiscardo). One then enters a magnificently proportioned atrium, which is one of the glories of Romanesque architecture in the South of Italy. The wide open area is enclosed by a random yet splendid selection of classical columns, above which arches are formed in the Arabo-Sicilian style rising high off stilt-blocks. Above the sturdy construction of these arches there is a miniature arcade enclosing galleries and the effect is to give a special elegance to the whole. There are several Roman sarcophagi placed at wide intervals within the portico of the atrium, which were used in medieval times as the tombs of important personages. The fine twelfth century campanile stands separately from the cathedral.

A statue of St. Matthew by Matteo Bottiglieri (1733) greets us as we approach the main doorway of the cathedral and high up on the façade an inscription records that the church was built by Robert Guiscard at his own expense in honour of the patron of the city. The main portal is original and is richly decorated in the Romanesque manner, while the doors themselves were cast in Constantinople, slightly later, in 1099. Unfortunately the niello-work in silver which we have noted in doors of the Duomo at Amalfi is here missing. Just inside the entrance there is a fine thirteenth century mosaic showing a portrait of St. Matthew.

The inside of the cathedral will be a disappointment for those expecting a continuation of the Romanesque style so evident outside, and for this the severe damage caused by the earthquake of 1688 is largely to blame. The transept is now quite out of alignment and the floor rises to the east. The subsequent restoration has left a blanket of drabness over large areas; classical columns are now encased in massive piers, and the whole style of the interior is quite altered, though the overall proportions remain the same. I was interested to see however, that in many places the covering plaster and rubble have been chipped away to reveal tantalizing glimpses of the capitals or the fluting of the ancient columns. At the time of writing this work is only at a rough stage, and it will be interesting to see how far it can be extended. It does not seem likely due to the presumed instability caused by the earthquake, that there will be a restoration as complete as that undertaken in many great cathedrals in Apulia, but any relief from the monotony of the present overall style will be greatly welcomed.

There are several things of interest and beauty in the cathedral. Outstanding among them are the two beautiful ambones and a Paschal candlestick, all of the twelfth century, decorated in mosaic in the manner of the *marmorani Romani*—the Roman marble-workers of the twelfth and thirteenth centuries—yet containing typical Saracenic-Sicilian and Byzantine motifs. The two ambones are placed in the nave before the choir, which here has retained its original position in front of the high altar. A stairway leads from the choir to each pulpit. The larger of the two ambones, on the right, is supported by 12 granite columns, while the other rests on four columns of rare Oriental granite. It is interesting to compare these ambones with those at Amalfi and Ravello.

The east end of the cathedral terminates with three apses all containing either restored eleventh-century or modern mosaics. The chapel in the right-hand apse, decorated by Giovanni da Prócida, is also known as the Capella di Gregorio VII. Gregory's throne is known as the Cappella delle Crociate, because knights on their way to the East on crusade were blessed here. The tomb of Pope Gregory VII lies beneath the altar, and for this reason the chapel is placed in the middle of the central apse. It was used during the consecration of the cathedral in 1084.

A flight of steps off the right aisle (note the unusual Roman bas-relief of a ship unloading) leads to the crypt, almost a church in itself, profusely decorated in polychrome marble by Domenico Fontana in the style of Florentine mosaic. The vaulted ceiling frescoes by B. Corenzio are of about the same period—the early seventeenth century. The remains of St. Matthew lie beneath the main altar and are thought to have been brought here by Prince Gisulph in the year 954.

The cathedral museum (Museo del Duomo) contains some exhibits of outstanding interest and beauty and should not be missed. In particular here, we can see an altar-front (*paliotto*) consisting of 54 scenes from the Old and New Testaments carved in ivory. This remarkable work illustrates a variety of styles—Provençal, Byzantine, Arabo-Sicilian and typical Romanesque. A number of artists were involved, and the various pieces were probably originally bound together with silver. Artistically, the works are of no special merit but of extraordinary interest. It is easily the largest known work of its kind: even so it is incomplete since four other panels are in museums outside Italy. Other outstanding exhibits in the museum are an *Exultet* roll of great beauty with miniatures of the thirteenth century, a cross inlaid with gems—the gift of Robert Guiscard, and various religious paintings, one attributed to Roberto Oderisi, a follower of Giotto, which with another, the 'Coronation of the Virgin' by an unknown master of the fifteenth century, were brought here from Eboli.

On the opposite side of the cathedral to the Museo del Duomo the long frontage of the Bishop's Palace faces the southern flank of the Duomo, looking extraordinarily graceful now that it has been stripped of its superfluous accretions to reveal the thirteenth century arcading. Permission may be granted to enter and see the part that is now used as a study-room for old manuscripts—a *salone* of splendid proportions which is given added dignity by magnificent ancient columns from Paestum supporting the upper structure.

A visit to the Museo Provinciale in the Via San Benedetto, not far from the Duomo, is well worthwhile. It has only been open for a few years and is thus still at an active stage of development, but eventually it will occupy the whole site of the old Benedictine monastery. The museum building has been cleverly constructed to incorporate a few of the arches of the old Norman palace the Castelnuovo, built to replace the Lombard castle, the substantial ruins of which are a prominent landmark high up on a hill behind the town. The exhibits in the museum will grow in number as the important current excavations in the province progress, but this is inevitably a slow process. One of the treasures of the museum is a splendid bronze head of Apollo which is of Greek workmanship of the first century B.C.

Although not notably well off for accommodation, Salerno has a selection of hotels in all categories, including a Jolly Hotel, and for those deciding to stay in the town there is a wide choice of excursions available: the Amalfitan coast, the mountain scenery of the interior, Pompeii, Herculaneum and Paestum are all within easy reach. Additionally, in the summer months, a boat leaves daily for Capri, with incomparable views to landward of fishing villages and hill-towns, and the mountains that form the Sorrentine peninsular. Yet nearer than all of these is the small town of Cava de' Tirreni, and the nearby Benedictine abbey of Trinita della Cava which achieved the pinnacle of its fame during the second half of the eleventh century, when the influence of Desiderius, Abbot of Montecassino, was at its height. A visit to the La Cava is stimulating both visually and aesthetically, since the monastery is set in beautiful countryside.

To reach the abbey it is preferrable to have the use of a car, but in fact there is a bus connection between Cava de' Tirreni and the small village of Corpo di Cava, where the abbey is situated, and public transport between Salerno and Cava de' Tirreni is frequent.

The town of Cava itself is attractive and has a distinct air of prosperity. It has long been so, for in the eleventh century when the town was ceded to the abbots of La Cava by the Lombard Prince Gisulph II, the town carried on a prosperous trade in silk via the port of Vietri, which was free of customs duties. Nowadays the wealth derives from the large number of summer visitors attracted by the lovely countryside and the excellent sporting facilities. Architecturally the town has considerable charm, in particular the main street, the Corso Italia, with its elegant deep porticoes and balconies, and a profusion of flowers and plants hanging from the arches or entwined in the railings overhead.

The abbey itself is about 3½ kilometres from Cava, and as the looping road climbs steadily so the views become more splendid, and one can see that the town of Cava and the main road passing through it are in a valley with mountains of over 3000 feet on either side. The village of Corpo di Cava and the abbey stand at a height of rather over 1250 feet. The village is pleasantly simple—rustic even—and it comes as a surprise to turn a corner in the small piazza and find the Albergo Scapolatiello. This ancient hostelry is now a most comfortable hotel, furnished with taste and style, where one can enjoy a magnificent view from the terrace while taking one's meal. The food is unpretentious and good, and the inn has a high reputation with Italians. It would make an ideal place to stay for those interested in exploring the lovely wooded hilly countryside surrounding it, though a car would be desirable for longer excursions. The prices are reasonable, especially outside the high season.

The abbey of Trinità della Cava rapidly achieved power and prestige after its foundation in 1011 by St. Alferius, a member of a noble Salernitan Lombard Family. Alferius, as a young man came under the influence of a monk from Cluny, St. Odillon, and in the course of time he retired from the world and lived in a cave near where the monastery buildings now stand and became renowned for his piety. Waimar III then gave him sufficient land to build and support a monastery, which flourished, and the monastic church was consecrated by Pope Urban II in 1092. After Montecassino, it became the most powerful and pre-

stigious monastery in Italy. Some idea of the huge following that this
Cluniac community had in the twelfth century is shown by the fact that
when the Benedictine monastery of Monreale was founded by King
William II of Sicily in 1176, the hundred monks that were spared to
colonize the new monastery came from La Cava. Nowadays the community is very small, considering the size of the monastic buildings, yet
the education of boys is still undertaken by the monks in addition to
their other duties.

The buildings of the monastery are almost landscaped into the side
of a valley, with a fast running stream 100 feet or so below, and they
overlook high wooded hills on the other side. It is a most peaceful spot.

A guide always accompanies visitors to the monastery, and he may
be summoned by a bell. Especially interesting is the thirteenth century
Little Cloister which lies off the chapter-house; many elements from
different styles combine here: Byzantine, Lombard, Romanesque and
Gothic, and the same can be said of the Capella del Crocifisso. In one
chapel there is a beautiful marble *paliotto* (altar-front) from the altar
consecrated by Pope Urban II in 1092.

The Museum, the Archives and the Library form notable parts of the
monastery, and of these the most important are the archives. There are
a vast number of items—some 40,000 parchment rolls and upward of
60,000 manuscripts on paper. Many of the Diplomas and Papal Bulls
relate to the early and medieval history of Italy. One of the diplomas,
dated 1120, with a golden seal, is from Roger II of Sicily granting to the
monastery several lands in Sicily together with some Saracen slaves.
Another, from Baldwin VI, King of Jerusalem, grants freedom of
navigation to the ships of the monastery; (the abbey's ships, with a
monk always as captain, were for many centuries prominent in the
Mediterranean, and made a substantial contribution to the wealth of
the monastery). A Lombard document of 792 is a deed of gift by which
a husband assigned a part of his property to his wife on the morning
after the wedding; (possibly this was a common practice). These precious collections make the abbey one of the most important
repositories of early medieval documents in Italy.

The Library contains much material of great value, including an
eighth century Visigothic Bible by the hand of the monk Danila, which
is a fine example of the decorative art of the period; the *Codex Legum
Langobardorum* dated 1004, containing a more complete digest of
Lombard law than any other in existence; a beautifully written quarto
manuscript of the Old and New Testaments after the reading of Vig-
ilius who was Bishop of Thopsus at the end of the fifth century; and an
eleventh century copy of the *De Temporibus* of the Venerable Bede.

Returning to Salerno gives us an opportunity of taking a closer look at the small town of Vietri sul Mare which is a centre of the ceramic industry. It is a pleasant town with lovely views towards the sea and the mountainous shores of the Sorrentine peninsular. Many shops and stalls along the roadside sell ware or colourful majolica tiles from the famous local workshops, and one of the factories has its entire façade covered with coloured glazed tiles in case anyone should doubt its function! There are some interesting individual houses with unusual stucco-work.

Spread out in a rough triangle contained by the Monti Picentini, the Monti Alburni and the Cilento mountains, the wide Piana del Sele is, as the name implies, watered by the broad and lazily flowing River Sele, and it was here at the mouth of the river, about 25 kilometres south-east of Salerno, that a group of Greek adventurers erected a Sanctuary in honour of the Argive Hera. As to when this event took place, and as to who was responsible, there is no knowing . . . but if we are of a romantic turn of mind, we can take the word of Strabo and believe that the leader was indeed Jason, leading the Argonauts, in which case the dedication was only fit and proper since Hera was the protectress of the Argonauts. We can come to other more prosaic conclusions, with a certain historical justification. Life had already flourished in pre-historic times on the left bank of the Sele—as proved by paleolithic and bronze-age objects excavated in recent years—and yet suddenly had died out. Then, at some time during the second millenium B.C. a group of merchant adventurers, probably from the Aegean seeking valuable metal ores, or in the course of general trading, had dropped anchor in the calm waters at the mouth of the Sele (ancient Silaris) and were the first to appreciate fully the great possibilities of the site as a trading post. They were followed by other sea-adventurers, including Greeks, but it was not until many centuries later that the idea was taken a stage further and a permanent settlement established at the mouth of the river (Foce del Sole) and full use made of the very fertile plain and varied surrounding countryside.

The mists of anitquity now begin to roll back, and we commence a period of some historical certainty. The new colonists came from Sybaris, on the Ionian shore, and settled in number during the first decades of the seventh century B.C., though some might have arrived as early as 700 B.C. The colonists were energetic and able, and transformed the settlement, so that by the second half of the seventh century the city of Poseidonia (known to us as Paestum) was well established, possessing a definite religious and political character. Whether the first colonists arrived with the idea of trade uppermost in their minds, whether it was a simple case of over-spill from the parent-city, or whether it was the result of political or religious differences among the Sybarites is not clear; but it is certain that by the first half of the sixth century Poseidonia was the most powerful of the Sybarite colonies, and during its golden age, from 560 to 440, it ranked high among the great trading cities of the Greek world. During much of that time it stood alone, since Sybaris was destroyed by Croton in 510 B.C. Not least of the reasons for this prosperity was the highly lucrative trade Poseidonia enjoyed with the Etruscans, who had moved into Campania in the sixth century and had become established over a wide area of the plain of Silaris on the right bank of the river. When the Estruscans were defeated by the Syracusans at Cumae and withdrew from this area, the void was filled by the Poseidonians who thereby greatly strengthened their position. It enabled them to substitute the products of the other cities on the Ionian Sea for those of Sybaris and to become the great trading link between the south and the Italic states and Etruria in the north.

Yet when the fall came it was sudden, for Poseidonia was conquered by the Lucanians in about 400 B.C., and its name was changed to Paiston, thought to be very close to the name of the pre-Sybarite settlement. Little is known of the period of a century and a quarter that followed, before the Romans forced Paiston out of the Lucanian federation in 273 B.C., except that it was a flourishing city, almost certainly due to trade. In July 1969 a farmer uncovered the limestone roof of a Lucanian tomb that contained frescoes in the early classical style (now removed to the excellent modern museum), and a vast acropolis of painted tombs was subsequently discovered only a few hundred yards outside the walls. It is almost certain that immensely important archaeological finds will result as the acropoleis of Paestum are systematically excavated in the years to come. Already there have been rich discoveries of household objects and treasures.

Under the Romans, Paestum (as it was re-named) developed strongly: baths, a Forum (probably constructed over the Greek Agora), additional temples and an amphitheatre were built, while housing development, though important, was more in the nature of rebuilding and restricted to the area enclosed by the Lucanian/Greek walls. Paestum remained loyal to Rome even under the stress of the Punic Wars when most Lucanian cities deserted her, and in return the Romans bestowed privileges on the city, one of which was the right to coin its own bronze money—at least until the times of Tiberius. The economic decline of the Roman Empire saw the end also of Paestum as an important city. The authorities could not afford the costly maintenance of continuous drainage, and the river Salso which passes close by silted up and caused widespread flooding; the fertile plains of old became a marsh, and malaria threatened to wipe out the population. A small Christian community clustered in dwellings around the church somehow survived, but in the ninth century A.D. they were driven into the hills by Saracen raids and settled at Capaccio Vecchio, taking with them the cult of St. Maria del Granato. And even to this day the locally venerated image of the Virgin Mary holds in her hand a pomegranate, just as Hera did at the dawn of civilized life on the banks of the River Sele. In the eleventh century the Normans removed many of the columns and marbles for the rebuilding and decoration of the cathedral of Salerno and associated buildings, and the long centuries of the Middle Ages and the Renaissance found the once famous city forgotten by the world of learning.

It was not until the seventeenth century that the name of Paestum re-appeared in Neapolitan literature (a lone scholar, the Neapolitan humanist Pietro Summonte had mentioned it in 1524). By the middle of the eighteenth century drawings and prints of the Paestum monuments began to appear and to attract enterprising and daring travellers to cross the malarial swamps by way of the state road (now the ss 18) that Charles III had built in order to study the temples. The French architect Soufflot (1750) followed in the footsteps of the Neapolitan Gioffredo (1746), and the splendid work of Saint-Non drew the attention of scholars all over Europe, including that of Wincklemann. The most famous of the early travellers from Northern Europe was Goethe who was overwhelmed by the impact of the great Doric temples: 'I found myself . . . thanking my guardian angel for having allowed me to see these well-preserved remains with my own eyes. Reproductions give a false impression . . . It is only by walking through them and round them that one can attune one's life to theirs and experience the emotional effect which the architect intended.'

One can reach Paestum either from the inland main road ss 18, or the Autostrada del Sole that links with it near Battipaglia. Another and more direct route is to take the coast road that hugs the shore of the Gulf of Salerno and crosses the River Sele very close to the scanty remains of the Sanctuary of the Argive Hera, a few hundred metres inland. All the valuable scupltures found here have been removed to the museum at Paestum.

The coastal road is flanked for long dull stretches by extensive plantations of the Australian eucalyptus tree, planted presumably towards the end of the nineteenth century in a forlorn attempt to provide an antidote to the *malaria*. However they do serve to freshen the air, and to act as a wind-break, and must have made some contribution to the elimination of the swamps later drained properly to rid the area of the scourge of the anopheles mosquito. Along this road too one finds a large hotel complex well set back, and self-sufficient in every aspect—

especially the social and sports side—an independence which is becoming a distinct trend in the south. But it is disappointing to see what is happening at the Lido di Pesto; in the space of only five years the whole area surrounding the archaeological site has been developing into a tourist slum; hotel accommodation here must be in danger of seriously outstripping demand.

Fortunately when we reach the archaeological precincts the entire area is refreshingly free from commercialism. The main road passes through the ancient walls at Porta Aurea, the north gate, with three others at the east, the south and the west (Porta Sirena, Porta Giustizia, and Porta Marina). The walls are just short of five kilometres in length and excellently preserved in the main. The lower courses, the original Greek walls, are composed of huge blocks of squared limestone, with smaller blocks above where the Lucanians added to and, strengthened them. The arch of the Porta Sirena is splendidly preserved, as are some of the towers, such as the Laura Tower, that fortify parts of the wall. The main glories of Paestum are of course the three Greek temples that make a journey to the site one of the highlights of a visit to Italy. Of the three, the middle one, the Temple of Neptune, is considered to be the finest surviving example of Doric architecture either inside or outside Greece. The descriptions that follow though not intended for scholars of classical architecture, may be of interest to those readers who would like rather more information than is commonly given in the tourist brochures; these temples at Paestum are unique and deserve a proper appreciation.

The oldest of the temples is the building that is commonly known as the Basilica, an error that originated during the very early excavations when it was thought that the monument did not have sufficient religious presence to qualify as a temple, and must therefore be a profane public building. Perhaps also the fact that this Doric temple has an odd number of frontal columns (nine instead of the usual six or eight) contributed to this belief. Certainly it is highly unusual, almost unique, for a Greek temple to have an odd number of columns on the short sides and this, together with the fact that all the columns are closely positioned, and have broad capitals with the cushion (*echinus*) wide and compressed, helps to date this temple to an early period—around the middle of the sixth century B.C. There are 18 columns to each long side (including the two at the angles) and so the total does add up to an even number—50—a large number for a building that measures 24.50 by 54.30 metres. All the columns both of the outside colonnade (*peripteros*) and the *cella* have a marked *entasis*, that is, a swelling of the outline caused by the convex curves of the sides; the shafts taper by as much as a third from the lower diameter to the top. This is another sign of the early date of the temple. A feature, shared with the Temple of Ceres also at Paestum, otherwise unique among all Doric temples, is that the necks of the capitals above the fluting of the columns are decorated with beautiful designs of rosettes, lotus flowers and palmettes. The marked originality shown here by architects of the Western Greeks in Italy was later to be abandoned in favour of the designs produced by the perfectionists of fifth-century Greece, (as will be seen a little later when we describe the Temple of Neptune). The dedication of the 'Basilica' is not known with certainty, but it is the opinion of leading authorities that the temple was most probably dedicated to Hera in about the year 550 B.C.

Only 40 metres away rises the most famous temple at Paestum, and the best preserved Greek temple anywhere—the Temple of Neptune, or Poseidon, but probably also dedicated to Hera. However, before describing it, it is better perhaps to take the temples in chronological order, and take a look at the most northerly of the Paestum temples— the Temple of 'Ceres' which stands a considerable distance away (about 600 metres) from the other two. Although built only about 30 or 40 years later than the 'Basilica', the Temple of 'Ceres' is a considerably more refined building. For one thing the *entasis* of the column is much less marked; and the columns are more spaced out, there being six frontal and 13 side columns evenly spaced. The more subtle tapering and spacing of the Doric columns gives a lift and harmony to the whole, and make the columns appear more slender than in fact they are. It is easily the smallest of the three temples measuring 32.88 by 14.54 metres. The dedication to Ceres which has been accepted as a convenient label is almost certainly wrong; most likely it was to Athena.

Here again we find marked unconventionality; the *cella* was entered through a prostyle porch or pronaos, this being formed by four columns along the front and two at the sides, and the especially interesting point here is that the columns were of the Ionic order. Thus in this temple, for the first time in the history of Greek architecture, two different styles were intermingled. Nothing remains of the pronaos or *cella* except the bare foundations, but the place can easily be distinguished; however two of the Ionic capitals may be seen in the museum.

For the convenience I will retain here the traditional name given to the latest as well as the finest of the three great monuments of Paestum—the TEMPLE OF NEPTUNE. In fact it was almost certainly dedicated to Hera, and at least one leading Italian authority refers to it as Hera II, to distinguish it from the 'Basilica'. Yet in most publications it is still called the Temple of Neptune to avoid any confusion, which is perhaps sensible. There is little doubt that buried somewhere at Paestum or its environs there are the remains of an actual temple dedicated to Neptune (Poseidon) since the sea-god must have had this honour bestowed on him by the Greeks, having named their city after him. It is thought by some archaeologists that the temple may be found in the vicinity of the Porta Marina (large areas within the city walls have yet to be excavated) while others think that a likely place may be somewhere on the headland by Monte Tresino, near the small town of Agropoli, where sailors could have seen the temple and used it as a landmark when approaching from the south.

The first thing that strikes one about the Temple of Neptune is its wonderful state of preservation; the entire series of 36 Doric columns of the main colonnade and the metopal frieze are still standing, and the cornices are in a near-perfect state. The roof, of course, has gone, but the two pediments have only comparatively small portions missing. As a result the unity and grandeur of this marvellous building can be seen without any effort on the part of our imagination; and the inspiration of the unknown architect is at once communicated as we view it from various angles—from afar and from close up. It takes a little time to appreciate fully the subtleties and refinements of this building, but the time spent will be fully repaid, offering some of the most pleasurable moments of our entire visit to southern Italy.

The temple measures 24.26 by 59.98 metres (79½ by 196¾ feet) and is the largest of the Paestum temples. It is a Doric temple with six frontal and 14 side columns (including those at the angles) and is clearly much influenced by contemporary architecture in Greece. Like the Temple of Zeus at Olympia, begun in about 470, the Temple of Neptune has a porch and an *opisthodomus*, each with two columns *in antis*, and a *cella* with two rows of smaller Doric columns, seven in each, above which, on the architrave are mounted two further rows scaled down and tapered in proportion. In fact the similarity between the two temples is quite remarkable, though not total, since the Temple of Zeus is considerably larger and had only thirteen columns along the flanks. Moreover, in the Temple of Neptune the architect has shown his independence by increasing the fluting of the external columns to 24 (from the canonical 20) while the smaller columns of the *cella* have 20 and the upper columns 16. The 14 columns of the *cella* have all survived, but only ten of the small upper ones. The columns and pilasters of the pronaos and of the *opisthodomus* (at the front and rear ends of the *cella*) have survived in good condition. It would be interesting to know what personal contact, if any, the unknown local architect at Paestum had with Libon of Elis, the architect responsible for the Temple of Zeus; the two temples were almost exactly contemporary and overlapped in the course of building since 'Neptune'

10 The wonderfully preserved 5th century B.C. Greek temple of Poseidon at Paestum, near Salerno

11 Terracotta *acroterion* from Locri in the museum at Reggio di Calabria

12　Inside the Temple of Poseidon, Paestum, looking towards the mountains of Campania

was almost certainly started between the years 470 and 460 B.C. and finished between 450 and 440.

It is a matter of opinion which is the finer—the Temple of Concord at Agrigento, or that of Neptune at Paestum. My view now is that the latter takes the honours. It is noteworthy however, that some of the refinements seen in the Temple of Neptune, such as the narrowing of the spaces between the last two columns on the flanks at all four corners, were borrowed from Sicily. However other subtle details seen in the temple, such as the inward inclination of the end columns to compensate for the cumulative visual effect towards the corners, of the tapering shafts, spring not from any one source but from the ingenuity of the fifth century architects as a whole. Later these refinements were to be developed much further, as in the design of the Parthenon.

Another interesting comparison between Paestum and Agrigento is that both temples were built of local stone. Seen in the natural colours of the stone, their appearance now is very different from their original aspect, when the stone-work would have had a veneer of stucco comprising finely crushed marble and plaster, and the whole would have been painted. The designs are entirely lost, though some of the pointed terracotta ornamentation from the façade and from the frieze of Temple Hera I (the 'Basilica') has survived and can be seen in the museum. The museum also contains clever mock-ups of pediments and friezes colourfully painted and incorporating original material.

Between the early decades and the end of the sixth century, magnificent works were found at the site—a statue of Zeus, a female bust with swastika decoration, a terracotta of Europa astride a bull, and a very fine fragment of a female head in marble—and all these can be seen in the museum. The latter is modern, very well designed and laid out, and should not be missed on any account. It contains several priceless paintings from Greek and Lucanian times, as well as a wealth of good Roman sculpture, including some excellent copies of Greek originals by masters such as Praxiteles and Lysippus. The discovery of the Greek paintings in the Tomb of the Diver in 1968 created a sensation, and they are still considered to be some of the most celebrated paintings of antiquity, though in themselves not great works of art. The fact is that particular interest has been shown in these since practically no Greek paintings on flat surfaces have survived—all the more regrettable since it was an art form at which the Greeks excelled.

There are many other fascinating sites to explore in the archaeological zone and there are surely, few more beautiful places in which to potter around classical ruins, the site itself pleasantly planted with shrubs and trees, the backdrop formed by the lovely Cilento mountains and the distant Monti Alburni across the plain. The classical buildings or remains of greatest interest are: the underground *sacellum* (probably consecrated to the deities of fertility); the Forum—the Roman Temple of Peace of Imperial times; the Boulenterion, a place of assembly of the 4th century B.C.; the Gymnasium; two great swimming-pools (*piscenae*) constructed of large blocks of stone with floors of waterproof beaten clay, one only discovered in 1969; the Via Sacra and the Via Porta Marina, which cross at a point just south of the Forum; the Greek and Lucanian city walls; and finally, the Roman Amphitheatre, only half of which is excavated, since the modern road cuts across the archaeological site, and the extensive part to the east is as yet untouched.

7. The Hinterland of Campania

The Region of Campania is not small. Along its length, from the border with Lazio at the River Garigliano, to the town of Sapri 205 kilometres south-east, it takes in a sequence of alternate plains and mountains, and has a coastline, after Pozzuoli of great variety.

The beautiful and fast-developing coast between Agropoli and Sapri will be described in the next chapter, and here we will concentrate on the wide plain of the Volturno River which spreads out from the long gently curving coastline between Formia and Pozzuoli, and, among others, takes in at the foothills of the Appenines, the villages and towns of Sessa, Teano, Capua, Caserta and Nola. Also, far into the mountains, there is the interesting old city of Benevento which merits a visit.

Our first route will be along the State road 7 *bis* to Aversa. Anyone who has followed the fortunes of the Normans in the South of Italy in the second decade of the second millenium of our era, will know that it was at Aversa that the Normans made their first substantial territorial gains, and the town became an entrepôt for Norman adventurers seeking their fortune in the South. The country was assigned to the Norman leader Rainulf by the Duke of Naples, Sergius IV, in the year 1030, in return for his alliance against Pandulf IV, the Lombard prince of Capua. This act speaks volumes for the determination and ferocity of the small band of Norman warriors, whose fighting skills especially from the stirrup, and general horsemanship, were in a different class to that of their contemporaries. Their efforts in hostile surroundings enabled them to carve out a dukedom for their leader Robert Guiscard by the year 1057—which his nephew Count Roger II was able to raise to the stature of a kingdom in 1130; this, the kingdom of Sicily, became arguably, the most powerful state in the western world, and it included, with the exception of Benevento, all the territories of Sicily, Campania, Apulia, Calabria, Molise and Abruzzo.

The Cathedral of Aversa, dedicated to St. Paul, is a fine building, originally the inspiration of Count Richard I, and was begun in 1053. Disappointingly, of the original Norman work only the eastern part has survived due to damage by earthquake and fire, but what remains is attractive and interesting and illustrates the usual diversity of styles found in typical early Norman buildings in Italy. There are other interesting churches in Aversa, such as the Annunciata with many fine paintings and works of art, and the small fourteenth century church of S. Maria a Piazza which contains some beautiful early frescoes, probably by Andrea Vanni and his pupils. The castle which Count Rainulf built was destroyed by an earthquake and the one we see is a rebuilding on the same site by Alfonso I of Aragon.

It is no great distance from Aversa to Caserta, about 18 kilometres by the shortest route. This town is now the capital of the province of Terra di Lavoro, and achieved a dramatic leap in status—from that of a small country village to a royal town—when in 1752 King Charles III of Bourbon chose this spot for his Royal Palace; it is this enormous building which gives fame to the place today.

At the outset Charles, who seldom did things by halves, decided that his new palace would rival Versailles in size and magnificence. To bring his ideas to fruition he appointed Luigi Vanvitelli, a Neapolitan, as chief architect. But in the end their plans proved to be too ambitious, and Vanvitelli's original design was never completed in its entirety, nor was the colossal building fully furnished as hoped. Even so the result is awe-inspiring. The palace has been called by Rudolf Wittkower 'the overwhelmingly impressive swan-song of the Italian baroque'—an apt description.

Vanvitelli was of Dutch extraction and this may help to explain his passion for geometrical neatness and precision. Orderliness is the key to the plan of the Royal Palace. Its size may be judged by its measurements—600 by 500 feet—containing a total of 1200 rooms. It is strictly rectangular in outline and has four large courtyards formed by the exact crossing of the internal sections. The entrance is a brilliant piece of architectural planning. The visitor on entering looks through an immensely long high monumental passage which cuts right through the building and allows a view of the lakes, lawns and gardens that extend for miles at the rear. Half-way along, at the crossing, one enters an octagonal vestibule, from which ascends at right angles, the largest ceremonial staircase in Italy—a single flight at first, which splits into two on reversing, and leads under a screen of three stately arches into a vaulted octagonal vestibule corresponding to the one below. From here doors lead into the State Rooms and into the chapel, the latter markedly similar to the one at Versailles. The State Rooms are sumptuously decorated as might be expected. The furnishings in the Appartamento vecchio, first inhabited in 1780, are in the style of Louis XV and XVI, and there are also most elegant examples of French furniture in the King's bedroom in the Appartamento nuovo (new apartment) and in Joachim Murat's room. The bedroom of Francois II is a really beautiful example of interior decoration in the grand style.

Vanvitelli was also responsible for the lay-out of the park, consisting of lawns, lakes, gardens, a waterfall and fountains, and woods which extend a great distance behind the palace. Water is a feature of the design of the gardens and had to be brought by tunnels and aqueducts all the way from Monte Taburno, a distance of 25 miles. The fountains were designed by Vanvitelli's son Carlo, who however was not responsible for the rather poor statues.

It is only a short run from Caserta to the delightful small hillside town of CASERTA VECCHIA, but without a car it is an awkward place to get to, since buses are very infrequent. However a special effort is well worthwhile. The town stands at a height of about 1360 feet, commands magnificent views across the Terra di Lavoro; and is in itself a place of extraordinary interest. Walking through its narrow streets one gets a real feel of a small medieval town. The reason Caserta Vecchia remains so unspoilt is that it has to a large extent been abandoned in the last two centuries for the favoured royal town on the plain below, so there remain untouched many ancient buildings both ecclesiastical and secular. The centre of attraction is the really fine cathedral of S. Michele that dominates the main square. It is of Norman inspiration, and was built between 1113 and 1153 by Bishop Rainulf and his successor Nicholas. The design of the building has a marked similarity to the Apulian-Romanesque cathedrals which adorn in such quantity the great plain of Apulia. It has a nave of majestic height from the sides of which slope away the roof-lines of the aisles; above an otherwise plain west façade, the gable is decorated with a blind arcade of interlacing arches and the motif is repeated at a lower level on the magnificent campanile. The projecting beasts above the three doorways, a bull, a centaur, and a horse are characteristically Apulian. The cupola above the crossing is exceptionally fine; it is octagonal in shape, and has interlocking blind arches and multi-coloured stone decoration such as can be seen in Sicily at the Cathedral of Monreale (exterior of the apse) completed about 30 years later.

The inside of the cathedral has been beautifully restored. The 18 columns of the nave are from an ancient classical site contrasting with the fine eighth-century pulpit. There are many things of interest in the church including some early carvings, and a fourteenth-century fresco of the Madonna and Child.

The thriving town of S. MARIA CAPUA VETERE takes its name from the basilican church of S. Maria Maggiore, which almost alone survived the devastation caused by the Saracens in A.D. 840. It is built on the site of ancient Capua, of Etruscan origin and Roman fame. (The modern town of Capua four kilometres to the north-west has quite different origins.)

The Roman remains at S. Maria Capua Vetere take the form of a colossal amphitheatre, a Mithraeum, and just outside the town on the road from Caserta, two well-preserved and very large Roman tombs, probably both of the second century A.D. The amphitheatre is a structure of enormous size, elliptical in plan and originally four stories high; it was built in travertine and brick by Augustus (exact date unknown), restored by Hadrian, embellished by Antonius Pius, and subsequently used as a quarry by diverse building contractors. Before the construction of the Colosseum it was the largest amphitheatre in Italy. The nearby Mithraeum, which is about ten minutes away on foot, is interesting. It consists of a vaulted underground chamber, with a lively painted representation on the end wall of Mithras killing the Bull. It is one of the best preserved Sanctuaries in existence dedicated to the Persian god Mithras.

The cathedral church of the Collegiata di S. Maria was originally built in the year 432 over Christian catacombs. In 787 the Lombard prince Arechi II added two outer naves so that the present church is very large. Unfortunately alterations and additions in the last few centuries have not added to the beauty of the interior, but for all that, it is an impressive building.

The small village of S. Prisco is only about a mile away from S. Maria Capua Vetere and the short detour is well worthwhile in order to see the chapel of S. Matrona which is in the church of S. Prisco. The chapel contains beautiful sixth-century mosaics which somehow escaped destruction by the Saracens.

Another diversion, of particular interest to those who enjoy medieval architecture, is the church of S. Angelo in Formis. It is situated in the village named after it to the north-west of Monte Tifata and only about six kilometres from S. Maria Capua Vetere going due north. S. Angelo is a most attractive eleventh century (1058–78) triple-apsed Romanesque church, built under the Normans but inspired by Desiderius' new church at Montecassino. The view from the back of the piazza in front of the church is splendid. The five almost pointed arches of the portico are supported by four solid columns on which are set carefully matched ancient Corinthian capitals. There are fragments in the colonnade that come from the temple of Diana Tifatina which was originally sited here. In 1072 Prince Richard of Capua formally gave the church and monastery to Abbot Desiderius of Montecassino, and the architrave of the portal bears an inscription to this effect. In the lunette there is a most colourful representation of St. Michael. There is little doubt that the architectural arrangement at S.

Angelo—the oriental-style arches with a high central arch, the decorative lunette over the doorway, the Basilican interior frescoed in the Byzantine style—was directly influenced by Abbot Desiderius' new church at Montecassino (we can see the influence too at Salerno, Ravello and Amalfi). In fact the style which is often known as Norman-Sicilian, and was indeed practised widely in Sicily in the twelfth century, had its origins at Montecassino under the great abbot a century earlier, and is faithfully reflected here at S. Angelo in Formis. Inside the church the walls of the nave are decorated with a magnificent display of frescoes by the Montecassino school showing scenes from the Old and New Testaments, and in the main apse, Christ enthroned with angels.

Modern Capua (as opposed to the ancient town) is a mere six kilometres from S.M. Capua Vetere on the main westward road, the ss No. 7. Actually it is early medieval in origin having been founded by the Lombard Count Lando in 856 as a place of refuge for those who had lost their homes when Old Capua was destroyed by the Saracens. It fits neatly into a loop of the river Volturno at a place where there are two bridges, one Roman and one modern. It was the original site of the Roman town of Casilinum. There are several interesting churches and non-ecclesiastical buildings in Capua, notably the church of S. Marcello Maggiore, originally ninth century rebuilt in the twelfth and subsequently restored on several occasions; the Palazzo Fieramasca; the church of the Annunciata in the main street (Corso Appio) originally of the thirteenth century, rebuilt in the Renaissance and baroque styles, and now completely restored after severe bomb damage; Frederick II's remarkable Capuan Gate—an intended imitation of Roman models; and the Arch of S. Eligio (thirteenth century). Northwards along the Via Duomo we reach the most important monument in the city, the cathedral church dedicated to St. Stephen and St. Agatha, and founded by Bishop Landulf I in 856, the same year as the founding of the town.

The Duomo suffered terrible damage from bombing in 1942 but has since been restored as nearly as possible to the original structure, thus removing most of the accretions of 1724 and 1850. Fortunately the beautiful campanile survived the bombing; it dates from the ninth century and incorporates fragments of classical and medieval marbles. One of the greatest treasures inside the church is a thirteenth century paschal candlestick of glorious workmanship; and there are further treasures in the sacristy: an Exultet with miniatures of the eleventh century, examples of Islamic crystal, and some very fine works of art in gold.

The visitor to Capua should try to make time if possible to visit the museum—the Museo Campano—which is far above average for a provincial museum. It is housed in the mainly fifteenth-century Palazzo Antignano, and is not very large, having about 30 rooms on two floors. Among precious objects that may be seen here are a selection of beautiful Etruscan bronzes, some Byzantine reliefs, a good collection of ceramics, and Roman mosaics of excellent quality, and Romanesque sculpture from Frederick II's Capuan Gate.

The town of BENEVENTO, archiepiscopal see and capital of Benevento province, is 62 kilometres from Naples, and may be reached by car along the pleasant route that takes in the small towns of Acerra, Arienzo and Monte-Sarchio, and which makes it way through the defile known as the Caudine Forks—traditionally held to have been the spot where the Romans were so humiliatingly defeated in 321 B.C. during the second Samnite War. Benevento has a population of about 60,000 largely supported by the marketing of agricultural produce, and by the manufacture of biscuits, chocolate, and the popular liqueur Strega (Benevento has a long tradition of involvement with the activities of *Streghe*—witches). It is also an important centre of communications for both road and rail.

Benevento is a very ancient town of either Oscan or Samnite origin, but it did not come into prominence until the period of Roman occupation. A Roman colony was planted there in 268 B.C. and it was then that the name of the place was changed to Beneventum from the inauspicious Maleventum of old. Fully appreciating its key position, the Romans developed the town and it became of strategic importance as a junction of the Via Appia and the Via Latina. At the time of the Emperor Trajan, the town was used as a starting point for the great military road, the Via Traiana, which extended to Brindisi in Apulia, and to commemorate this event the splendid Arch of Trajan was created in the year 114; it remains today in excellent condition in spite of earthquakes and the appalling destruction the town suffered from bombing during Hitler's War. Undoubtedly the town's most important period after the decline of the Romans was the long and remarkable Lombard rule of nearly 500 years from 591 until 1081, when it fell to the Normans. It was then immediately turned over to the Papacy, and with only one interruption (during the French occupation at the time of Napoleon) remained as a Papal State until the unification of Italy in 1860.

The major remains of the Roman period which can be seen today are the Arch of Trajan (just mentioned); the Theatre; and the Ponte Leproso which carried the Via Appia across the River Sabato. There are also some Roman relics, mainly inscriptions, in the Museo del Sannio. Trajan's Arch, closely derived from the Arch of Titus in Rome is a majestic monument, solid, sober and severely classical. Almost the entire surface is covered with well-executed reliefs of a symbolic and allegorical nature, the meaning of which is not always clear. The arch is made of local stone and faced with Parian marble. It is almost exactly contemporary with another splendid Trajan Arch, that of Ancona (A.D. 115) and although better preserved, lacks the latter's elegance and comparative simplicity.

The Roman theatre is sizable and in a fair state of preservation thanks to modern restoration, though in fact mush of the upper level is in a ruinous condition. It was built under the Emperor Hadrian but enlarged by Caracalla at around the year A.D. 210, enabling it to hold up to 20,000 spectators. The lower tier of seats has been renovated and the theatre is used for concerts and drama.

We are certainly fortunate that the Lombard epoch is represented by a monument of such outstanding interest as the Church of Santa Sofia. It was begun by Gisulph II and completed in 762 by Prince Arechi II. The front of the church is plain but very pleasing, with a subtle interplay of concentric convex and gently concave lines. The main blind arch over the beautiful thirteenth century doorway is carried by two almost matching antique Corinthian columns, the discrepancy brilliantly compensated for. The proportions of this façade are masterly.

The inside is surprising for the design is anything but simple. The ground-plan is part circular, centred on three round apses, and part stellar-pointed. In two of the apses there are remains of eighth-century frescoes. The drum is hexagonal, and is supported on rounded arches over an inner circle of six antique columns, and an outer circle of pillars—the whole connected with intricate vaulting to the main walls. The vaulting was under repair at the time of my visit—part of a major renovation—and I was not able to study the vaults in detail. However it is clear that this is a building of original and daring design, and it would be fascinating to know from where the architect drew his inspiration. A Roman model such as Constantia's mausoleum (A.D. 350) might have guided him; but in fact the arrangement at S. Sofia is far more ambitious and brings to mind the advanced ideas of Borromini, 900 years later.

The cloisters of S. Sofia are of extraordinary beauty. They were built much later than the church, in the middle of the twelfth century. Small rounded arches are raised high on slender columns in Moorish style, and cushioned by unusual trapeziform imposts. The Lombard carving of the imposts is of a very high order—imaginative and bold. It is interesting to compare this large cloister with that of Monreale in Sicily—another Benedictine monastery—though stylistically it is quite different. At Monreale the arches are pointed and the paired columns alternately decorated in polychrome mosaic, while at S. Sofia with one or two exceptions the single marble columns are plain and straight-shafted. Both are architectural works of distinction on a grand scale, and it is a joy at S. Sofia to wander round these peaceful garden cloisters and to study the carvings at leisure.

The old monastic buildings—the monastery once came under the authority of Montecassino—have been skilfully converted into the Museo di Sannio and display a varied collection of antique works, especially from the Samnite territories. An interesting relief shows a Samnite gladiator in action (first century B.C.) from Benevento. Other notable works include a Lombard golden cross of the seventh century, and a fourteenth century sculpture of the Madonna and Child—a charming piece by Nicola da Monteforte.

The Cathedral of Benevento was so badly damaged by Allied bombs that a complete reconstruction had to be carried out after the war, and in the circumstances a good job was done, though inevitably the interior is now lacking in character. Luckily considerable portions of the façade survived and the entire campanile, which is plain but handsomely proportioned. The cathedral was built in the thirteenth century, and the stylish façade is doubtless influenced by Pisan work, with blind arches rising high from ground level, above which are more deeply recessed arches with rose windows inserted in three of them. The famous bronze doors of the Duomo were so badly damaged in the raids that they have been placed in the rebuilt Archbishop's Palace which is to the left of the cathedral. The library in the Palace where the bronze doors are kept, also contains some beautiful specimens of manuscripts written in the Beneventan script, a well-rounded hand, vernacular in its origins (seventh century) but which developed at Montecassino to the level of calligraphy. It was widely admired and copied and remained popular until the thirteenth century.

The town of Avellino lies about 33 kilometres due south of Benevento and the road follows the valley of the River Sabato through attractive countryside. Avellino itself, the provincial capital, is of no great architectural interest having suffered much from earthquakes, but it enjoys a glorious position in the hollow of the mountains. The most interesting nearby place is the Abbey of Loreto just outside the village of Montevergine, which stands at a height of 1263 metres several kilometres distant from the abbey. The monastery was begun in 1119 on the site of a ruined temple and prospered under both the Norman and Angevin royal houses.

A town, one of the many in Italy, where piety and pageantry go hand-in-hand is Nola—just off the main road (No. 7 *bis*) and the autostrada (A.17) between Avellino and Naples. The occasion for this fiesta is the annual celebration of the return of St. Paulinus to Nola, after capture and imprisonment by the Goths in the fifth century. St. Paulinus, who became Bishop of Nola in 409, was converted when he visited the grave of St. Felix who was buried at Cimitile—the cemetery of Roman Nola. As a result he expended much time and energy as well as his private fortune on the building of a cathedral at Nola where the relics of St. Felix would rest, and also an aqueduct. His feast day on June 22nd is marked by a spectacular outburst of emotion and exuberance and takes the form of the 'Dance of the Lilies', the 'lilies' being in fact eight lofty wooden steeples. They are made locally and represent bunches of lilies to welcome their bishop home. Around these symbolic structures dance huge crowds of men and boys to the strains of a band, and the festivities terminate with the solemn procession of the silver statue of the saint from the cathedral, led by the bishop to the sound of the triumphant bells of the Duomo.

8. From Agrópoli to the Gulf of Policastro

There are three ways of reaching the Gulf of Policastro from the Naples/Salerno area: the fast route follows the Autostrada A3 through the Vallo di Diano as far as the Valle Noce—Maratea exit, where it joins the ss 585; a slower route passes through the beautiful mountainous countryside of the Cilento along the ss 18 and joins the coast about ten kilometres before Sapri; and the third follows the coast road, No. 287, shortly after leaving the environs of Paestum, and this has the advantages of taking in some beautiful small seaside towns and villages where facilities for tourists are now becoming available. In addition the coastal route allows one the opportunity of visiting the extremely interesting recent excavations of the ancient Greek city of Elea (modern Velia) without a major detour, since the road passes very close by. Unfortunately for much of its length the road winds and twists in a series of sharp bends, the surface is rough at times, and it is subject to landslides—but these disadvantages do not outweigh the pleasure of this route, provided one has ample time.

The first place of note is the small town of Agrópoli—Byzantine in origin—which stands on a promontory with views over the wide Plain of Sele. The town was vulnerable to Saracen and Corsair raids and suffered much. There are two beaches at Agrópoli and a small selection of hotels of the unpretentious kind. Fourteen kilometres further on, the attractive and popular seaside resort of S. Maria di Castellabate is fast developing, with camping, hotels and good bathing. High up on the hill overlooking the resort is the village of Castellabate which grew up around the castle, built in 1120 for the abbots of La Cava. As we have already seen the community developed a lucrative maritime trade in the Mediterranean. Here they operated from the small ports now known as S. Maria and S. Marco.

The road then cuts across a plain leaving Punta Licosa and its lighthouse about four kilometres to the west, before joining the coast again and passing through the fishing villages of Agnone, Acciaroli and Pioppi. All these have now become small resorts and the visitor is welcomed on entry and bidden farewell on exit, in four languages, as if to prove to the local tourist-board that they have not missed a trick here. The bathing conditions along this attractive stretch of coast are variable, but there are considerable stretches of sand near the Marina di Casal Velino for those who like a beach.

The ruins of the ancient Greek city of Elea are only about four kilometres from the last-named resort, lying just off the junction with ss 447 which comes in from the left. It is here that some of the most important excavations in Southern Italy in recent years have been carried out. Since 1962 enormous progress has been made and continuing work will bring to light many aspects of the life of the city as yet unknown. Elea or Hyele was a Phocaean foundation. The colonists arrived at this spot not directly from their mother-land in Ionia, but via Alalia in Corsica where they had settled in 560 B.C., maintaining close relations with their sister-colony at Massalia in the south of France. Rivalry with the Carthaginians and Etruscans led to war, and having been overwhelmingly defeated at sea they were obliged to quit Corsica and find another home. After a period of refuge in Rhegion (Reggio di Calabria) they moved north up the coast and discovering an easily defensible promontory at the mouth of the Alento river, founded their new city of Elea in 535 B.C. The colony flourished, mainly because of trade with Massalia, though it was never to achieve the prosperity or importance of its near neighbour Poseidonia. Indeed the fame of Elea was mainly due in ancient times to its school of philosophy—called the Eleatic School—which was in sympathy with the Pythagorean school in Croton. The founder of the Eleatic School was Parmenides and his work was carried on by Zeno, whom Aristotle called the inventor of dialectic.

We know very little at present of the early history of the colony, and although we have no evidence of wars with the Etruscans it is inconceivable that the Eleans were not engaged at some time. Etruscan power was at its height in the sixth century B.C. and their movement south into Campania had taken them as far as the banks of the River Silarus (Sele) as we have seen. In about 272 B.C. Elea became an ally of Rome, and after the Social Wars was made a *municipium*. It remained a place of some importance under the Romans (re-named Velia). It is almost certain that in Roman times it was more noted as a resort (it was visited by Cicero and Horace) rather than as a commercial centre, and indeed it was the shift in the direction of trade to the Adriatic ports, especially Brundisium (Brindisi) and the great network of roads that supplied them, that spelt the end of Velia as an important trading port, just as it did to Paestum. The parallel between the cities is even closer, since it was the silting up of the rivers Alento, and the smaller Fiumarella that finally sealed the fate of Velia, although we know it was still trading in Byzantine times. A medieval watch-tower was built over the remains of a Greek temple on the acropolis.

It has been stated by some academics that the site of Elea remained lost until it was re-discovered by the great French archaeologist and traveller Lenormant in 1883. However this does not fit the account that Crauford Tait Ramage gives of his visit to Velia in his book *The Nooks and By-Ways of Italy* (splendidly edited by Edith Clay and re-titled (1965) *Ramage in South Italy*). Ramage was travelling in 1828 and this is his account:

> I was curious to see what time and the more destructive hand of man had left of this once-famous city. I reached the ruined castle, now called Castellamare della Bruca, evidently a fortress of the middle ages, of considerable strength before the invention of gun-powder . . . The city was placed behind it, partly along the top of the ridge and partly in the plain below. The walls may be traced imper-fectly for a circumference of about two miles, constructed of large squared blocks of stone.

So it is clear that substantial remains were in evidence in his time, which to a classicist such as Ramage with a deep knowledge of the Greek civilization in Magna Graecia, was of extraordinary interest.

Present excavations are making great strides towards revealing the lay-out of the Greek city. At the time it was built—in the sixth and fol-lowing centuries B.C. the sea came far closer to the promontory on which the town was sited and there were two sea-gates, one to the north and one to the south which are now land-locked. The major walls of the city ran inland to a high point (Castellaccio) and then south to the sea. Not all have yet been excavated. The acropolis was at the high-est point to the west and overlooking the sea, and was thus in a natural defensible position. It was here that Ramage saw the medieval tower, and here archaeologists have revealed the foundations of an Ionic temple, possibly as early as the end of the sixth century B.C. However the most important find has been the recent discovery of the gateway known as the Porta Rosa, a key defensive point on the road which joined the north sea-gate—the road itself passing under another line of defensive walls running along the ridge. The Porta Rosa is in a mar-vellous state of preservation, having been most skilfully excavated and freed from the mass of earth and rock caused by landslides which have badly hindered further excavation works. It is a splendidly constructed gateway (with a relieving arch above the main one) and is proof that the voussoir arch on a monumental scale, was being built by the Greeks as early as the fifth century B.C. It is considered by experts to be the most remarkable gateway in Magna Graecia.

Other important finds at Velia are the remains of Hellenistic dwellings near the south sea-gate; traces of the agora; an archaic gateway of the sixth century; parts of the sacred area with small temples; a small Hellenistic temple (re-worked in the first century B.C.); the remains of a large fifth-century altar; and various *insulae* of the Roman period. There is little doubt that continuing work at the site holds out exciting prospects.

After Velia the road passes through the villages of Ascea and Pisciotta and both these places have their own marinas. This part of the route is especially beautiful. After the Stazione Pisciotta-Palinuro, a new road has been constructed which hugs the shore as far as Palinuro (No. 447r.) and saves a long and twisting route inland to Foria and back to the coast. This excellent road is continued after Palinuro as far as the Marina di Camerota (No. 562) and eventually links up with the main road to the south, ss 18, 2½ kilometres after the small resort and fishing village of Scário—the first village we come to on the actual Gulf of Policastro.

The stretch of coast just mentioned on either side of Palinuro, deserves a rather fuller description since it is clear that strenuous efforts are being made here to develop these parts into a major tourist area. There is no reason to doubt that these efforts will bear fruit; the whole of this coastline is studded with interesting caves, the bathing is good, communications are now first-rate and hotels (and a holiday-village) have been built. Two of the caves, the Grotta Azzurra and the Grotta dell' Arco are celebrated local attractions, the former near the end of the famous sickle-shaped point of Capo Palinuro. Ramage was taken by a fisherman to see the Grotta Azzurra, called then La Grotta degli Stucchi, and it is still necessary to bargain with a boatman to reach it, since it is inaccessible by land. The name Palinuro is retained from legendary times when it seems that the Cumaean Sibyl promised that the cape should eternally preserve the name of Aeneas' helmsman, Palinurus.

Important excavations near Palinuro in recent years have brought to light tombs dating from the sixth century B.C., which may not have been those of a Greek settlement but perhaps indigenous peoples who had come under Hellenistic influence.

Our route, having linked with the ss 18, runs along the northern shore of the Gulf of Policastro until it reaches the summer resort of Sapri, which in recent years has developed considerably and can now offer a wide range of hotels, pensions, and camping facilities. The resort possesses a long gently curving sandy beach for good family bathing. Once past Sapri we enter the Region of Basilicata which has a small portion of coast on the Tyrrhenian Sea (only about 20 kilometres) but the visitors to the small resorts included in this stretch, such as Rotondella, Aquafredda, Certusa, Fiumicello, Santa Venere, and the Marina di Maratea, must enjoy some of the most glorious views to be found along any stretch of coast in Italy. Beyond the gulf the mountains to the north rise in a long line, the distant ones a pale grey-blue, and those close up to the coast clearer and more colourful and soaring to a peak in the superb majestic form of Monte Bulgheria. The coastline too is attractive and interesting, with plenty of variety for those who wish to swim either under or over the water. The beaches tend to be on the small side, and the sand is usually grey, but the scenery is delightful. The hotels vary from modest family concerns to outright luxury—such as the Santavenere Hotel at Fiumicello, Maratea Porto.

The scenic attractions of this coast, the joys of swimming in its clear unpolluted sea and the big improvement in road communications is sure to mean a large increase in visitors in the coming years, and it is devoutly to be hoped that the authorities at Potenza will not allow these glorious shores to be spoilt by over-development as happened long ago on the almost equally attractive Costa Brava. The little port of Maratea, as far as I could judge from a short visit, it's quite unspoilt and has considerable charm. The more ancient town stands on the hillside above at a height of about 1000 feet.

Those who have travelled by the inland route will have seen the great range of mountains comprising the Lucanian Appenines which stretch far to the east. Regrettably the scope of this volume does not allow me to describe in any detail the wild and often most beautiful interior of the Basilicata (Lucania), nor to include a description of the two provincial capitals Potenza and Matera. The former, in any case is of very little aesthetic interest due to bombing and earthquakes, and it might well appear to be a modern city. However the Provincial Museum is interesting and there are adequate hotels. Some of the Lucanian mountain scenery is superb, such as Monte Sirino, over 6500 feet, near Lagonegro—and the truly majestic Pollino range which forms at the south of the Region the barrier between Basilicata and Calabria.

Part II
CALABRIA

9.   Cosenza and the Greek Sila

Cosenza is the capital of the northern of the three provinces of Calabria, and is a flourishing town, though it remains something of a mystery as to why this should be. Compared with the advantages that
Reggio di Calabria has—with its main-line railway link, the sea-port
and airport—it would not appear to have much to offer, but the fact
remains that whereas in recent years Reggio has remained static,
Cosenza has boomed. In 1965 the population was 82,000, but now
must be a great deal more. The development was particularly noticeable when recently I visited the town again after a gap of five years.
New suburbs are rising up fast and large, modern, well-run and comfortable hotels such as the second category Hotel Europa (just outside
the city at Roges) are being built. It is sensible to reserve rooms in
advance at such hotels.

The autostrada A3 passes very close to Cosenza, increasing its
importance as a centre of communications, but Cosenza's wealth
comes from being the market-place for the agricultural produce of the
highly fertile valley of the Crati, in which it is situated, and for the
uplands of the Sila. Naturally its importance is enhanced by its
administrative responsibilities as the provincial capital.

The part of the valley in which Cosenza stands is like a wide shallow
bowl, and the splendid mountains that surround it are far enough away
to give glorious views on all sides, and do not appear oppressive. The
placing of the city is at the confluence of the rivers Crati and Busento,
and it is on the southern side of the Busento that the older and more
interesting parts of the town are to be found.

The city has suffered extraordinary misfortunes during its che-
quered history. Once the chief city of the Brutii, the Saracens took the
town at least twice in the process of warring with the Byzantine Greeks
in the tenth century, and in 1050 it fell to Robert Guiscard but
remained the administrative centre of northern Calabria as it had been
three centuries earlier under the Lombards. In the last 200 years it has
suffered five major earthquakes and was the target of Allied bombs
during the preliminaries to the invasion of Southern Italy in 1943. But

the town has shrugged off misfortune, showing the same character and resilience as Messina, another southern city battered by fate.

The Duomo is an important monument from the Norman era. It was begun in 1185 in the Romanesque style, though completed in the Provencal Gothic style in the following century. At some later period the interior was baroqued, and although much of this decoration was removed in the restoration of 1947, the interior is disappointing. In the Archbishop's Palace behind the Duomo, is kept the cathedral's most precious treasure—the reliquary crucifix presented by Frederick II when he attended the consecration of the cathedral in 1222. It is a most beautiful gold cross in the Byzantine style, with miniatures painted on enamel at the four corners, and lettering in Greek, and may well have come from a Sicilian workshop.

The Norman castle (remodelled by Frederick II) is set high on a hill overlooking the old town. Beyond the Busento the modern suburbs of the newer town stretch into the distance. All around there are marvellous views. Gissing had called at Cosenza on his travels with a pagan pilgrimage in mind, for it was here that Alaric, King of the Visigoths died and was buried with the spoils of Rome deep in the bed of the Busento River, to frustrate all future treasure-seekers:

> Ever since the first boyish reading of Gibbon, my imagination has loved to play upon that scene of Alaric's death. Thinking to conquer Sicily, the Visigoth marched as far as the capital of the Brutii, those mountain tribes which Rome herself never really subdued; at Cosentia he fell sick and died. How often had I longed to see this river Busento, which the 'labour of a captive multitude' turned aside, that its flood might cover and conceal for all time the tomb of the Conqueror! I saw it in the light of sunrise, flowing amid low, brown, olive-planted hills . . . The Crati, which here has only just started upon its long seaward way from some glen of Sila, presents much the same appearance, the track which it has worn in flood being many times as broad as the actual current.

For those people who are touring Southern Italy today, Cosenza is a very convenient base for exploring the great plateau of the Sila, which is the outstanding physical feature of the upper half of Calabria. These days a great deal of attention is focused on the Sila as a tourist attraction, with every justification, for it is both unusual, and in parts incredibly beautiful. It is unusual because the scenery is quite different in character to the mountainous country to the north and to the south of it. The Sila consists of a great table-land of granite, measuring 65 kilometres from Corigliano in the north to Taverna in the south, and 38 kilometres east to west from Savelli to Spezzano—these distances being as the crow flies and certainly not as the donkey walks. While it is roughly correct to call the Sila a table-land, 'highlands' would perhaps be a better description, since the Sila does have several peaks of which Botte Donato at 1929 metres (c. 6500 feet), Monte Gariglione, 1765 metres, and Montenero 1881 metres, are some of the highest. The fact that the rock is granite makes a considerable difference to the topography since this rock holds water well, unlike the porous limestone of the Appenines. Thus from time immemorial the Sila has been famous for its forests and in particular the magnificent Sila pine, and its timber has stacked the ship-building yards of the Greeks, the Romans, the Byzantine Greeks, the Normans, the Hohenstaufens, the Spaniards, the French and the Bourbons. In addition the felling of timber by German merchants took place on an enormous scale at the end of the nineteenth century—to the despair of Norman Douglas. So it is not surprising that the impenetrable forests have vanished and with them too the bears, the brigands and most of the wolves that made the Sila a place to be feared rather than admired.

It was not long ago, at the turn of the century in fact, that wolves were a serious menace. Norman Douglas wrote in *Old Calabria* 'They tell me that there is a government reward for every wolf killed, but it is seldom paid; who ever has the good fortune to kill one of these beasts carries the skin as proof of his prowess from door to door, and receives a small present everywhere—half a franc, or a cheese, or a glass of wine.'

In the admirable *Handbook for Travellers in Southern Italy* (John Murray 1853) Octavian Blewitt observes:

Eastward of Cosenza, beyond the dense cluster of villages which cover the hills on the right bank of the Crati is the vast tract of mountain and table land still called by the ancient name of *Sila*. This remarkable tract is less known and explored by travellers than any mountain district in the south of Europe ... Many of the higher peaks of La Sila are covered with perpetual snow. The upper range of hills is clothed with impenetrable forests of firs; the lower ranges abound in oaks, beeches and elms, and present a succession of rich pastoral plains intersected by beautiful ravines and watered by copious streams. These table lands are used by the agriculturists of the south as the summer pastorage of their flocks. At the breaking up of winter not only the shepherds but many of the landed proprietors themselves remove to La Sila from all the neighbouring towns.

I have quoted the above passage at length not only because of its admirable description of the area, but because it makes an interesting comparison with conditions today, a century and a quarter later. We know now that the climate on the Sila has changed. This must be due to deforestation, for there is no longer perpetual snow on the peaks, and now the streams are not nearly so evident. Clearly, in the middle of the last century it was both colder and wetter, which must have been due to the presence of the great forests that would not long remain a feature of the Sila. Today really substantial progress has been made to re-forest the land, and re-afforestation schemes have full regional and governmental backing. It will be interesting in a decade's time to compare the rainfall in 1946 with that of 1986, by which time many of the post-war plantations will be reaching maturity, or at least have attained substantial growth.

The Sila is divided into three areas, namely Sila Greca in the north, Sila Grande in the middle, and Sila Piccola in the south, and it is mainly the Sila Greca which will be described in this chapter though the road we will take to reach it traverses the Sila Grande. Actually the name Greek Sila is probably a case of misinterpretation in distant times, since it was probably thought that the language spoken by the foreigners inhabiting the small towns such as San Demetrio Corone, Spezzano and S. Sofia d'Epiro was Greek. It was an understandable error since most of the immigrants from the East had indeed been Greeks, and the fact that the language spoken was Albanian made it no more intelligible. Moreover when it was discovered that the newcomers practised the Greek rites of the Catholic church, that settled the matter—they were Greeks; and among the more isolated villages I am sure that this is the view still held. (To complicate matters there is a town of more substance on the edge of the Sila Greca—Rossano—which has been strongly associated with Greeks, in this case the Byzantines.) An explanation as to why the Albanian colonies became established in the Sila (and in Sicily) will be given a little later.

The road we will take from Cosenza to bring us up to the Sila passes through the small town of Spezzano della Sila (to distinguish it from Spezzano Albanese on the northern fringe of the Sila Greca) and along the whole of this route one enjoys magnificent scenery. The pleasure is increased by the splendid driving conditions of the super-highway, only recently completed, which is so well engineered that it is unnecessary to change down from top gear even in a small car, provided one keeps up a brisk pace. It is exhilarating to drive fast up this road with the air becoming fresher every minute, the trees changing from olives and carobs to oaks, chestnuts and beeches once the higher levels have been reached, and with wonderful and constantly changing panoramic views as the highway gently curves its way into the mountains, tunnelling where necessary, or riding on concrete stilts high over valleys. Soon the dust and congestion of the main streets of Cosenza seem half a world away.

By the time one reaches the Lago di Cecita the view has become somewhat less than spectacular, and the road, by now the old ss 177, runs along the shore of the lake. This is not my favourite among the three great lakes of the Sila (Lago Arvo and Lago Ampollino being the others) but it is very pleasant for all that to be driving along a great expanse of water at a height of nearly 4000 feet. None of the lakes are natural; they act as reservoirs, and supply water-power for electricity, but they have now had the time to acquire the natural look, and indeed are well stocked with fish. About this lake Douglas wrote in 1912: 'The lake is to revolutionize the Sila; to convert these wildernesses into a fashionable watering-place. Enthusiasts already see the towns growing upon its shores—there are visions of gorgeous hotels and flocks of summer visitors . . .' He of all people would surely have guessed the reality in the event, as opposed to optimistic speculation, for the wheels of change grind exceedingly slowly in the deep South. As far as the Lago di Cecita is concerned the 'gorgeous hotels' are notable for their absence, and long may it remain so—though there is scope, of course, for carefully planned tourist villages such as can be found on the banks of Lake Ampollino, which will be described later.

After passing the north-eastern corner of Lago di Cecita, the road turns due north, becoming a humble mountain road until after about three kilometres it arrives at a junction. At this point I was in something of a quandary, for although wishing to visit Rossano, the incredibly twisting route of No. 177 from this juncture to Longobucco was decidedly off-putting, as time was not on my side given the number of places I planned to visit during the day. Glancing at the map (Touring Club Italiano folio 23/24) I decided to take a chance with time and proceed through Acri, Bisignano, S. Sofia d'Epiro and S. Demetrio Corone before linking up with the fast ss 106 near the Ionian shore, to visit Corigliano and Rossano, then double back on the same road and join up with the autostrada A3 back to Cosenza.

It should be remembered when touring in the Sila that appearances on the map can be deceptive since it is so often impossible for the map-maker to show the actual number of bends. Accordingly one nearly always finds oneself behind schedule. Even so, on the descent to Acri I decided to stop the car at a convenient place off the road and relax for a few minutes on foot with the sun and the wonderful mountain air on my face. From where I stood, the view overlooking a deep valley towards Serra Crista d'Acri was magnificent. Above the road-cutting, the pink rock flecked with white contrasted with the deep greens of thickly growing chestnut trees. It was early autumn, in a few weeks time the colouring would be superb. The freshness of the outside air and the heady aromatic scent of herbs enhanced by the sun acted like a tonic. It was an effort to return to the car.

Acri is a sizable market town of about 25,000 inhabitants and gives one the impression of a certain affluence. It even has a small 4th category hotel. When I was passing through, a street-market was in full swing which retarded progress.

The town of Bisignano about 13 kilometres from Acri is only about a third of its size, but in olden times was far more important. As early as the year 743 it was an episcopal see. The present cathedral is Norman in origin but so badly damaged by earthquakes that little of the original fabric remains. There are several churches of interest in this fortress hill-town which, being built on the spur of a hill at about 1100 feet commands magnificent views across the valley of the River Duglia. Despite the earthquakes, the over-riding impression one gets, is of great antiquity. The streets are sometimes so narrow that it is only just possible to squeeze a car through, between the severe stone walls of houses.

From Bisignano to S. Sofia d'Epiro is a distance of 15 kilometres, and it is fairly laborious driving without the compensations of especially fine scenery. Santa Sofia is however a delightful place, though being a small country town it shows little signs of prosperity. And yet there is nothing of the harshness of Bisignano about it, and there are no obvious signs of poverty, either in the buildings or among the people themselves. I spent a very pleasant hour exploring the town, and as this is the first of the 'Albanian' towns which we shall visit, now is a good opportunity to explain how it was that the Albanians came to these parts.

To do so it is necessary to go back to very early times. The Albanians in the western Balkans were a remnant of the old Illyrian population, but their actual origins remain a mystery. The fact that the Albanian language is the only surviving example of the so-called Thraco-Illyrian (Indo-European) group of languages points to extremely obscure origins, but past attempts to link them with the Etruscans (Tirane/ Tyrrhenian–Tosk/Tusci) must fail since the Etruscan language is certainly not Indo-European. After the division of the Roman Empire, the lands inhabited by the Albanians became provinces of the Byzantine Empire, but in A.D. 640 the northern parts settled by the Gheg communities, were invaded by the Serbo-Croats and remained under their rule until 1360; as a result, many of the inhabitants were driven into the mountains.

It was in the middle and southern parts of the country inhabited by the other major language group, the Tosks, which became the real centre of international interest, and between the tenth and the fourteenth centuries this part of the Balkans was fought over by all the

powers in the area—Bulgaria, Serbia, the rulers of South Italy—
(including the Normans who had a tremendous struggle with the
Byzantines)—the Greeks of Epirus, and Venice. The reason, of
course, is obvious when looking at the map: the coastline from
Durazzo to Epirus with its many small ports commands the Strait of
Otranto, (the distance between Italy and Albania across the water is
only 75 kilometres). For a short period, central Albania including
Durazzo passed into the hands of the Angevin kings of Sicily, and later,
Stefan Dusan (1331–58) styling himself Emperor of the Serbs,
Greeks, Bulgars and Albanians included all Albania in his short-lived
empire. However, on the death of Dusan and the break-up of the Ser-
bian empire, Albania came under the rule of local chieftains among
whom there was much rivalry. Included among them was the family of
Castriota which ruled the territory of Durazzo and Kroia.

By the end of the fourteenth century a far greater power than any
before was threatening Albania and indeed the whole of the Balkans—
the Ottoman Turks, fast growing in military strength and in political
confidence. The weakness of Albania after the withdrawal of the foreign powers and the subsequent anarchy under local rulers would, in the
normal run of events have meant an easy conquest for the Ottomans,
and it must have been a shock for them to come up against a leader who
was to hold them at bay against enormous odds for 24 years.

George Castriota, the Albanian national hero, better known under
his Turkish name, Skanderbeg, was one of the hostages demanded by
the Ottomans (generally sons of the Chieftains) after they had
occupied the country in 1385 and he began his career at the Ottoman
court. He was converted to Islam, rose by merit to become an important general, but deserted in 1443 and returned to Albania to lead a
successful revolt, at the same time reverting to the Christian faith. His
many qualities won him widespread support including that of the
Kingdom of Naples, the Papacy and the Republic of Venice, while the
skill and disciplines he had learnt in the Turkish army enabled him to
fight off the invading Ottoman troops even with their greatly increased
strength and confidence after the fall of Constantinople in 1453. His
heroic defence of his land must surely put him in the same category as
another hero of those times, John Hunyadi from Transylvania, who
after Mahomet II had invaded the Balkans with an army of 200,000
men, decisively defeated the Turks at Belgrade in 1456 and so
stemmed the tide of Ottoman expansion for a considerable period.
Clearly Skanderbeg has always been considered a hero not only by his
own people but by all the Christian states who benefited from the
tying-up of the Turkish troops for so long a time. Almost certainly as a
result, southern Italy was spared a major invasion by Ottoman troops

(Otranto was invaded in 1480 by Mahomet II but only as a limited action in support of his temporary ally Venice).

The death of Skanderberg in 1468 was a mortal blow to the Albanian national cause. A rapid re-conquest by the Ottomans followed and there began a large-scale Islamization that was to last 450 years. Huge numbers of Albanians especially the Greek-Orthodox Tosk-speaking peoples from the south emigrated to southern Italy, Sicily, southern Greece, and Romania, or took to the mountains and joined Roman Catholic Ghegs in the north rather than submit to the Ottomans and lose their faith. At the beginning of this century it was estimated that there were 72 Albanian enclaves in southern Italy and 8 in Sicily with total population of about 200,000. The figure may not be far short of this today, and a great many more live in other countries—in the Balkans and America. Indeed it is estimated that the overseas population is very close to the present population (2,500,000) of Albania, an accurate reflection of its traumatic history.

It has been characteristic of all Albanian communities overseas that they have jealously preserved their language, customs and traditions. The land they were offered in southern Italy was nearly always mountainous and the conditions hard, and a tremendous amount of work was needed to clear the forests and to cultivate the land in order to support themselves. Once settled they were very often cut off, and there was no incentive to learn the native language, and for many generations they knew only their own. Even to this day the Albanian language survives in these hill-top villages and towns, although in present times the inhabitants are bi-lingual, which is just as well since the Albanian language must rank among the most difficult in Europe. (Norman Douglas, no mean linguist himself, was appalled by its difficulty and after five days study could not construct the simplest sentence correctly.) At one time Albanian had 30 different alphabets each with nearly 50 letters, but in modern times the language has been modelled on Tosk. A large number of words have been borrowed over the centuries from Italian, Turkish, Modern Greek, Serbian and Latin, though surprisingly practically nothing of ancient Greek.

One of the main reasons for the widely divergent Albanian dialects was the absence of a literary culture. The earliest printed works in Albanian are those of the Catholic missionaries, one of which (possibly the first) was the *Dictionarium Latino—Epiroticum of Bianchi* published in 1635. It is noteworthy that the most celebrated Albanian writer, Girolamo di Rada, was born in Italy not Albania—to be precise in Macchia in the Greek Sila. He was the son of an Orthodox priest, and after an education in Naples, he retired to the village of his birth and dedicated himself to writing—in prose and poetry—for the cause of his beloved country. Norman Douglas, a great admirer, wrote of him 'He it was who divined the relationship between the Albanian and Pelasgian tongues; who created the literary language of his country and formulated its political ambitions' and added, 'He was the Mazzini of his nation'.

Although one might justifiably feel that Douglas was rather carried away in his eulogising at least one cannot fault his sentiments. But in fact probably the earliest literary work of merit in Albanian is the eighteenth-century poetry of Gjul Variboba, again a Calabrian, and again from the Sila Greca, this time the small town of S. Giorgio, to the east of a cluster that includes Vaccarizzo and S. Cosmo Albanese, and about 20 kilometres from the most important of these Italo-Albanian towns, S. Demetrio Corone.

It was to San Demetrio that I drove after my short visit to S. Sofia d'Epiro, and the first important building that one passes on the outskirts of the town is the celebrated Albanian College, once the heart of Albanian intellectual life, which was founded by Ferdinand of Bourbon in 1794 on the site of a dissolved Basilican monastery, and includes some of the original fabric. The church of S. Adriano standing to the right of the college is interesting. It was rebuilt in 980 after an early church founded by St. Nilus of Rossano was destroyed by the Saracens. It is basilican in plan and mainly a mixture of Byzantine and Romanesque of which twelfth century Norman work predominates. The pavement in mosaic and *opus sectile* was executed in Norman times and depicts lions, leopards and serpents, and was thought by the French scholar Bertaux to resemble the one which once lay before the high altar at Montecassino.

For anyone knowing the historical background of San Demetrio and especially its exalted position in the intellectual life of the overseas Albanians, the town today comes as something of a shock. It is a sad place really—dusty, down-at-heel, lacking any apparent vitality. One wonders, while strolling through its undistinguished streets, whether this is due solely to poverty. It is difficult to say, but certainly there is nothing of the 'poise' that can be seen in its near neighbour S. Sofia, no hint of liveliness. Yet paradoxically when I met and spoke at some length to a small family group and some friends, I found them to be vivacious, lively and very good-humoured, bearing out all I had read about these Albanian (Tosk) communities. (It seems that the Ghegs of N. Albania show opposite characteristics—dour and hard, in common with their historical background.)

I was fortunate to have met these people, and it came about in the following way. I had just left the parish church in the centre of the town (interior design according to the Greek rites) and was inspecting the outside when I was hailed by a man in a boisterous, if not exactly provocative way, who demanded to have his photograph taken. Nothing unusual about that—one is always being waylaid by children and sometimes by adults—but in this case his uninhibited manner was due, it was easy to see, to an overlong session at a nearby wine-bar (it was a Sunday). The pleasantries over, I tried to slip away —but without success; *all* his friends (and there were a few standing around) must have their photos taken too—this exhortation to the reluctant bystanders at a pitch of voice that must have carried across the Crati valley to the Pollino mountains beyond. Well, this too was easily accomplished. But that wasn't the end of it. The foreigner had a car, in that case he must come at once to Macchia where the wife and family were waiting: he would show me over his beautiful town—far finer than anything San Demetrio had to offer.

While inclined to agree that the beauties of S. Demetrio were strictly reserved for the scenic glories of its views, I was not at all eager to fall in with the plans of my new acquaintance. Macchia I knew to be only a few kilometres away, yet it was not the distance but the doubtful prospect of ever shaking off the man from Macchia that made me hesitate. Seeing that I demurred, the man became more insistent, more demonstrative, ever more exaggerated in his description of the wonders of Macchia . . . and I was on the point of despairing of ever getting rid of him when I was rescued by a family who came out of a nearby house to find out what all the noise was about—a man and his wife and their daughter. They seemed to know the man from Macchia, at any rate they soon quietened him down, and after introducing themselves, we started a most friendly conversation. They had never met an Englishman before, and indeed foreigners in S. Demetrio are, it seems remarkable for their absence. They were clearly pleased to talk with one, and with a freedom and unself-consciousness that is notably lacking among southern Italians when they talk to strangers. This was especially true of the girl, aged about 20.

Moreover she spoke in English, and so confidently and correctly that I asked her if she had ever been to England.

She smiled: 'Oh no, I have never been out of Italy.' I must have shown my surprise for she said, 'Why do you ask?' 'You speak very well. Have you been studying English long?' 'For about two years—and a little at school.' I complimented her and asked her whether she still spoke Albanian regularly?

'Yes, of course; I speak it all the time with my family. We are brought up speaking both our own language and Italian.' It occurred to me then that for someone who was able to master Albanian, English would present few problems. She was a local schoolmistress, but English was not her main subject. I told her that I had just come from Santa Sofia and mentioned that I had seen only two of the women there dressed in the colourful Albanian costumes, both of them elderly. I asked her whether young women ever wore the costumes today. She laughed: 'Only when one gets married—as a wedding-dress.' I said I thought that was a pity, but to her the matter was uninteresting. She wanted to know about England, and whether we would stay in the Common Market. Her interests were wide-ranging and she obviously felt rather isolated: 'There is nothing to do here' she said, gazing about her, 'we might be cut off from the world'; but there was no bitterness in her voice and clearly she did not expect to escape from her restricted way of life. We spent some time chatting and eventually the time came to say goodbye. Her father told me that there was no hotel in San Demetrio but directed me to a *locanda* where I could get a meal, and where I was glad to find shade from the heat of the early afternoon sun.

It is about 45 kilometres from S. Demetrio Corone to Rossano along the route I took, via the valley of the Mizofato Torrent and Corigliano Calabro, and, due to shortage of time, I was not able to do more than a brief reconnaissance of Corigliano by car—up to the top of the long main street and back. Even on such a brief acquaintance it had every appearance of being an interesting and lively small town with some elegant buildings, and a handsome church—St. Anthony of Padua— with its cupola of polychrome majolica, situated at the foot of the hill. The aqueduct which bestrides the main road is actually medieval in origin, though it might appear Roman, and used to supply water to the castle.

Corigliano and its more famous neighbour Rossano stand on high ground at about 800 feet at the foot of the Greek Sila overlooking the Ionian Sea. It is 17 kilometres between the two towns, the last six of which wind in a series of tight bends up to the hill on which Rossano is built. One is tempted to use the word picturesque when describing the older parts of Rossano, but that would give quite the wrong emphasis. It is above all a place of character, a combination of old buildings and narrow streets which would have been even more evident but for the destructive effects of an earthquake in 1836, which levelled to the ground half of the houses then standing.

During the centuries of Byzantine rule in the south of Italy— between the eight and eleventh centuries—Rossano was both a formidable citadel and an important centre of Byzantine culture. Even after the Norman conquest Byzantine influence predominated, for the Normans not only tolerated, but later under their Kings positively encouraged Basilian monasticism, indeed several new foundations came into existance. Of the ten convents that came into being in the orbit of Rossano, the most important was that of Santa Maria del Patire (Patirion), a description of which will be given later.

The main purpose of my visit to Rossano was to see the celebrated Purple Codex—a unique and most beautiful work. But before visiting the cathedral museum where it is housed I decided to seek out the little church of S. Marco, which is one of the best and earliest examples of Byzantine church architecture in the south of Italy. It was built in the tenth century in the form of a Greek cross inscribed in a square. Restoration and redecoration was in progress when I arrived, so it was not possible to judge whether religious services still take place since nearly all interior movables had been stripped. Presumably they do. Looking up at the five little cupulas from the small piazza outside allows one to see how closely comparable S. Marco is to another beautifully preserved small Byzantine church—the Cattolica of Stilo (which will be described in chapter eleven).

Stimulated by this short visit, I retraced my footsteps and succeeded in getting lost in the network of old streets before finding my way back to the piazza and the steps which lead down to the cathedral. This was damaged in the earthquake of 1836 and the façade is modern. I was fortunate in being able to see the Purple Codex, since I had arrived outside the normal hours of viewing, but one of the cathedral clergy kindly opened up the small museum and personally showed me the holy book.

According to Norman Douglas the *Codex Purpureus Rossanensis* was not identified until as late as 1879 (by Gebhardt and Harnack) but certainly its importance was recognised long before. Ramage was shown the Codex in 1828:

> Signor Masci accompanied me to the house of a canon of the church of Rossano, who possessed a manuscript of the Gospels of St. Matthew and St. Mark in Greek characters, illuminated with small figures at the beginning of each chapter. It is in excellent preservation, and must be of an early date, though I could not discover how it had come into his possession.

In fact the Purple Codex dates from the middle of the sixth century and is the best preserved of the two surviving illustrated gospel texts in Greek of this period. It consists of 188 pages, but is far from complete, since several folios are missing and also the canon tables. The illuminations, sometimes occupying the whole page, are of a high standard and clearly the *Codex Rossanensis* was in the luxury class. The superior quality parchment is painted purple, the script worked in silver and gold, and no modern reproductions that I have seen have been able to capture the subtle colour tones of the original illustrators. It is almost certain that this beautiful work was produced at Constantinople and may well have formed part of an imperial gift to a new monastery. It is a mystery how it came into the hands of the clergy of the cathedral of Rossano, and only speculation to believe that it might once have been in the possession of the monastery of Patirion (S.M. del Patir).

The ruins of the monastery and the restored church of Santa Maria del Patir stand at an elevation of about 1900 feet at a remote spot nearly seven kilometres south of the main road between Rossano and Corigliano. From here one has a magnificent panoramic view of the plain of Sibari, the Pollino range of mountains and the gulf of Taranto. The name Patir or Patire derives from the local pronunciation of the word Pater (Father); (the convent was called 'monasterium Sancti Patris' when the control of its famous library passed into the hands of the Vatican in the seventeenth century). The monastery was a late foundation in the years of Norman rule, being founded by the Blessed Bartolomeo di Simeri in 1101. It followed the Rule of St. Basil and soon prospered, benefiting from grants of land and generous timber rights. In 1806 it was suppressed and allowed to fall into decay, a process completed by earthquakes, so today we see only the ruins of this once proud convent and it is fortunate that the church itself has been restored. It is a basilica in the oriental style with three semi-circular apses.

We will conclude this chapter with a description of the region which forms a sizeable chunk of land between the Ionian sea and the Tyrrhenian—the major part of it comprising the wide and fertile plain of Sibari until the barrier of the mountains of the Catena Costiera are reached in the west.

The distance between the Tyrrhenian at Punta di Cirella, and the Ionian sea at Sibari is only 58 kilometres, but there is not fast road linking them at this point. It may be thought surprising that there is so little in the way of towns or villages in the extremely rich Plain of Sibari, watered by the rivers Crati, Coscile and Esaro, but this is a legacy of the times within living memory, when these low-lying areas were plagued by malaria, so that villages and towns were built on high ground in an attempt to escape the fever. The most prominent of these are Spezzano Albanese and Terranova da Sibari to the south and the much larger town of Castrovillari to the north.

Thus at Sibari itself there are merely a few buildings clustered round the station, though there are now developments taking place not far away at the Bagamoyo beach where the white sandy shore curves round in a gentle arc. On a clear day the distant mountains at this point form a spectacularly beautiful background—the panorama covering well over 180 degrees. At the height of summer however, heat-haze or humidity can effectively blot out this marvellous view, and the late spring or the autumn are the best seasons for enjoying the many scenic wonders of southern Italy. The name Sibari derives from the ancient Greek city of Sibaris which was wiped out after the defeat of its army by the men of Croton in 510 B.C. A further and more detailed account of the fate of Sibaris, and a wider discussion of the Greeks of Magna Graecia will be reserved for a later chapter.

The town of Castrovillari, snugly sited at the foothills of the towering Pollino mountains, need not delay us much. It is an important centre of communications as well as being the market-town for a wide surrounding area, and its prosperity is evident in the solidity of its nineteenth-century buildings. It possesses two good hotels, a motel, a well-preserved Aragonese castle, and a famous sanctuary built by the Norman Count Roger I in 1090 and dedicated to S. Maria del Castello; it has been restored on two occasions since, and little of the Norman work remains.

The Pollino range of mountains straddle the neck of land between the Gulf of Taranto and the Tyrrhenian Sea in a magnificent arc looming high, majestic and bare as one climbs towards them from Castrovillari. They form in effect the boundary between Basilicata and Calabria, the high peaks being from east to west, Monte Sparviere, La Falconara, Dolcedorme (the highest at about 7500 feet) and Coppola di Paolo. The road or autostrada (A3) we can take to bring us to a linking road to the Tyrrhenian coast, passes close to the last-named peak, and then we descend on a small tortuous mountain road and across the River Lao to arrive on the coastal plain at Scalea.

About 15 kilometres north of Scalea the rapidly expanding resort of Praia a Mare is typical of the many sea-side holiday places that have been developed along this beautiful coastline in recent years. At the time of writing Praia has no less than seven second-class hotels, seven of the third category and four of the fourth—three times the number of a decade ago when the total was six. The scenery is splendid here with the mountains and hills dropping sharply to the shore where there are long stretches of sandy beaches.

The coastal road from Praia to Scalea passes close to the shore, then cuts across the low-lying Cape Scalea before reaching the attractively situated town with a fine view of the sea, the mountains and the plain at the mouth of the River Lao. Ten years ago the Marina of Scalea had only one little inn with six rooms, but now it has five hotels, one of which is partly air-conditioned and offers accommodation for 154 people. There is a ruined castle at Scalea, with main steps leading up to it through the narrow streets of the old town and hence its name.

The small towns of Cirella, Diamante and Belvedere Marittimo between them possess several hotels, among them a good Autostella A.C.I. at Cirella with 90 double rooms. Continuing further south and still on the coast road (ss 18), the town of Cetraro is a much larger place with a population of over 10,000. At this point we are within 22 kilometres of the town of Paola, where a good road, the ss 107, curves in easy gradients through and over the mountains to the autostrada, or the main road (ss 19) to Cosenza.

Paola used to be a port of call on the voyage from Naples to Messina, the steamer lying off-shore, and it was here at the turn of the century that Gissing alighted on his romantic journey to the Ionian shores. He was eager to get started and didn't stay long enough to visit the place for which the town is most noted—the Sanctuary of St. Francis. Paola was the birthplace of S. Francesco, who in 1474 founded the order of the Minim Friars (*Minimi*—the least of the Brothers) whose rules were similar to those of the Franciscans—only stricter—and whose motto is *Caritas*. At the peak of its influence in the seventeenth century there were 9000 friars in the order. The Basilica was built in 1452 and incorporated an earlier chapel dedicated to St. Francis of Assisi; it was restored in 1555 after having been sacked by corsairs. The buildings are extensive and are delightfully situated in a fold in the hills just north of the town.

Continuing on the main road south for another 26 kilometres and always accompanied by the railway, we arrive at the pleasant small town of Amantea. This now has several hotels, mainly in the third and fourth category. A decade ago there was only one; (the small village and marina of Fuscaldo six kilometres north of Paola can beat this: from no hotels at all in 1965 to seven now, including the vast Sangrila Residence with 452 beds: one wonders how many are occupied outside the short season.) Amantea is rather smaller than Paola, with about 11,000 inhabitants, and like the latter has an upper and a lower town. The small fifteenth century church of S. Bernardino da Siena is of above-average interest. Over the five pointed arches of the portico there is a medieval cross made from plates of colourful majolica, and inside there is a beautiful marble group of the Madonna and Child by Antonello Gagini, made in 1505. A. Gagini was a member of a Lombard family of sculptors whose distinguished works can be seen in many parts of southern Italy and Sicily.

10. Catanzaro & the Sila:
the Gulf of Squillace

The quickest way of reaching Catanzaro by car from Cosenza is to take
the autostrada A3 to S. Eufemia Lamezia and then the fast state highway No. 280 which follows for a long way the valley of the river
Lamato in an easterly direction, before linking up eventually with the
southern by-pass of Catanzaro.

Not only is the autostrada A3 an extremely fast road, it has been
landscaped so well that for the greater part of the way one can enjoy
magnificent scenery and far more generous views than on the other
roads. The highway has been carefully engineered and the grades are
so gradual that it is not ever necessary to change out of top gear, so that
both fast and enonomical motoring is possible. In addition, south of
Salerno the autostrada is toll-free (at the time of writing) presumably
in order to encourage tourists to the resorts of the *mezzogiorno*. A
word of warning may not be out of place here: the views, the effortless
speed and the wonderful road-surface of the autostrada sometimes lull
one into a mood of unwatchful complacency. Always keep an eye on
the rear-mirror; it is surprising how quickly cars doing 120 mph plus
can descend on one.

For those visiting Catanzaro for the first time by car my earnest
advice is to time your arrival before nightfall, since the one-way system
here could only have been devised by someone with a strong sadistic
streak. I admit I hold a biased view of the *circumvallazione* operating in
the city. I arrived after dark at the height of a thunderstorm of tropical
intensity that broke three months' drought and it took me an hour to
find my hotel, having been three times misdirected. In daytime however, the approach to Catanzaro from the Lido is certainly dramatic for
it is perched high on a bluff at 1100 feet, between the gorges formed by
two mountain torrents, the Fiumarella to the west, and the Musofalo to
the east. Describing his approach at dusk George Gissing wrote:

> Very beautiful was this long, broad, climbing valley, everywhere
> richly wooded; oranges and olives, carb and lentisk and myrtle,
> interspesed with cactus (its fruit, the prickly fig, all gathered) and

with the sword-like agave. Glow of sunset lingered on the hills; in the green hollow a golden twilight faded to dusk.'

The accommodation that had been booked for me and which I had all but despaired of finding, was in fact the Motel AGIP, situated on the southern side of the high viaduct that straddles the gorge of the Fiumarella. Motels owned by the petroleum companies in Italy have a high reputation and the one in question was no exception—well-managed, comfortable, and with a good restaurant. Catanzaro is a noticeably go-ahead place and is well provided with hotels, including two in the first category, one of which is a Jolly Hotel.

A very short diversion here to elaborate on Jolly Hotels. This organisation blazed the trail in providing good hotel accommodation in the south of Italy. Long before hotel development on a large scale began in recent years (officially encouraged by loans and grants), Jolly Hotels were providing hotel accommodation, nearly all in the first category, which never fell below a high standard of comfort, cleanliness, and pleasant interior decor.

Modern Catanzaro cannot by any stretch of the imagination be called beautiful, its cubic modern buildings utterly lack any distinction. Gissing wrote, 'Impossible to find oneself at Catanzaro without thinking of earthquakes' and this is the clue to the absence of virtually any building of merit. One frightful shock-wave at the end of the eighteenth century left hardly a building standing. One of the few strong enough to withstand the shock—the Norman castle—was later pulled down to accommodate a major road improvement.

There is a lively atmosphere in Catanzaro and a feeling of confidence which succeeds in transmitting itself to a stranger. The narrow awkward streets of the older parts, all hills and corners, are packed with cars day and night until quite late, and sometimes even the elaborate one-way system fails to cope with the traffic. Parking in the centre of the town is difficult, and it is best to go on foot whenever possible.

Here is not the place to go into detail, concerning the unfortunate dispute between Reggio di Calabria and Catanzaro over which city should represent the Region of Calabria as its capital. In any case it is history now. Catanzaro's claim was successful—a decision which will surprise no one who knows both cities—in spite of all Reggio's natural advantages.

Catanzaro is not one of the very old foundations of Calabria, having been founded by the Byzantines at the end of the ninth century during the time of Nicephorus Phocas' vigorous reconquest of the country from the Saracens and Lombards. At a very early date the manufacture of silk became an important industry. Silk-weaving on an industrial scale was introduced into Sicily by Roger II who captured a complete silk factory on one of his expeditions against the Byzantine emperor. Jews played a leading part in the trade (as they did at Trani) and at one time there was a ghetto behind the present Palazzo Fazzari. The skills of weaving and dyeing in the city reached such a height that Catanzarese weavers were summoned to Tours and Lyons in 1470 to teach the secrets of their art to the French.

A tour of the city's churches and other monuments need not delay us long; as the admirable Mr. Blewitt succinctly put it in 1853, 'The churches present little call for notice' and promptly went on to describe the castle. The neo-classical cathedral of the nineteenth century was largely destroyed by Allied bombs in the last war and has been rebuilt in a more modern style, but inevitably suffers from lack of character. The small church of the Osservanza possesses a sculpture by Antonello Gagini, and a very realistic painted wooden carving of Christ nailed to the Cross (1650) by Fra Giovanni da Reggio. The basilica of the Immacolata, rebuilt in 1765 and many times restored since, contains some examples of the rare works of the Neapolitan painter and modeller Caterina de Julianis (1695–1742); her technique was to model the figures in wax and then colour them. The spacious interior of the chiesa del Rosario (or the church of S. Domenico) is in the shape of a latin cross, and contains a marble statue of the Madonna and Child by Francesco Cassana.

The church of the Immacolata, facing Corso Mazzini, is in the very heart of the older town and just south from here the Via Giovanni Jannoni leads to the Provincial Museum and the delightful public gardens of the Villa Trieste. These overlook the valley of the Musofalo Torrent towards the high hills, capped in dark green, of the Sila and it forests. The gardens are peaceful, and contain many interesting shrubs, plants and trees, and the panoramic views are magnificent. The small museum, reached from within the gardens, was in the process of re-arrangement during my visit, but I was shown some of the more important objects including a fifth century Hellensitic helmet from Tiriolo, a marble head, and an Athena in terracotta from Locri. The collection of Greek and Roman coins is above average for a provincial museum, and the small art gallery has some interesting paintings including a Madonna and Child signed by Antonello da Messina and dated 1508.

One of my first actions in Catanzaro was to take up an introduction I had been given, to someone living in the city, and it was decided that it would be a good idea for me to see something of the Sila Piccola and the Sila Grande while I was staying in Catanzaro. My new acquaintance soon had an itinerary planned, and we decided to leave early the following morning on a tour that took in the small town of Taverna in the mountains, the tourist village Villagio Mancuso, Lake Ampollino in the heart of the Sila, the highland town of S. Giovanni in Fiore, and finally the long descent to the sea to Crotone, before returning along the southern highway ss 106 to Catanzaro.

It was a fine morning as we left behind us the city suburbs and climbed towards the hills, and the air soon had freshness, and the light a brilliance which is typical of these southern mountain regions. Hardly less exhilarating were the wide sweeping views of the landscape, the greens becoming lighter and fresher as beeches and chestnuts began to predominate over pines and olives. The first place of any importance we came to was Taverna, very pleasantly situated on the side of a hill with wonderful views. An ancient town, perhaps of Greek foundation, Taverna is especially noteworthy as being the birthplace of Mattia Preti (1613–99), the 'Cavaliere Calabrese' who followed Ribera as the leader of the baroque school of Naples. Four of Taverna's churches contain works by Preti, in particular that of S. Domenico which has a large number, the best known of which is perhaps the painting of St. John the Baptist.

Beyond Taverna the road climbs in a tortuous fashion, reaching the Villagio Mancuso at a height of just over 4500 feet. Standing among pines and firs and a mile or two further on, is another holiday resort, the Villagio Racisi. At the time of writing there is one large second category hotel and several third category hotels and pensions at these two resorts, plus a village of chalets at Il Rosetto. It is a little over 17 kilometres from Villagio Mancuso to Lake Ampollino—a beautiful stretch of water about 4200 feet above sea-level with mountains forming a back-drop to its tranquil surface. Dark pines and firs are continually forming a silhouette against the brightness of the water as the road weaves and curves along the southern shore of the lake. My companion showed an admirable tolerance of the pale-skinned cattle that wandered at random along the road and rebuked me for showing irritation at the hazards they caused. The matter was jokingly but firmly put in perspective: 'After all, it is their countryside' she said, 'It is we who are in the way.'

We decided to stop for lunch at an hotel which is close to the shore at the eastern end of the lake beside the Villagio Palumbo, a development on a considerable scale, comprising self-contained holiday flats and chalets. It also gave us an opportunity to stretch our legs while inspecting the new flats which are built of wood and concrete, and though not unpleasing in style, have a deadening uniformity. Fortunately they are fairly competently landscaped and lie well back along the track which leads south from the lake and are not too obstrusive. There is considerable sport to be had in these parts—good fishing in the lake and shooting for woodcock and other wild fowl, and also for hare and a certain amount of wild boar. The tourist villages are very popular with summer visitors, and the sporting season extends well into the autumn. By winter however it can be very cold at these altitudes, and normally snow lies deep on the ground.

Having turned the corner at the eastern end of the lake, the road eventually breaks away from the shore and heads north for another 12 kilometres until the town of S. Giovanni in Fiore is reached. The little research I had done into this, the largest town in the Sila, was not exactly exciting: 'The narrow streets and hovels of this town are infinitely depressing' (Peter Gunn); 'a large sleepy village that has nothing attractive about it except its name' (Leslie Gardiner); 'San Giovanni is as dirty as can well be; it has the accumulated filth of an Eastern town, while lacking all its glowing tints or harmonious outlines' (Norman Douglas). The latter did however speak well of its women: 'it would be difficult to find anywhere an equal number of handsome women on such a restricted space. In olden days it was dangerous to approach these attractive and mirthful creatures; they were jealously guarded by brothers and husbands. But the brothers and husbands, thank God, are now in America . . .'.

Pressed a little for time, we did not stop in S. Giovanni; certainly the appearance of the town would seem to have smartened up a little since the above-quoted reports, but during our slow progress through the streets I cannot remember seeing a single memorable building . . . or woman for that matter. But of course when Douglas was travelling in Calabria in the first decade of this century, many of the womenfolk in the towns and villages wore their distinctive costumes, and nothing was better suited to cover up any little defect in feminine beauty. Today's dreary uniformity in dress favoured by country people tends to exaggerate any shortcoming.

A short distance north of S. Giovanni, the town road joins the main road ss 107 between Cosenza and Crotone, which bisects the Sila plateau from west to east. A little further on, this road connects with a newly built super-highway which curves in gentle gradients through the mountains, following roughly the direction of the old road, but incomparably superior in every way. For nearly 30 kilometres this new road allows one to keep up fast average speeds and even after it has linked up with the old road again just after crossing the River Neto, high speeds can be maintained. Thus we made very good time to Crotone.

The difference in temperature between the highlands of the Sila and the shores of the Ionian Sea is of course very marked. It was distinctly hot and lacking in shade at Crotone, and also humid, whereas up on the Sila the air had been fresh, with the forests and meadows softening the brilliant light. But in its own way Crotone is not lacking in character, especially the southern part of the town with its yacht harbour and wide expanse of sandy beach. The city is very ancient in origin, having been founded by an Achaean colony in 710 B.C., but I would like to reserve a discussion of Greek Croton to a later chapter, in the context of the cities of Magna Graecia as a whole, except that here I shall give a brief description of our visit to the sole remaining Doric column of the Temple of Hera Lacinia at Capo Colonna.

From the glory and might of Greek times to the dejection and lassitude of the last years of the nineteenth century when Gissing saw Crotone make a melancholy record in which malaria as much as maladministration had played a leading part. Poor Gissing, laid low at his hotel with a progressively debilitating disease which was to cause his early death, even his superabundant enthusiasm failed him:

> Any northern person who passed a day or two at the *Corcordia* as an ordinary traveller would carry away a strong impression. The people of the house would seem to him little short of savages, filthy in person and in habits, utterly uncouth in their demeanour, perpetual wranglers and railers, lacking every qualification for the duties they pretended to discharge . . .

And yet such is the change of mood, that having described his recovery he was able by the end of the chapter to write:

> Brute races have flung themselves one after the other upon this sweet and glorious land . . . Tread where one will, the soil has been drenched in blood . . . An immemorial woe sounds even through the lilting notes of Italian gaiety . . . A wandering stranger has no right to indulge a contemptuous impatience . . . Listen to a Calabrian peasant singing as he follows his oxen along the furrow, or as he shakes the branches of his olive tree. That wailing voice amid the ancient silence, that long lament solacing ill-rewarded toil, comes from the heart of Italy herself, and wakes the memory of mankind.

These words bring back memories of life in Mediterranean lands, in Spain, in Italy, in Sicily, only a couple of decades ago, when there was indeed grinding poverty, when often the hard and monotonous life of a farmer and his wife was unrelieved by television, running water, or even electric light.

Of course, Crotone has greatly developed since Gissing's time; the elimination of malaria opened the way for a rapid expansion of its industrial activities. It is now an important manufacturing centre with a population of about 45,000. The largest single industry is Montedison's fertilizer and chemical plant, part of a major and continuing investment in the south, which will make the Crotone complex the most important inorganic chemicals site within the Group. To keep pace with these developments the 'new' port is being considerably enlarged (Crotone is the only port between Reggio and Taranto) and it will be able to berth large ocean-going vessels.

Hotel accommodation at Crotone is reasonable, if not exciting, and includes the Hotel Costa Tiziana (out of town at the end of the long sweeping beach that stretches out towards Capo Colonna). The town has suffered much damage from earthquakes which is reflected in the architecture of the cathedral 'an ugly building, as uninteresting within as without,' Gissing calls it. Its prize possession is the 'Black' Madonna, otherwise called the 'Madonna di Capo-Colonna' which is annually carried with much ceremony to the sanctuary on the cape on the second Sunday in May, returning by sea and escorted by a long procession of boats. The town itself is busy and lively, but not particularly interesting. Easily the best parts can be found in the older quarter of the town between the massive castle—built by Don Pedro da Toledo in 1541 as a defence against Turkish invasion—and the Duomo. The new museum, situated near the castle in Via Risorgimento, is beautifully arranged and contains Pre-historic, Greek and Roman objects found in the district and in the territory of Croton, as well as from the Sanctuary of Hera Lacinia. There is also a good collection of coins.

The road that leads to Capo Colonna passes the cemetery by the sea-shore and continues for about 11 kilometres until it reaches the sickle-shaped cape. There is a lighthouse at the point, and also a chapel. The solitary column which survives of the once magnificent Doric temple at this site (marking the shrine dedicated by Hercules himself, it was believed) should make a rather pathetic picture: it stands on a shaky-looking base and is itself incomplete with half its capital missing. But oddly enough it is a moving sight. We saw it with no one else for company on a sunny afternoon, with a wind getting up and ruffling the magnificent expanse of blue sea that more than half encircles it. It requires little imagination to realise what a tremendous impact the temple of Hera Lacinia must have made. No sanctuary in Magna Graecia had greater sanctity than this temple. Even as late as the sixteenth century 48 columns were thought still to be standing, but an ambitious prelate, a Bishop Lucifer, true to his name, pulled them all down save one and used the material in the construction of his palace. When this in turn was destroyed in the earthquake of 1783, the stone was used to strengthen the mole of the old Port. The shrines in the temple were enriched by offerings from all parts of Magna Graecia, and according to Cicero, when the painter Zeuxis was commissioned to adorn the temple walls, he was allowed to choose five of the most beautiful girls of Croton as models for his picture of Helen of Troy—the women of the city having an unrivalled reputation for their beauty.

On our return journey to Catanzaro we decided to make a slight diversion to the headland beyond Capo Rizzuto, in order to see the romantic view of the Aragonese castle, guarding the coast on a tiny island just off-shore which it wholly occupies. It made a beautiful sight in the evening light with the sea just swirling over the sandy bar that separates the castle from the rocky shore, making it impossible to visit. A few light fishing-boats had used the bulk of the old fortress as a protection against the stiff southerly breeze and had tucked themselves under the ramparts in the calm water. There is a small village here and a second category hotel in the vicinity. Only about 16 kilometres away on the coast near Isola di Capo Rizzuto, there is a large tourist village—the Hotel Villagio Valtur—that can accommodate nearly 900 people.

Leaving Le Castella we rejoined the main coast road ss 106 and continued past open rolling country with the mountains always in the background, until we reached Catanzaro Lido. This, a popular holiday town, has developed considerably in recent years, but it is a long way from being my favourite seaside resort on the Ionian shores. Here the ss 19 links the Statale Ionica with Catanzaro and we turned north for the city as the sun was beginning to set behind the Calabrian Appenines, having completed a round trip of 240 kilometres.

My companion suggested that on the following day we should make a short tour of the resorts and other places of interest on or overlooking the gulf of Squillace, a suggestion to which I readily agreed. We again took the Statale Ionica and our first call was at the Roccelletta del Vescovo di Squillace, also called S. Maria della Roccella. This very interesting ruin is set back a little from the road on the right, 1½ kilometres from Lido di Catanzaro, on private property—but there is no difficulty in getting permission to view it. It is immediately apparent that this was at one time a major church; the scale is very large and the fine reddish-brown Roman type bricks are beautifully worked. It was once the second largest church in Calabria (after the cathedral of Gerace) but expert opinion differs as to when it was built, adding greatly to its interest. Lenormant placed it among the first churches of Christendom; E. Caviglia assigned it to the sixth century; but I would tend to agree with the majority opinion of today in thinking that it is Romanesque, built under the Normans in the eleventh century (or twelfth), mainly because it was characteristic of the Normans to build these huge basilicas (there are many examples in Apulia and Sicily), while the Byzantine churches in the south were on a much smaller scale.

There is not much of interest architecturally in the small market-town of Squillace, which stands at about 1000 feet in the hills over-looking the gulf. However the views from the ruined Norman castle (now a jail) are superb. A quiet little town of only about 3000 inhabit-ants, it nevertheless boasts a sizeable cathedral—standing at a slightly lower level to the main piazza—which suffers from lack of character having been rebuilt after the earthquake of 1795.

Returning to the main coast road we drove on and reached the Lido of Copanello ahich, together with the Lido di Squillace and the Lido di Golfo, make use of the excellent beaches and splendid bathing along this part of the shore, up to the Point (Punta di Staletti) which juts into the ocean. The Lido of Copanello and the cluster of buildings above are now referred to as Staletti, and in the course of only four or five years the hotel accommodation has been greatly improved without spoiling the physical appearance of these open beaches: thus we now have the first category Hotel Villagio Guglielmo with 288 beds, and the Vitale Club Hotel, a modern hotel in the second category with 50 rooms.

South of Punta di Staletti and beyond the next little bay, we arrived at the beautiful sweeping line of the coast that curves in a gentle arc to the small town of Soverato (pop. about 6000). Here, one can sense, is an up-and-coming resort. Indeed it is extraordinary that such a beaut-iful spot has been so little developed—(one can imagine what the Span-ish would have made of it!). Soverato to my mind, is one of the most attractive places along all the coasts of Southern Italy: it can justifiably call itself the 'pearl of the Ionian'. Pleasant gardens come close up to the excellent beach of fine white sand that continues for several kilometres round the shore. Across the wide expanse of the bay there is a superb view towards the mountains. If I am not mistaken Soverato will become, within a few years, the Alassio of the south. One can only hope that the planners will show discretion. Of course, development there is bound to be—the bathing and underwater swimming are superb here, and the sea clear and fresh, in marked contrast to the pol-lution at the resorts of the northern Mediterranean.

11. From Stilo to
Serra S. Bruno and S. Eufémia

A pleasant round trip from Catanzaro takes in the small towns of Stilo
and Serra S. Bruno and includes some very fine mountain scenery.
Joining the Statale Ionica at Catanzaro Lido, one drives south past
Punta di Staletti and Soverato and along the beautiful coast road close
by the sea, that passes by the small marinas of Badolato and S.
Antonio. After about an hour's run from Catanzaro one reaches Punta
Stilo with its in-shore lighthouse, and Monasterace Marina, where the
ss 110 links with Stilo and the mountains beyond. Between the last-
named places is the site of the ancient Greek city of Caulonia.

The road to Stilo slowly ascends the delightful valley of the Stilaro
fiumara and then climbs more steeply in a series of bends to the little
town that stands at about 1200 feet on the flank of Monte Consolino.
Stilo is an agreeable small country town, but few strangers would find it
worth a special visit, were it not for the unusually interesting Byzantine
church of the Cattolica which stands on the side of a hill, beneath a
sheer cliff-face, overlooking the town. It is reached by way of the main
road to Serra S. Bruno, and it is is sign-posted, pointing to the right;
here a road in a very poor state of repair leads up to the gates of the
church grounds. These are kept locked and it is normally necessary to
find the custodian with the keys, which in my case was unnecessary
since a small boy ran off to let her know of my arrival.

La Cattolica is a gem of a little church. It was built in the Eastern
style by the Byzantines, conceivably as late as the twelfth century (the
experts differ about this: a leading authority dates it to the tenth century). The brickwork has mellowed to a warm reddish-brown which is
very attractive. Its shape is distinctive, almost Georgian/Armenian,
being square, with five circular cupolas each capped with radiating
roof-tiles, the roofs overlapping the drums like so many tin-helmets.
The middle cupola is taller and bigger than the other four at each
corner. There are fairly substantial remains of Byzantine frescoes in
the interior—one of which shows St. John Chrysostom, and another,
St. John the Precursor, in the iconographical style of the eighth century. Stilo was a centre for Basilican monks and hermits from early

113

times, and there were Greek churches here earlier than the Cattolica. If, as seems likely, the Cattolica was built in the tenth century, the monks may have arrived from Sicily, having been forced to leave by the Saracens, as it is known that several communities emigrated from the island for this reason.

I had arrived at Stilo fairly early in the morning, but already it was getting warm before I left for the mountains and the town of Serra S. Bruno. The route over the mountains provides some glorious scenery and since it winds and twists to a height of well over 4000 feet, the air becomes very fresh and cool and clear, even though the sun remains hot. The countryside is well wooded, with oaks and chestnuts becoming increasingly common and at the highest levels great woods of beech. Some of these are well on the way to maturing and are being thinned, while at other stretches huge areas are being planted with saplings, the beeches mixed with fast growing conifers—spruce or pines—which encourage the growth of the hardwoods as they compete for light in the years ahead.

Serra S. Bruno owes its fame to the existence, since 1090, of the Certosa di S. Stefano del Bosco—being founded by the head and founder of the Carthusian Order, St. Bruno, on lands granted by Count Roger the Norman. The Charterhouse, which is reached along a fine avenue of magnificent, fully matured black poplars just before reaching the town, was closed to visitors on the day of my visit, it being a Sunday—so I had no option but to walk around its walled gardens observing what I could from the outside. In fact due to the frightful damage it sustained during the earthquake of 1783 nearly all the buildings are comparatively modern. The cloisters and chapels were built in 1900 to the design of French architects, though traces remain of the church of 1595 in the façade. It should be noted that women are not permitted to enter the precincts.

The little church of S. Maria del Bosco is reached by continuing along the road past the Certosa for about one kilometre. Here the road ends and there is parking space and a refreshment room. Not far from the lake there is a small octagonal building largely in ruins, within which one can see S. Bruno's tomb surmounted by his effigy. Here, in a clearing in the woods, the saint lived and died.

There is some fine wooded country beyond the chapel, and I spent an hour walking up a long path through the trees, with a stream running down the valley never out of ear-shot—a very lovely spot with splendid unspoilt woods and the song of many birds—so rare in Italy. Here they must have sanctuary from netting, trapping, shooting or other forms of destruction.

Serra S. Bruno has no pretentions to being other than a small market town and is notably lacking in hotel accommodation. However it is a good deal more lively than many other country towns I have visited in southern Italy, and maybe this is due to the fresh keen air of its altitude (2600 feet). Moreover its houses have character, several of them with wrought-iron balconies, and there are as many as four churches of above-average interest, a large number for a small provincial town. Almost certainly this is due to the stimulating presence of the Certosa, which, until 1765 held the town in fief. The Carthusians encouraged many artists, sculptors and engravers to work with them, some foreign and others from the locality, such as the Scaramuzzino and Barillari familes. Wood-working was the specialist craft of the local artists as seen in the fine wooden pulpit in the Chiesa Matrice (1795). This church also contains four marble statues from the Certosa, with interesting low-reliefs by an artist who signs himself 'David Muller 1611', and was probably trained in Flanders. Other examples of fine woodwork can be seen in the doors of these churches. The interiors are very gay, bright and cheerful with plenty of light and a profusion of coloured stucco and interior decoration—exactly as one would expect in small country churches like these.

There was a procession in honour of the Blessed Virgin Mary being led by a priest and a bag-piper going from church to church, which only had modest support, and far more interest was centred round the usual Sunday fair taking place in the wide main street. For my part I searched in vain for a *trattoria,* and in the end had to be content with a snack-bar.

Leaving Serra S. Bruno I continued on the ss 110 and made for the Tyrrhenian, descending all the way beyond S. Nicola da Crissa in a series of loops, and eventually arriving at the coast where the autostrada A3 passes close by the railway station for Pizzo. From here I took the long straight ss 18 across the rich agricultural lands of the plain of S. Eufémia with its extensive citrus plantations, as far as the road junction with Catanzaro.

My main reason for visiting the S. Eufémia area was to see for myself the progress that had been made in building the new international airport. This will fit neatly into the rectangle formed by the sea to the west, the river Lomato to the south and the two directions of the main road on which I had just travelled. No one I had spoken to during my travels had been able to give me a definite answer as to when the airport would be ready for operations: some said 1976, others 1977 and a cynic at Cosenza thought it was highly unlikely it would ever be finished. My view is that to forecast any time before 1977 would be optimistic. Of course the airport is of enormous importance to the future prosperity of the *mezzogiorno,* since it will open up all the resorts of the deep south which at present are poorly served by the sole international airport in the south (excluding Sicily), 409 kilometres away from S. Eufémia at Naples, itself not a large airport. The days of the packaged holiday by direct flight to S. Eufémia Lamezia, from England, France, Germany, Scandinavia or the United States cannot be far away.

Before heading north for the hill-towns of Sambiase and Nicastro I drove thought the small town of S. Eufémia Lamezia where there is a substantial modern hotel, with rooms all fitted with bath or shower, in the Station square. Hitherto the importance of S. Eufémia has rested mainly on the fact that it is on the main line from Rome to Reggio and is the junction for Catanzaro, but with the opening of the airport the whole of this area will be transformed and additional hotel accommodation will certainly be provided—especially as there is a fair-sized industrial estate being built alongside the airport.

The country towns of Sambiase and Nicastro stand at about 550 feet and 700 feet respectively, on the side of the high hills that rise to the north at a height of over 3500 feet at Monte S. Maria. From the road that links them one has splendid views to the Tyrrhenian Sea over the Plain of S. Eufémia—(also known as the Plain of Maida in English history books after the town of Maida that lies 15 kilometres to the south: it was here that a small British force under Sir John Stuart defeated the French army in Calabria during the Napoleonic Wars—commemorated by the name given to a new London suburb, Maida Vale). Nowadays the two towns and the surrounding district are known collectively as Lametia Terme, and are sign-posted as such, which can be confusing—(I see that the spelling Lamezia Terme is still used on the T.C.I. Touring Map).

Here for the sake of identity I will retain the individual names: Sambiase is a centre for the wine trade and is a busy little town specializing in the local red wine that takes its name from the town. About four kilometres away are the ancient mineral springs called Terme Caronte; to the best of my knowledge there are no hotels in Sambiase. At Nicastro however, three kilometres further east, there is every sign from the many new buildings that the town is booming: there is a choice of hotels. It is a lively place—the market for the rich surrounding countryside, producing citrus fruits, vegetables, wine and olive-oil, and there is also a centre for light industry such as pottery and the weaving of rugs and shawls. It would be surprising if tourism were not shortly to be added to this list. One of the pleasantest aspects of these parts, is that one can still see the beautiful traditional dresses of the womenfolk. They feature typically, a long red underskirt which reveals an inch or two of white petticoat and pleated overskirt pulled back to form a bustle; generally a black shawl or mantle is worn round the shoulders.

Sundays and feast-days often bring out more elaborate versions of these traditional dresses, bringing welcome flashes of colour and gaiety to the normally sombre clothes worn by the country people.

12.   The Gulf of S. Eufémia and the Gulf of Gióia

The Gulf of S. Eufémia sweeps down in a gentle curve, with only the mouth of the river Lamato and the tiny resort of Maida Marina to interrupt its placid shores before the town of Pizzo is reached, just as the coast begins to bend towards the west. Pizzo, high on its commanding rock 350 feet above the sea, has a choice of second and third category hotels. It is one of the centres for fishing tunny and swordfish which are a special feature in these waters between April and July. Pizzo is medieval in origin, and the Castle, built by Ferdinand I of Aragon in 1486, is now in use as a Youth Hostel. There are attractive coves for bathing between the rocky headlands along this beautiful coast.

The road between Pizzo and Vibo Valentia has some beautiful views over the coast on one side and the hills inland on the other, and after about ten kilometres one reaches the town. Vibo Valentia has every appearance of being a go-ahead and progressive city. Being 1800 feet above sea-level the town commands glorious views in fine weather, towards Sicily and the Lipari Islands. The castle is at just about the highest point on a hill overlooking the centre of the town, a substantial but disappointing ruin, though the views both seaward and inland do much to compensate. Vibo Valentia grew up near the Greek city of Hipponion, the sparse ruins of which lie about a mile to the north-east quite near the cemetery. Hipponion was founded by the Locrians in the fifth century B.C. and a Roman colony was established in 192 B.C. when the name was changed to Vibo Valentia; subsequently the town flourished. It suffered much however at the hands of the Saracens in the tenth century, and it was so reduced in importance that it was necessary, in effect, for Frederick II to re-found the city; in 1235 he gave his new town the name Monteleone. It rapidly recovered importance, and during the period of Murat's rule it was a town of 20,000 inhabitants and the capital of the province. Yet, true to its fluctuating fortunes throughout its history, Monteleone had to suffer another setback, for as a punishment for its support of the French regime, the Bourbons reduced its population to less than half, and transferred the provincial capital to Catanzaro.

13   Fine Lombard carvings in the cloisters of the 8th century Lombard church of S. Sophia, Benevento

14 The coast-line near Praia a Mare, Cosenza, Calabria

15 The late-Byzantine church of La Cattolica at Stilo, Calabria

The name Monteleone was not replaced by its Roman name until 1928, at a time when the Fascists were keen to recall the ancient glories of classical times. The modern town has little need of such a psycholigical boost, but the name, with its ringing and rhythmic sound certainly suits the style of the place. One has a distinct feeling that Vibo Valentia will make the most of the opportunities that undoubtedly will be coming its way in the years ahead. Already, in respect of hotel accommodation it is well provided for, with three modern second-category hotels and several of a lower grade, some at the Marina about 11 kilometres away; the latter is certain to be developed.

Walking about the town one is constantly reminded of its former status: there is a solidity about the buildings, and the town has a distinct poise and dignity. The gardens below the main street are attractive, with some splendid fully-matured firs, the great arms branching out like Hebrew candlesticks.

The large church of the Collegiata was founded perhaps as early as the ninth century, but earthquake damage necessitated a complete rebuilding between the years 1680–1723. Inside one is greeted by a rather incredible combination of pink and white stucco and other interior decoration, but it is cheerful and bright and the proportions are good. There are some fine things in the church—a very good altar in rare dark marbles in the left transept, a superb early crucifix perhaps of the fifteenth century, and some striking pieces of sculpture attributed to the Gagini brothers.

From Vibo Valentia I turned towards the sea and picked up the coast road No. 522, which hugs the shore and passes through the resorts of Briatico and Parghelia before reaching Tropea—a distance of about 32 kilometres. It is extraordinary to think that only six or seven years ago there were no hotels rated above the fourth category along this entire stretch of coast, including Tropea—which only had one. Now this coastline is being transformed—though fortunately by no means spoilt—by the addition of some superior modern hotels. At Tropea the situation has improved out of recognition: now, just outside the town at Locca, there is the very well-appointed and expertly managed Hotel Rocca Nettuno, with large private grounds, a private beach, a swimming pool and other facilities, which can accommodate 500 people. This hotel is surely a pointer of things to come in many other parts of southern Italy; it represents a substantial investment, in this case from overseas, with generous financial support from the Italian authorities. In addition to the Rocca Nettuno there are three other modern hotels in the town.

Tropea is a most picturesque old place, compact, and with narrow ancient streets which are squeezed into the limited space provided by a small plateau, which ends abruptly with high cliffs. It is a town of character, possessing palaces, churches and a delightful small cathedral. The bathing is first-rate, with fresh clear water. There are long stretches of sandy beaches, with a church and other buildings of the old town perched at the very brink of the sheer cliffs providing a dramatic focal point as viewed from the beaches on either side of the promontory.

The cathedral is reached by way of the Via Roma; it is a delightfully quiet corner of the town with a small turning-point at the dead-end beyond the church, with views across the valley towards Parghelia. The cathedral is basically an eleventh century Norman building which suffered at the hands of the rebuilders after earthquake damage in the eighteenth century. Now however, it has been very well restored to its earlier simple style. It is basilican in form with three apses concluding a main aisle and two side aisles. The cathedral contains some works of art of above-average interest: the 'Black Crucifix' a fine piece of carving in wood of the fifteenth century; a marble statue of the Madonna by G. A. Montorsoli (1555); and a painting in the Byzantine style, possibly of the fourteenth century, called 'Madonna di Romania'. Also, in the passage leading to the Sacristy there is a beautiful tomb for the Cazetta family executed by Gagini.

The See of Tropea is one of the most ancient in Calabria and goes back to the year 499.

There are many churches and palaces in Tropea that deserve unhurried exploration; in particular the churches of S. Francesco d'Assisi, the small church of S. Maria dell' Isola, and the Palazzo Toraldo with its extremely rich collection of fourth and fifth century Christian inscriptions, held to be the finest in Calabria.

Leaving Tropea by the scenically beautiful road to Caria on my way to Nicótera, I decided to take a roundabout route which would give me a chance of seeing a few of the villages, some large, some tiny, that cover the south-eastern slopes of the wide plateau between Milleto and the coast at Tropea. For most of the run between Caria and Mesiano the land is level at about 2000 feet, and the change in the air and vegetation is noticeable. At Mesiano I took the road to the south through the villages of Pernocari, Rombiolo and Mandaradoni, to name only the larger ones, and arrived eventually at Nicótera. Olives and nuts appear to be the main produce of the land in these parts, and the numerous villages tucked into the folds of the hills seem to be very poor and the male inhabitants almost without exception, either too old or too young to be working. There was a depressed air about all of these places, but it is almost impossible to judge the degree of poverty of these southern villages without intimate knowledge of them, and judgement from the driving seat is more than usually hazardous. If, as one suspects, the numerous inhabitants find it difficult to earn a living from the soil, why should there be such a profusion of villages—no less than ten along the 16 convoluted kilometres between Mesiano and Nicótera? Perhaps it was weariness as much as poverty that showed in the lined faces of the listless men I saw sitting in groups, on the stone steps outside their houses in these straggling villages.

The driving conditions along the route I had travelled after leaving the plateau road, were anything but relaxed and it was a relief to take a rest at the superbly positioned hill-town of Nicótera on the Gulf of Gióia. This small town, so attractive from a distance, especially looking up at it from the sandy southern shores of the gulf, is something of a disappointment at first hand, but it is interesting nonetheless.

The cathedral of Nicótera has a notable 'Madonna della Grazia' by Antonello Gagini, some good low-reliefs, and a sixteenth century wooden crucifix. A finer crucifix (fifteenth century) can in fact be seen in the Church of Gesù e Maria.

There is a good beach at Nicótera, and the sandy shores stretch for 14 kilometres or so, past the small villages of S. Ferdinando and Eranova to the Marina of Gióia Tauro. About midway along this coast there has now been built a Club Mediterranée tourist village. The bathing here is splendid, with the views toward Nicótera and the massive headland that turns the point at Capo Vaticano adding a welcome new dimension to the flatness of the shore. I did not know of the existence of the club before I spotted it from a vantage point in Nicótera, since it is too new to have been included in the guide-book I was using. At the time of writing it is the only tourist development along this lovely coast between Nicótera and Gióia.

From the Club Mediterranée I took the long straight road back to the highway ss 18, and, by-passing Rosarno, crossed the wide plain of Gióia—or Rosarno, as it is sometimes called—making for Palmi. The plain of Gióia is the richest olive-growing district in Italy, the olive-trees of such enormous size that collecting the olives is a more than usually difficult operation and can only be done with the aid of ladders. The fruit of these trees is a large black olive of prime quality. One can only appreciate the extent of these olive groves when one has driven past them, mile after mile. The endless ranks of splendidly kept trees may not make for variety, but they are immensely impressive.

It so happens that this is the part of Calabria that has been selected for the siting of a large steelworks, near Gióia Tauro. It is interesting that even amongst those to whom I have spoken who have been most critical of the efforts of the Cassa per il Mezzogiorno (the government agency responsible for supplying capital for the development of the

South), none have had a good word to say about this project. A man in an official position in Reggio, when talking about it threw up his hands in dismay: 'Fancy putting down a great steelworks in such beautiful countryside' he exclaimed, 'it will be a terrible eyesore!' He was referring of course to the lovely combination of mountain, plain and sea, which can be enjoyed from so many vantage points in a wide sweeping arc from Nicótera through Laureana, Maropati, Taurianova and Monte S. Elia at Palmi, from which a steelworks will stand out like a sore thumb. Nevertheless the plans seem to be set, though at the time of writing work has not commenced. Perhaps there will be opposition by local vested interests, similar to that which has delayed progress on the new airport at S. Eufémia. The decision to build at Gióia does seem a strange one.

About 20 kilometres south of Gióia, Palmi stands in a commanding position about 750 feet above the sea, with beautiful views from the belvedere of its attractive gardens in the direction of Capo Barbi and along the superb shores of the Costa Viola. It is a prosperous country town, showing signs of rapid development, and being so close to the autostrada its importance is sure to increase. It might well form the centre of a revitalized tourist industry for this district, but to date little has been done. Part of the difficulty is the terrain, since the mountains sweep right down to the shore along the rocky coast between Palmi and Bagnara. But a start has been made in the town itself and there are now three small modern hotels, graded II and III, and four simple ones in the fourth category. Palmi has its own small marina three kilometres away, south of Capo Barbi. From the belvedere of Monte S. Elia, just off the main road (ss 18) south of Palmi, there is a tremendous view which on a clear day takes in the nearer slopes of the Aspromonte, the Straits of Messina, the Monti Peloritani in Sicily, Mount Etna, and to the north-west, Strómboli and the nearer of the Aeolian islands.

13.   Reggio di Calabria and its environs

From Palmi one can join the autostrada A3 for the route south to Reggio, and this is advisable if time is short, since the coast road by the nature of the terrain makes for a slow journey. However later in the chapter we will take this road from Reggio, and visit Villa S. Giovanni, Scilla and Bagnara as well as other smaller places along the coast.

The Autostrada del Sole is throughout its length a remarkable piece of engineering, but nowhere does the spectacular nature of the road strike one more forcibly than during the stretch between Bagnara and Scilla. Hugging the side of the mountain and supported on great concrete stilts, the road gradually descends towards Scilla, and one looks down from a great height almost vertically to the coastal towns and villages far below. The road cuts through large chunks of mountain on at least seven occasions, and the cost of tunnelling alone for this short stretch of about 14 kilometres must have reached an astronomical figure. In general the layman cannot begin to comprehend the engineering difficulties and costs of this incredible road. Certainly the Calabresi I have spoken to have shown no appreciation of it; one is more likely to hear grumbles at the alleged length of time it has taken to complete. One despairs of ever hearing any credit given by southerners to the efforts by the State to improve conditions in the South. And yet in the field of communications great progress has been made—not only with the outstandingly good new roads, but also with the railways. I remember several years ago travelling to Sicily by train from Rome and seeing the work being done to lay a second track throughout the very long route, often in appallingly difficult terrain, involving the construction of a great deal of new tunnelling. The work has now been completed.

The difficulty about trying to write objectively about Reggio di Calabria is that one is constantly making comparisons with the city across the straits that has shared with it so many disasters, and this is hardly being objective. Moreover for those who know both cities the comparison is not at all favourable to Reggio. Earthquakes in 1783 and 1908 (to mention only the most disastrous) destroyed practically every building standing at those times in Reggio, so that, with rare exception, there is left now nothing of architectural importance; it is a city of low, uninspired and in many places downright ugly, functional, shock-proof buildings often in concrete. And with the passing of its buildings of merit there seems to have passed too a large part of the spirit of the people. Defeatism is in the air in Reggio; one senses a feeling of disillusionment—a weary acceptance of the inevitable that is close to despondency. It is an ennui of the corporate spirit that leads to inaction, whereas decisions are called for. In fact Messina suffered far greater losses than Reggio in the 1908 disaster (100,000 died compared with 5000) and the catalogue of disaster in its history exceeds that of the Calabrian city. And yet today in Messina we find a vitality and optimism that is quite absent in Reggio. One might even say that the most outstanding aspect of Reggio today is its view across the straits to Etna, the Peloritani mountains and Messina. But enough of comparisons.

This is not the place to go into detail about the troubled times that resulted from the decision to transfer the capital of the Region of Calabria from Reggio to Catanzaro. Yet it is necessary to record the fact, since it explains a lot of the bitterness that one finds today in Reggio, based as it is on allegations of political graft and favouritism. If only the Reggians can get over their disappointment, there are enormous opportunities in the field of tourism in their own province that can absorb their energies. There is much to be done.

The town of Reggio with a population of about 160,000 lies on a north-east to south-west axis and consists almost exclusively of extremely long parallel streets, making for considerable monotony. For example, Corso Garibaldi with its extension Viale Giovanni Amendola is over three kilometres in length and the roads parallel to it almost as long and just as straight. The only pleasurable street to walk along is the Corso Vittorio Emanuele, separated by long pleasant gardens from the Lungomare Matteotti, and from the latter promenade, on a fine day, one can have glorious views across the straits to Sicily. Reggio has a fair-sized port, though not deep enough to take really big ships, and it is from here that both the ferry steamer and the Aliscafi hydrofoils leave for Messina.

The one large monument to escape total destruction during the earthquakes is the impressive Aragonese castle, set in its own attractive grounds in the southern part of the city, not far from the cathedral. The latter, a post-1908 reconstruction, is totally devoid of architectural merit.

Without doubt the pride of Reggio is its very fine archaeological museum, housed in a modern building overlooking the Piazza Indipendenza at the bottom of Viale G. Amendola. The most important exhibits in the extremely valuable collections are from Locri, but also to be seen are many finds from other parts of southern Italy from the Palaeolithic to the post-Roman periods. The famous votive plaques or *pinakes,* concerning the cult of Persephone are extraordinarily graceful. They came from the sanctuary to Persephone at Mannella, Locri. The *pinakes* are made of clay and were originally painted, and the low-reliefs show scenes such as the goddess's robing and hairdressing, the bridal procession, the preparation for the marriage bed, and Persephone with Pluto seated together receiving gifts from other deities—all compositions of artistry and grace and full of interesting detail. The majority of them date from the fifth century B.C. Among the most important exhibits are the famous group of the Dioscuri (late fifth–early fourth century B.C.) excavated in fragments by Orsi and Petersen; some important terracottas from the revetment of the Temple of Casa Marafioti, Locri; and the terracotta *acroterion*—a nude youth astride a horse, his feet supported in the hands of a sphinx below; this is fifth century, also from the temple of Marafioti. The museum is in the course of rearrangement, and soon a very rich collection of finds from Reggio, Hipponium, Caulonia, Croton and Sybaris (to mention the more important) will be exhibited in more spacious surroundings on the first floor, where there will also be on show an extremely valuable numismatic collection and a display of Lucanian pottery. The Museo Nazionale at Reggio ranks in importance above all other archaeological museums south of Naples, with the exception of Taranto, and it does seem remarkable that it is so little patronized by Italians. However the lack of crowds ensures an atmosphere of relaxation and calm in marked contrast to the streets outside. There is no more pleasant place to pass the time during the heat of the morning—but it should be noted that the museum is closed all day on Mondays.

Hotel accommodation in Reggio has shown a steady improvement in the last ten years with the addition of four hotels, two in the second category and two in the third. Reggio has one first category hotel, the Excelsior, with a delightful view from the front rooms of the palm trees, holm oaks and flowering shrubs and trees of the gardens along the Lungomare Matteotti, and across the straits to Sicily. A festa was in full swing during my stay in the city and a large stretch of the Viale Giovanni Amendola was given over to roadside stalls. It was an entertaining diversion to wander past these stalls at night, watching the wonderful displays of virtuosity by the salesmen as they tried to entice a few *soldi* from the deep pockets of the wary country-folk, of whom huge masses had descended on Reggio from the surrounding villages. The electric light bulbs hanging by strings over the stalls, the general hubbub of the cheerful crowds, the despairing blasts on the horn as drivers vainly attempted to pass through the packed road, the shouts of laughter or yells of pain from children depending on whether they were enjoying themselves or being walloped by exhausted parents—all the excitement, brightness and *joie de vivre* of the occasion, made up for the poverty of what was on offer.

I was fortunate in having been introduced to people in Reggio during my recent visit, who were to make a great difference to the enjoyment of my stay and to my knowledge of the city and the neighbouring towns and villages. Soon after my arrival my new friends suggested a trip to Gambarie and Rumia, the resorts of the Aspromonte. We left early in the morning and took a secondary route into the mountains, passing the small villages of Trizzino and Terreti. This road is hard work for the driver, but allows the passengers magnificent views. Unfortunately our view towards Sicily was obscured by heavy humidity, but the mountain scenery is lovely, with the changes of vegetation and woodland showing a sequence of citrus, olives, chestnuts and finally beeches, with mountain flora replacing cactus and agarves. There are also magnificent woods of tall mountain pines in the highlands.

Our first stop was at Gambarie (altitude 4428 feet), a resort that has grown in importance in recent years. There is a selection of hotels here including the Grande Albergo Gambarie (Cat. II) and a variety of attractive villas of the chalet type, with corrugated-iron roofs. It is both a winter and summer resort with ski-slopes on the side of Montalto, complete with chair-lift. There is a small shopping area here and tourist bars, but one feels that much more could be made of this place as a holiday resort. The views are spectacular, the air bracing in the summer and brisk in winter with always some warmth in the sun. The failure to develop Gambarie would appear to be caused as much by lack of drive as by lack of resources. One can imagine what the Norwegians or the Austrians would have made of it!

Only a few kilometres away from the town is the beautiful small lake of Rumia, its still water reflecting the green, thickly wooded higher slopes of the Aspromonte. A new large second-category hotel has been built here, but is not available for public bookings since the entire building is at present occupied by the unfortunate people who lost all their possessions when their village was obliterated by a landslide; they are being cared-for and maintained by the Provincial government.

Landslides are in fact commonplace in the south of Italy, doubtless due in part to deforestation in times past, but also because of the violence of the storms of rain and wind that hit these upper slopes. No one who has experienced a heavy storm in these mountains can ever be surprised at the possible consequences. In addition, the rock formations are often so sheer that it is remarkable that soil and timber can cling to them, and quite understandable that they are often carried away, leaving the stark dramatic rock formations that one sees in so many places in southern Calabria, for example at Pentedattilo, where the village huddles at the foot of the great rugged bare crag looming above, so as to form almost a part of it.

Before returning to Reggio along the main road through the villages of S. Stefano and S. Alessio we decided to visit the so-called Mausoleum of Garibaldi—the site of the wounding and capture of Garibaldi by government troops on 29 August 1862. This may seem to be an extraordinary event to those who know of Garibaldi only as the hero of the *risorgimento;* it was a direct consequence of the impatience of the national leader who raised an army of 3000 volunteers, in order to invade the Papal States and bring them into a United Italy, in spite of the opposition to this move by Rattazzi the Prime Minister.

On the return journey to Reggio we passed again through glorious scenery, the road eventually, after innumerable twists and bends arriving at Gallico Marina, about eight kilometres north of the city. As we crossed the plains near Reggio we passed groves of citrus fruits, including terraces of the remarkable bergamot orange—this is the only place in the world where this fruit is grown, such is the unique combination required of soil, irrigation, sunlight, and air, and temperature-variation between night and day. The essence of the bergamot, formerly squeezed out by hand by the local womenfolk, is used as a base in the perfume industry. It combines well with other essential oils, and is considered an indispensible product for the manufacture of really high quality perfumes and toilet waters. The immediate neighbourhood of Reggio is of additional importance to the world's perfume manufacturers, since it is here that 40 per cent of the total acreage of jasmine is grown.

The coast road to the north from Reggio passes several local seaside resorts such as Pentimele, Gallico Marina and Catona on the way to Villa S. Giovanni, and while only of passing interest to the sophisticated traveller they all have one feature in common—a beautiful view across the Strait of Messina. I saw these small resorts in the early autumn, outside the season (which ends on 31 August for Italians) and it may not be fair to judge them in the condition I found them—but one gets the strong impression that all these Reggian sea-side places could be considerably smartened up. Once in Villa S. Giovanni however, the scene changes at once; there is a sprightliness and bustle about this lively place which is in marked contrast to Reggio (crammed though the latter is with traffic) accounted for by the fact that it is the ferry

terminal for the heavy rail and road traffic that crosses from the mainland to Sicily. Indeed the atmosphere in Villa S. Giovanni is much
more in accord with that of Messina across the Strait. Because of its
importance as a communications link this small town is very well-off
for hotels.

At the small fishing-cum-tourist village of Cannitello, two
kilometres round the headland, I was able to inspect a swordfish
fishing-boat pulled up on the beach for repair, but minus the
immensely long cat-walk from the prow, from which the fishermen are
able to see and harpoon the fish. However the extremely tall mast was
in position making the boat look more than ever ungainly. Apart from
the obvious question of stability, these craft can only be sailed in very
calm conditions, for then the spotter at the crow's nest atop the mast
can see the swordfish in the still clear water. Normally when out fishing, all motion is severely restricted, since swordfish are very nervous
creatures and any quick movement frightens them off. Great skill and
patience is called for by the men, and the work can be hazardous. The
pescespada fishermen are a breed apart.

About eight kilometres further along the coast, the large fishing village of Scilla is most beautifully set into the curving hollows formed on
either side of the dominating rock that forms the headland. On the
south-western side there is a splendid long beach (*la spiaggia delle
sirene*), and on the other side, the fishermen's dwellings come right
down to the water's edge, making a most picturesque scene from above
of brown-tiled roofs and weathered white-washed walls against the
blues and purples of the bay. Here, an occupant could literally cast a
hand-line from his living-room window. This part of the town is known
as the *Chianalea* and is where many of the *pescespada* fishermen's
families live.

The castle which crowns the high rock dominating Scilla—once
owned by the Ruffo family—has now been extremely well converted
into a youth hostel, and the views from here are quite splendid. This is
the rock—Scylla—identified by writers in antiquity, but feared by
Odysseus and his companions as a six-headed sea-monster with loins
girt with the heads of baying dogs. (There is a splendid statue of this
creature by Montorsoli in Messina). On the other side of the straits
lurked Charybdis, another monster it was believed, waiting to prey on
any who ventured too close. One can understand the fears of these
early mariners since the roaring of the whirlpool on the Messina shores
and the noise of the current and frequent rough water near the rock of
Scilla, must have easily aroused superstitious notions, especially in
misty weather. (It was no help that at this point Odysseus lost six of his
companions.)

Scilla, to all intents and purposes, is almost untouched by tourism. The broad sweeping beach of the *sirene* has only two small *pensioni* one of which, Matteo a Mare, is in the first category.

Another ten kilometres along the Costa Viola one comes to Bagnara Calabra, a town of about 12,000 inhabitants, a centre for the marketing of fish and for the fishing of *pescespada*. Bagnara is in a magnificent situation with folds of the mountains running steeply down to the sea. There is little finesse about the town; the smell of fish is in the air, and one sees fishing-tackle on all sides. When I was there, there must have been 50 or 60 small fishing boats pulled up on the beach. Tourist accommodation has increased only marginally over the past ten years.

It is a hard climb out of town before one reaches the autostrada, which at the Bagnara exit is at a considerable height. On the easy journey back to Reggio, I found myself reflecting on the attitudes of the people of the South to the huge amounts that have been invested in Southern Italy since the setting up of the *Cassa per il Mezzogiorno* 15 years ago. One can understand in a way why southerners are scornful of what has been achieved, since the building of roads—to take one example—does not in itself make any permanent impact on the unemployment problem. Indeed southerners consider that this improved system of communication only adds to the wealth of the industrial North, since the main industries to benefit are controlled from the North. The fact that these same roads will open up the South to tourism on a large scale in the years ahead is largely overlooked. In any case, it is argued, the profits from hotels will go into the pockets of the northerners who finance them, or overseas to the Germans or Swiss who can be tempted to take advantage of the generous grants and tax exemptions available; it is disregarded that tourists will spend money in the shops and bars. Even the really big projects such as the steel-works at Taranto, or the petro-chemical plant at Brindisi, are criticised because they are not labour-intensive—being very modern and largely automated.

It is unwise to generalise about political and economic problems in the South, but one thing seems clear: the gap in productivity between the north and the south of Italy has increased without a break since the unification of the country in 1870, and in spite of all the efforts to bring industry to the South in the past 15 years, the gap continues to grow. It is difficult to see how it could be otherwise since the North cannot be expected to wait until the South catches up—cannot halt its own momentum. Industrially, the North was infinitely more advanced than the southern kingdom at the time of unification and well placed geographically, was able to take full advantage of the stimulus of the First

World War. The South, between the wars, could never hope to come to terms with such a lead. A succession of governments, it would seem, showed unconcern. A commentator on the Italian scene has recently written: 'It is a common complaint by the Calabresi that under Bourbon rule they were neglected, under united Italy's House of Savoy they were driven to brigandage or enrolled to die in distant wars, and under Fascism they were sent to settle in the ephemeral African empire.'

The coming of the Common Market has only strengthened the position of the industrial North; and for all Italians living north of Gaeta, the *mezzogiorno,* (meaning here the lands of the old Kingdom of Naples) remains a 'problem' area. But a bigger problem is how to develop something approaching unity between the 'two nations', which in spite of all efforts and by whichever criteria are used, in customs, culture, and social habits, remain as separate as ever. It is a problem which would seem to be a long way from being solved and one which Italy is by no means the only country in the world to grapple with. Perhaps the wisest course is to strive not for unity, which because of the country's history would almost certainly be artificial, but for equality of opportunity. The latter may not be so far-fetched as many people think, especially if one day the clearing of the Suez canal opens the way for the products of industry in the south to the markets of the Middle East, with certain advantages in connection with geographical position and transportation costs. Such an event might provide the stimulus which the South needs if its industry is to develop on a scale to match the North.

14. From Reggio to Taranto: the Ionian cities of Magna Graecia

Reggio di Calabria is of very ancient origin. The old Greek city, called Rhegion, formed an important link in the chain of powerful cities and their satellite territories which dominated the Ionian shores. The whole of this Greek-controlled area of southern Italy came to be known as Magna Graecia—Great Greece. Some of the cities established on the Ionian Coast, such as Croton, Sybaris or Taras, in their prime rivalled any of the cities in old Greece in wealth and power, justifying the proud title. And these Greek colonies in Italy had more to offer than just luxury and wealth. Writing of the philosophers of Elea and Croton, D. Randall-MacIver says:

> It is a most remarkable thing that Magna Graecia should have produced almost simultaneously these two great independent school of philosophy, and it makes us reflect how much of our Greek legacy we owe to the colonists of the west. Without the orators, philosophers, scientists, and historians who were born or fostered in Magna Graecia, the ancient world, and we ourselves, would have been much poorer.

Rhegion itself never became one of the really powerful colonies (though defensively immensely strong) due to the fact that it did not possess any worthwhile land, and its importance lay in the fact that it controlled, with the city of Zancle (or Messana) lying opposite, the vital trade route from the Ionian to the Tyrrenhian Sea. Indeed in antiquity Rhegion was far more closely linked with Sicily than with Southern Italy. Its foundation followed very closely on that of Zancle, and a substantial number of the original settlers of both cities came from the same city in the mother-country—Chalcis in Euboea. In this manner the Chalcidians were able to ensure that no other people were able to assert a dominating influence in the Straits, and the same time could count on a profitable income from port dues, tolls, and, at times, trans-shipment facilities. The date of the foundation of Rhegion is generally thought to be 730 B.C. (or only a few years later) and followed very quickly after that of Zancle. It was the second oldest colony on the mainland of Italy, maintaining close ties with the oldest Euboean colony—Cumaeo.

During very early times Rhegion was on good terms with its neighbour Locri, but eventually relations deteriorated especially after Syracuse, intent on gaining a foothold on the mainland, made a formal alliance with Locri. Alarmed at the growing power of Syracuse and her allies, Rhegion entered into an alliance with Taras (Taranto), and remained in bitter opposition to Syracusan plans for expansion, which however did not prevail against the power of Dionysius of Syracuse, who in a long siege in 387–386 B.C. starved out the inhabitants and dismantled the walls. Rhegion however survived as an inhabited place, and 100 years later, under increasing pressure from the Lucanians and Bruttians, requested and received a Roman garrison. Thereafter under Roman protection the city recovered, and was able to contribute ships and men to Rome during the First Punic War, and was rewarded with certain privileges. At the time of Augustus new colonists were sent to the city, and under *pax Romana* it flourished, becoming Rhegium to the Romans—signifying a change in status as much as a change in name.

Today in Reggio very little survives of its ancient past. Not very substantial remains of the city walls can be seen near the Post and Telegraph building between Corso Vitt. Emanuele and the Lungomare, and there are foundations of a small Greek temple in Via Torrione. That however is the sum of it. Practically nothing can be seen of Rhegion's works of art, and not a line of her authors has survived. And yet we know that Rhegion had its own poets and historians and sculptors, one of whom, the sculptor Pythagoras was famous in his time. Such a void is odd, considering the discoveries that have taken place at Locri, which did not survive so long as Rhegion as a place of importance. Perhaps the long history of earthquakes and the subsequent rebuilding of what has remained throughout the ages a substantial town, has destroyed all hope of further major discoveries.

The road along the Ionian shore between Reggio and Taranto hugs the coast-line for the greater part of the way, and for almost the entire distance one is in sight of the railway line that was completed at around the turn of the century. When Gissing was travelling along this line, the road was probably little more than a dusty cart-track, but today it is a first class highway, and has been improved in many respects during the last decade or so. Journey times compared with many other roads in Calabria (excepting the newest) are fast, and it would be possible to cover the 451 kilometres between Reggio and Taranto in a day, if anyone should feel so inclined. That, however, is very far from what I am suggesting, since there are a number of places of interest that may be visited en route, so for the purposes of this chapter I shall adopt a leisurely tempo. As far as accommodation is concerned this coast has been transformed in very recent years, and details will be given at the appropriate places.

Once past the dreary industrial southern suburbs of Reggio and clear of the airport, the main road (ss106) sweeps in a grand manner past Punta di Pellaro, with lovely views across to Sicily, and on a clear day to Etna, and then passing very close to Capo dell' Armi, with its lighthouse, reaches Melito di Porto Salvo after 30 kilometres. At this point a road runs north across the Aspromonte to Gambarie. It was at Melito that Garibaldi landed with his 'redshirts' in September 1860 having overrun Sicily, and again in 1862. From the sea the whole of this southern promontory looks white, and it was known to the Greeks as Leukopetra. Melito is a small town but has only a very modest hotel, and from here to Brancaleone there are merely very small sea-side villages. A feature of this land, are the torrents and *fiumara* that take the autumn rainfall and the melting snow in spring from the slopes of Aspromonte. The torrents can have a savage water fall for short periods and cause much damage, but for six months in the year they are dry. Typical of the villages perched in the incredibly rugged foothills of these mountains are: Pentedattilo, with its extraordinary background of rock shaped like the five fingers of a hand; Bova, once a bishopric but now neglected and said to be, as a colony of a city of Magna Graecia, the sole remaining link with old Greece; and Palizzi; beautifully situated at the bottom of two perpendicular barren rocks, on the highest of which is perched the ruins of its castle.

Round the corner, past Capo Spartivento, the road turns northwards and soon reaches Brancaleone Marina where the beach is good, and inland the plain is planted with vines and fruit trees. Here there has been built a new medium-sized hotel (Altalia, Cat. II), and another at the next and larger town of Bovalino Marina (Orsa, Cat. II). These however are only small places, and it is not until we reach Locri that we find an attempt to develop tourism on a scale that is at all ambitious. A few years ago there were only two very humble hotels in Locri, but now there are three modern second-category hotels, one of which (Rachele) has 100 rooms. It is too early to make a fair appraisal of the attempts to make Locri into an attractive resort since everything in this respect is so new, but a good start has been made and doubtless will continue.

Of course, Locri starts with a big advantage in that the modern town is very close to the ancient Greek city of Locri Epizephyrii (to give it its full name), the ruins of which lie on the left-hand side of the road about three kilometres from the town as one approaches from the south. The ruins cover a very wide area and extend for a distance of 2½ kilometres back from the main road, and for this reason it is wise to study the plans and photographs in the excellent new Antiquarium, illustrating the history and development of Locri, before setting out on foot or by car (there are certain drivable tracks and paths).

It would be misleading to suggest that there is much to see now of what was once a great city. The Graeco-Roman Theatre (Hellenistic in date but much re-worked by the Romans) is perhaps the most substantial ruin; but the once splendid Ionic temple at Marasa has only one rather pathetic broken stub of a column of the many (17 side columns) which once supported a massive entablature and roof, including the central free-standing *acroterion,* which depicts a Nereid flanked by Dioscuri on horseback (now at the Museum of Reggio). However it is an enjoyable experience to explore this site: the whole area is now an orchard, olives and almonds mainly, and their beautiful shapes add colour and variety to what would otherwise be a somewhat desolate scene.

Perhaps the most interesting part today is the Centocamere, an urban area where excavations are currently in progress. Craftsmen must have lived here, since the remains of a pottery kiln have been found. It is here also that one can see stretches of the earlier walls. Of the later walls (perhaps third century B.C.) many hundreds of metres can be traced along the site. The absence of really intensive excavations at Locri is most marked, compared to the large resources made available for the work at Sybaris (and with such poor return), little has been attempted. I have not been able to discover the reason for this, which may be connected with the ownership of the land, but one day important finds are bound to be discovered here which will add to our knowledge of the history of Locri.

Though never in the same league, in terms of power and wealth, as Croton or Taras, Locri is one of the most interesting of the colonies of Magna Graecia. Locrians were despised by their neighbours, Rhegion on one side and Croton on the other, because of their supposedly bastard ancestry. The original site of the colony, planted or directed here in 673 B.C., was probably at the mouth of the Portigliola Torrent which runs close by the present south-western city walls—but shortly after arrival they moved to the present site, previously occupied by native Sicels for some centuries. This site extends to fairly steeply rising hills, and here the Locrians developed their city with three distinct parts— an upper, a middle, and a lower city. In the upper city there was not an acropolis, but a citadel in three parts crowning three hills—Castellace, Abbadessa and Mannella, which rise to about 500 feet. Religious life

16   A corner in S. Demetrio, an 'Albanian' small town in the Greek Sila, Calabria

17   The mountain village of S. Sofia d'Epiro on the edge of the Greek Sila

18   Dwellings in the *trulli* style near Alberobello

19   Fishing boats preparing to leave for the night catch from Monopoli, Apulia

was centred on Persephone, and a Sanctuary was built in honour of the goddess.

Due to the hostility of their neighbours, the early years of the Locrian colony were anything but secure, though they managed to subdue the Sicels. However in the middle of the sixth century an extraordinary event took place which enabled them to consolidate their position and even to expand, with a new colony at Medma on the Tyrrhenian coast of Calabria. This was the battle of the Sagras river, where a huge army from Croton, intent on destroying Locri once and for all, was defeated with enormous losses by a Locrian army of only 10,000 men, perhaps one tenth the number of their enemy. Clearly, it was argued at the time, such a stupendous victory could not have been achieved by mortal arms alone. Consequently stories have come down to us (from the pens of Locrian writers) in which we read of the sudden appearance of Ajax in the heat of battle (Leonymus, the Croton commander was felled by his sword), and even more significant, when the fortunes of the battle still hung in the balance, the arrival on each flank of the Locrian army of 'a young horseman of resplendent beauty and gigantic stature, mounted on a white horse'—clearly the eagerly awaited Dioscuri Castor and Pollux, at whose temple in Sparta the Locrians had offered sacrifice.

The appearance of the Dioscuri was one of the favourite themes of the artists of Locri, and it was only natural that images of the Divine Twins should have been placed on the roof of the temples at one of the gates of the city in commemoration of such a great victory. Whether this was the famous temple of Persephone is in dispute, and is doubtful. We do know however that the Sanctuary of Persephone was situated in the ravine between the heights of Mannella and Abbadessa. The spot which has given up such a priceless yield of treasures was in fact the burial place for the ex-votos from an earlier sanctuary, (from 650–450 B.C.) which had been deliberately broken up and carefully interred. There are terracotta figurines of goddesses and humans and animals, and the *pinakes* decorated in low relief, which Orsi found and patiently reassembled, and which now adorn the museums of Reggio and Taranto. The new sanctuary itself was found to be quite empty, but it is probable that the magnificent sculptures known as the Boston and Ludovisi thrones (the latter one of the outstanding exhibits at the Museo Nazionale Romano in Rome) came from the Sanctuary of Persephone.

The later history of Locri, centred on the alliance with Syracuse, has already been touched on, and suffice to say that under the protection of her powerful allies Locri became, in the fourth century, the most formidable power in Magna Graecia next to Taras.

One of the reasons that the Locrians clung to their site, even in the insecure early days, was that the advantages from the point of view of communications outweighed the disadvantages of its poverty in agricultural land. Just enough for their own needs, there was never an exportable surplus of corn—as at Metapontion and Taras—so the Locrians depended for their wealth on manufactured goods such as pottery, bronze objects—like mirrors, terracotta revetments, and a highly individual form of sculpture—at all of which they excelled. The city was well placed on the ancient east-west coast road (which bisects the site of Locri to this day and is still known as the 'dromos'); it was a 'port'-of-call for westward-bound ships en route for the Straits and the Tyrrenhian; and the Locrians had the use of an ancient communications route through the mountains via Taurianova, leading to the west coast near Hipponion.

The present road through Gerace, Cittanova and Taurianova in all likelihood follows the ancient track. Throughout almost the entire route from Locri to Gióia Tauro (ss 111) there is beautiful scenery, which at times—especially the first 34 kilometres as far as Cittanova— is spectacular and at times incredible. In 1847 Edward Lear made a drawing of Gerace, one of many to illustrate his immensely readable book on Southern Italy. These have often been taken to be wildly exaggerated, and I thought so myself when I first saw them. But when I arrived in southern Calabria and saw the mountains and the sometimes fantastic rock formations for myself, I realised that Lear's drawings were true to nature. What is missing in these black and white sketches is the colour and the wonderful luminosity of the light, perhaps the most characteristic aspect of this Southern Italian scene. Lear himself constantly remarks on the colour effects, and does, within the limitations of his medium, cleverly suggest the light by strongly contrasting highlights and shade. He wrote:

> *August 11* ... After siesta, drawing again. A beautiful trait of Gerace is its admirable colour; its white or delicate fawn-hued cliffs, and gray or dove-coloured buildings coming beautifully off the purple of the mountains.

The climb up to Gerace is abrupt, and alternate loops in the road bring one into view of the town securely perched on its immense slab of rock and looking well-nigh impregnable. Whether it was malaria, or the murderous attacks of Corsair raiding parties which forced the inhabitants of old Locri to found Gerace in the seventh century is debatable, but I suspect that both were responsible. For Lear, Gerace was 'by far the grandest and proudest object in general postion, and as a city, which we have yet seen in Calabria.'

Today Gerace, although possessing the largest cathedral in Calabria, is a sleepy little town, and as Leslie Gardiner says 'no more than a large, depopulated mountain hamlet sunbathing the years away and hoping for better times.' These however may be just round the corner, for the Costa Ionica is clearly going to attract a large number of tourists in the years ahead, and the Cathedral is one of the main cultural attractions for the whole area. As it is, the 75 years since the turn of the century have seen its population fall from 7,250 to just under 4,000. Standing at over 1600 feet it commands tremendous views, especially at the upper level of the town by the Norman castle, looking out over the sheer precipice towards the pass in the mountains to the northwest. The vast cathedral is not to everyone's taste: 'The green, yellow and white marble of this florid concoction comes from classical Locri' writes Leslie Gardiner, and wastes no time getting off the subject. But for all that, it is an interesting building. It is Norman in origin and was founded by Robert Guiscard in 1045, and later enlarged and restored by Frederick II in 1222. It was severely damaged by the earthquake of 1783. When Ramage visited the cathedral 45 years later it was still too badly damaged for public worship, and services were held in the crypt. The church is Latin-cross in shape with a deep central apse and two shallow side apses. The antique columns taking the load over the rounded arches are from Locri—a selection of *verde antico, giallo antico* and *breccia africana*, and some very fine fluted columns of white marble. The crypt is supported by many more ancient columns from Locri, and contains a painting thought to have been brought from Constantinople in 1261, called the 'Madonna della Deitra.'

There are two other churches of considerable interest in Gerace. S. Francesco, built in 1252, is now in the process of being restored; the main doorway is extraordinarily fine with most delicate carving, showing a marked Saracenic influence both in shape and decoration. On the right of S. Francesco is the tiny Byzantine-Norman church of S. Giovanello.

Five kilometres further along the coast brings one to Siderno. Here again, as at Locri, the ambitious efforts to transform this place from a slumbering sea-side town into a wide-awake modern resort are too recent to judge their success, but certainly there is a handsome modern *lungomare* at Siderno with young freshly planted palms along the sea front, and flowering shrubs, and a few years added maturity will make all the difference. In recent times a modern hotel with 66 rooms and part air-conditioning has been built (President—Cat. II), and there are also three modest hotels.

The next resort, 4½ kilometres further on—Marina di Gioiosa Ionica—is much smaller than Siderno but considerably more interesting as a place. For one thing the well-defined ruins of a Roman theatre have been excavated here, and there is a handsome sixteenth century look-out tower known as 'la torre Galea'. Of the two modern second-category hotels here one, San Giorgio, is large (88 rooms) and the other, Miramare, of medium size. A decade ago there was only one tiny inn with 11 rooms. At Roccella Ionica, seven kilometres further on, the situation has changed even more dramatically, for this small resort now has three modern second Category hotels with a total of 142 rooms and a brand new bathing station with all facilities. In the background, perched high on a formidable rock are the substantial ruins of the Carafa castle. This castle was instrumental in beating off a raid in strength by the corsair Dragut, its guns inflicting heavy losses on the invader's ships.

The whole of this coast is remarkable for two things, the number of forts or look-out towers that were built to watch these long, wide, easily invaded beaches, and the numerous *fiumare* that drain the foothills and high points of the Appenines. Shortly after leaving Roccella Ionica one comes to three of these *fiumare* the second of which the Allaro, is the River Sagras of antiquity, where the Crotoniates were routed by the Locrians. About seven kilometres inland from here is the town of Caulonia which became a fief of the Carafa family after the thirteenth century. It does not however mark the spot of the ancient Greek city of Caulonia, for this, as was stated briefly in an earlier chapter, was situated almost on the shore at a spot very close to Monasterace Marina, about 14 kilometres further east, just before Punta Stilo. The Greek town in time extended to three small hills, on the side of one of which is the modern lighthouse.

Ancient Caulonia was an Achaean colony which came within the Crotoniate orbit and was probably founded in the mid-seventh century B.C. Its territory was neither extensive nor very rich, though it was wealthy enough to finance and build a large Doric temple in the early part of the fifth century. Only part of the temple stylobate is extant, and parts of the town walls. The latter are unusual: there was no building stone in the district, so the Cauloniates used large smooth pebbles or stones from the river bed, held together with a kind of cement made from earth and strengthened with lime, and it says a lot for their building technique that this unique method has in part survived after 25 centuries of sun, wind and rain, to say nothing of man-managed destruction. The beautiful and advanced coinage of Caulonia between 530–510 B.C. (in particular a splendid incuse stater, depicting Apollo holding the lustral branch with a stag in the background) indicates economic security by that time. The city suffered defeat at the hands of Dionysius I of Syracuse after which its inhabitants were transported to

Sicily and the territory given to the Locrians.

The road from Monasterace Marina to Soverato heads due north and passes a number of miniscule marinas none of which have yet been developed. Shortly after passing Punta Stilo we cross the boundary into the province of Catanzaro and thereafter for about ten kilometres we have lovely views towards the hills and the villages of S. Caterina and Badolato. After crossing several *fiumare,* the road then passes through Soverato and curves round the beautiful bay to Punta dei Staletti with its cluster of resorts, which have been described in Chapter Ten. Having passed Catanzaro Lido we arrive, after 15 kilometres, at Sellia Marina from where there is a fine view of the coast, and here in recent years a large hotel has been built with 148 rooms (Triton, Cat. II). Returning to the coast road, and hugging the shore near the promontory at Le Castella, we then turn north again and cut the corner well west of the Lacinian Promontory at Capo Colonna, leaving the airport on the right.

A description has already been given of the modern town of Crotone in Chapter Ten, and here I would like to give a brief account of the foundation and history of the ancient city—Croton (or Crotona)—which ranked among the most important of all the cities of Magna Graecia. Croton, probably an Achaean colony, was founded in 710 B.C., and soon made good use of the only natural harbour between Taras and Rhegion, and also of the fertile low-lying plains that surrounded it at least as far as the river Neto. In its prime, the walls of the city extended for many miles (in Livy's time 12 Roman miles) and its territory at the time of its greatest expansion, probably stretched as far as the Tyrrhenian Sea. Yet practically nothing of substance survives, and the disappearance of the ancient city is very remarkable if we compare it, not with Sybaris where there is an explanation, but with Syracuse, where extensive remains of walls, fortifications and monuments can be seen today. One is left with unrewarding speculation as to how this immensely solid mass of masonry vanished without trace.

After an early set-back in its first major war—with Locri, as already described—the power of Croton grew steadily, and many decades were to pass before the quarrel with Sybaris erupted into a war, which in 510 B.C. ended in the destruction of the latter city. Recorded history about this matter is so sparse that few details have come down to us as to the nature of the quarrel and it is difficult to believe, as some scholars have suggested, that it was merely a case of typical Greek jealousy of their neighbours. Nothing but a deliberate action aimed to undermine the very security of Croton could, one feels, have forced on the Croton leaders the extreme steps that they took. After all, this was not just a punitive military campaign, but an act of annihilation. Sybaris was literally wiped off the face of the earth, and even the foundations of a once great city were buried, it was hoped for all time, under the river bed of the Crathis which was specially diverted from its course for the purpose. The human misery and suffering consequent upon this act of hatred can easily be imagined, and it is hard to believe that all this was because of mercantile rivalry.

Nevertheless, the consequence of the elimination of Sybaris was that Croton enormously increased in wealth and power. She gained a substantial part of the vast agricultural territories and much of the commerce that would have gone to her enemy. In addition Croton gained valuable new raw material from silver mines and forests, and as a result became the most powerful city-state in southern Italy. Yet by the end of the following century the dominance of Croton was over, brought about it would seem by luxury and decadence (calling to mind the main reasons for the fall of Akragas in Sicily). Indeed it is ironic that this should have come about, since it was the luxurious way of life of the Sybarites which the Crotoniates most despised. By the time the Romans planted a colony here in 194 B.C. it had ceased to be a city of any importance.

Croton is perhaps best known for the prowess of her athletes, of whom Milo was the greatest, winning innumerable victories in contests of strength, such as wrestling, at the Olympic Games. But there were other great Olympian victors from Croton, and Stabo tells us that Crotoniates could count more successes than any other single city; her athletics won the stadion seven times in the eight contests between 508 and 480 B.C. Milo was certainly an astonishing character, for he was even elected to lead the army of Croton against the Sybarites at the battle of the Crathis. The city was also famous for its School of Medicine, and its doctors acquired world-wide renown (especially Democedes, physician to the King of Persia). However more significant than her athletes or her physicians, was the remarkable school of philosophy founded by the greatest (adopted) son of Croton—Pythagoras.

It has been said that 'the great interest of Croton's history, if only we could know more of it, would lie between 550 and 408 B.C., especially when it was under the government of the Pythagorean brethren' (Randall-MacIvor). Pythagoras can be considered the first great philosopher of Greece; it was he in fact who coined the word 'philosopher'. His main doctrine was that of metempsychosis or transmigration of souls—not borrowed from Oriental countries, but originating from his own ideas. Pythagoras was also a leading scientist, metaphysician and mathematician, and it was he who discovered the essential mathematical quality of the musical scale. He can be considered one of the great geniuses of all time. He was idolised as the master giving 'final expression of eternal truth' during his lifetime, and worshipped as a god for many decades after his death. Yet he was driven out of Croton together with the oligarchical faction which he supported and had to take refuge in Metapontion; years after the master's death, his Brotherhood received a mortal blow when in about 450 B.C., leading members holding a meeting in Croton in the house of Milo, a disciple of Pythagoras, were massacred when his house was set on fire. The moral and political exclusiveness of the Brotherhood had brought them hatred and jealousy from their democratic opponents.

A description of the sole remaining column of the famed Temple of Hera Lacinia has been given in Chapter Ten, and here it is only necessary to add that this magnificent temple became the national sanctuary of the Greeks in Magna Graecia, who assembled there annually in large numbers to honour the goddess.

The main road ss 106 continues northward past Croton and soon crosses the broad River Neto. Three kilometres further on is the turning for Strongoli, close to which was sited the ancient Greek town of Petelia. The site has not yet been properly excavated. It was at Strongoli that the travel-worn and exhausted Crauford Tait Ramage found kind hospitality, after being brusquely received in Croton, and was much taken by one of the daughters of his host: 'the sparkling eyes of the younger sister proved the most attractive object of the company, and induced me to prolong our social meeting "to the wee sma' hours ayont the twal" '. And yet this incredible man was up 'before the stars disappeared, [and] as the sun arose was ascending the rising ground on which the village of Cirò was placed . . .'

The heroic self-discipline of Ramage is enough to arouse feelings of guilt as one speeds along the modern highway towards Ciro Marina, his book tucked in the car-locker, but few people these days would be able to spare the time he was able to take. Certainly the late twentieth century, whatever its other drawbacks, has compensations when it comes to travel.

The ancient name for the Greek town which lay in the area of Cirò Marina, Punta Alice and the small town of Cirò in the hills above, was Crimissa, and it was the chief of the small towns or settlements established in this district. A few hundred kilometres from Punta Alice there are the scanty remains of the foundations of the Temple of Apollo Alaeus, invisible in Ramage's day, but now revealed by P. Orsi, who found an important marble statue of Apollo (now in the Museo at Reggio).

The town of Cirò is now celebrated as being the production centre for the best known Calabrian wine, named after it, and the favourite of

Norman Douglas. He called it 'the purest nectar', and I would agree with this description only in respect of the white wine—a golden honey-colour, and served slightly chilled, delicious. Red Cirò is not so palatable to my taste.

Shortly after passing Cirò, the road joins company with the railway line, and together they sweep round past Capo Trionto and leaving Rossano (described earlier) to the south, curve back northwards past the ancient site of Thurii and enter the wide and magnificent Plain of Sibari. Thurii was founded by Athenians in the year 444 in part replacement for Sibaris, and Herodotus was one of the colonists. Even in those times the wine of this district was praised above all others of south Italy.

Sybaris before her fall in 510 B.C. was the wealthiest of all the Greek colonies in Magna Graecia and possessed a huge territory (roughly equivalent to the present province of Cosenza) with a total population of about 500,000. The native peoples who confronted the colonists on arrival, the Oinotroi, were peaceably inclined, and so the Sybarites were able to conquer a greater territory in a shorter time than any other Greek colony in Italy or Sicily. This, of course, brought them great riches, from corn, wine, timber, silver-mines and the favourable position at the narrow point between the Ionian Sea and the Tyrrhenian with well-trodden routes up the valley of the Crathis and through the mountains to Laos, Scidros and Poseidonia and thence to Etruria. The supposed idle luxury and wealth of its citizens has come down to us in the word 'sybarite', and indeed in the contemporary Greek world anecdotes circulated for centuries of the moneyed decadence of the city—needless to say highly colourful and exaggerated. Yet the mode of living that has reached us with some degree of authenticity, would appear to be little more than intelligent arrangements for a civilized existence in a mainly very hot climate: trees were planted in the streets for shade, no noisy trades were allowed in the centre of the city (as at Herculaneum later) and there were public baths—probably the first in antiquity. There was also a much greater social freedom between the sexes than was usual in the Greek world, (were they encouraged in this by their Etruscan contacts one wonders?) and they took much pleasure in dressing well and in good food and wine.

Sybaris is thought to have been founded by Is, an Achaean from the Peloponnese who arrived with a party of Achaean Troezenians in about 720 B.C. After its destruction by the Crotoniates it was rebuilt at least twice, the last time with Athenian help, but never achieved its former eminence, and later a fourth Sybaris was founded further south on the River Traeis (Trionto), the ruins of which have been uncovered. It is highly unlikely that the earlier re-buildings were on the original

site which, as we have noted, was utterly destroyed and the ruins subsequently covered over by many metres of mud and silt brought down
by the River Crati (now joined with the Coscile). This makes the
discovery of the remains of the original city of Sybaris an unusually
difficult project, for apart from the re-building, the city is thought
to have had several suburbs, yet the rewards in store for those who
succeed might be fabulous, though it is likely that the search will be
long.

A major victory has been won in recent years, to preserve this
extremely beautiful as well as important historical site, for a petro-
chemical complex which had been planned for Sybaris will be sited
elsewhere. But the huge grant of money voted by the Government for
the excavations, and the expertise and dedication of a team of Italian
scholars and American experts from the University of Pennsylvania,
have failed to produce anything of outstanding importance, although
they do claim to have discovered—at a site called Parco del Cavallo—
the archaic walls of the city, at a great depth, on the left bank of the
Crati, together with fragments of archaic sculpture. However, excavations are continuing, with the aid of modern scientific equipment
supplied by the Lerici Foundation.

There is very little in the way of tourist development at the locality of
Sibari (Stazione di Sibari) but a restaurant and bathing facilities can be
found at the Bagamoyo beach, where acres of very fine golden sand
stretch along the gentle curve of the shores of the Gulf of Taranto.
Here one can look back on a glorious backdrop of purple-blue mountains, the Pollino range still snow-capped in early summer.

The road and railway from Stazione di Sibari run in harness, hugging
the shore all the way from Villapiano Lido to the station for Rotendella
and Nova Siri, crossing the regional border with Basilicata at this point.
The road then bears inland slightly and heads for Policoro, having
bridged the river Sinni (ancient Siris) about four kilometres after the
border. Just outside Policoro is the site of Heraclea, a Greek city
founded in 433 B.C. on the site of one of the earliest cities in Magna
Graecia—Siris. It is not surprising that Siris was sometimes confused
with Sybaris by ancient writers, for the similarity between the two was
marked. Siris was colonised by Colophonians from Ionia, and thus
formed an Ionian wedge between two Achaean cities. The colony
flourished and soon became a rival to Sybaris, and second only to it in
wealth and luxurious living. A rival so potentially dangerous had to be
eliminated and this the Sybarites proceeded to do, with help from
neighbouring cities, and having sacked though not destroyed the city in
the sixth century, brought it under their economic and political direction. Siris as a place ran down after the destruction of Sybaris, and in

the year 432 B.C. Taras founded a new colony here and named it Heraclea.

Important excavations are taking place at Heraclea (Eraclea) which have already yielded rich finds, including a Sanctuary of Demeter and Kore—and there is every reason to be optimistic about future results since the site is far easier to work than Sybaris, and already air photography has revealed a substantial area of the town.

From Eraclea to Metaponto is a distance of about 23 kilometres, and at this point one is still just inside the boundary of Basilicata which has a width of only about 35 kilometres on the Ionian Sea. Metaponto was originally a Greek city, founded mainly by Achaeans, probably in the first quarter of the seventh century, almost certainly on the site of an earlier Greek settlement known as Metabos which might have been established in heroic times. The Achaeans called it Metapontion, and this became Roman Metapontum, and hence the modern spelling. Today it is one of the most rewarding sites to visit on the entire Ionian shore, since there are substantial remains above ground of one temple—the so-called *Tavole Paladine*—and recent excavations in the area of the Temple of Apollo Lycius have revealed part of the ancient city. Work is continuing and hopes are high of further important discoveries.

Metapontion was a small city in comparison with the giants of the age such as Sybaris, Croton or Taras, but it became very wealthy by virtue of its rich arable land (famed for the abundance of the harvests) and its horse-raising activities. Such was their prosperity from the cultivation of corn that the Metapontines took an ear of barley as the emblem of their city, dedicating it in gold to Apollo at Delphi, and using it on their coins. The silver stater incuse coinage of 510 B.C. has a simple but beautiful decorative motif of an ear of barley, and a later coin of high artistry by Aristoxenos shows on the obverse the head of Demeter wearing a corn-wreath (silver stater, about 380 B.C.).

After the destruction of Sybaris, Metapontion came increasingly under the influence of its powerful neighbour Taras, and when in 332 B.C. the Tarantines called in Alexander of Epirus to help them in their struggle against the native peoples, the citizens of Metapontion naturally allied themselves to him. When Alexander was killed near the city, he was buried there. The city was made a *municipium* by the Romans, but by the first century B.C. it was in decline, and by the second century A.D. all was in ruins except the town walls and the theatre.

I arrived in the area of ancient Metapontion in the late afternoon, and made straight for the Tavole Paladine (or Palatine) which, together with the modern Antiquarium, is on the left-hand side of the road about five kilometres beyond the turning for the Lido di

Metaponto. Tavole Paladine was the name given to a late sixth-century B.C. Doric temple, of which 15 columns survive. In all likelihood it was dedicated to the goddess Hera. The columns showed up well in the warm late afternoon sun, and one sees here the most impressive single classical ruin of the entire southern shores of Italy, though still far inferior to any of the temples at Paestum. There are beautifully kept gardens in the vicinity of the temple which add to the pleasure of a visit.

I cannot praise too highly the admirable Antiquarium, built in 1961, which is typical of the small modern museums and antiquariums in the South today. The exhibits are carefully arranged and beautifully displayed, and there are many items—vases, revetments, coins etc.—of great interest, but too many to identify here. It is especially helpful to have drawings to scale showing details of recent archaeological work, and in particular the 1973 excavations at the site of the Temple of Apollo Lycius.

Since the Temple of the Tavole Paladine was built in the suburbs of Metapontion, in order to visit the site of the ancient city one has to turn back south along ss 106 and head for the village of Metaponto, turning left along a rough road shortly before reaching the village. The excavations here, old and new, cover a largish area, perhaps 600 × 400 metres. The new diggings have revealed a wall in excellent conditon. The trench beside it was full of muddy water when I was there, and clearly, as at Sybaris, a watertable has accumulated since ancient times. A sophisticated arrangement of pumps was in operation trying to clear the water, or at least keep it under control. The older *scavi* show a rather random selection of tumbledown or sheared-off columns and general archaeological bric-a-brac, but are quite impressive. Remains can be seen here of the late sixth-century Doric temple of Apollo Lycius, and a theatre. Some of the lion-head waterspouts and terracotta revetments from the temple are in Potenza museum. The excavations here, because of the conditions, must be very costly, but if enough cash is forthcoming the next few years may well see startling results, for air photography has revealed a substantial area of the ancient city, which, grass-covered, lies not far below the surface between the rivers Bradano and Basento, as well as a large complex of buildings at the artifical harbour at the mouth of the Basento.

Great efforts have been made in recent years to make the Lido di Metaponto an attractive resort, with considerable success. There are now a number of modern hotels. Normally the bathing here is safe, and the sands are very fine. The town is set out like a small garden-city, with good roads, public gardens and many small villas built among pines and evergreens and a cheerful display of flowers.

After crossing the boundary with the Region of Apulia (the old spelling normal in English translations, will continue to be used instead of the official Puglia) the main road ss 106 bears inland and runs parallel with the shores of the Gulf of Taranto, leaving the Marinas of Ginosa (two hotels) and Castellanota (four hotels and one motel) about three kilometres to the east, connected by the main line between Taranto and Reggio. Before describing the modern city of Taranto in the next chapter, I would like to give here an account of its origins and its subsequent history in ancient times, condensed to the briefest outline since there is practically nothing remaining of the Greek city today. And because of modern overbuilding the prospect of any archaeological work in the future is very remote.

The area around Taranto was certainly occupied in pre-historic times, and by the thirteenth century B.C. Mycenaean imports began arriving at Scoglio del Tonno, and at Leporano on the southern coast beyond Capo S. Vito. Contact with the Aegean was probably unbroken until the arrival of the Greeks in strength under their leader from Sparta, Phalanthos, in 706 B.C., and the main party almost certainly found Greek traders residing in the area from a generation or two earlier. The colonists were Laconians, the only colony that Sparta founded, and it is possible that they settled at Satyrion for a while pending negotiations with the native Iapygians. The site chosen by the leader was the peninsular of land almost completely enclosing the Mare Piccolo (inner harbour) from the Mare Grande, the main outer harbour, protected from the ocean by the Isole Cheradi. This peninsular now comprises the Citta Vecchia. During the first two centuries of its existence the city of Taras was small though prosperous—from corn, wool, and olive oil—and it was not until the Tarentines suffered a disastrous defeat by the Iapygians in about 473 B.C. that a change of constitution introduced a moderate democracy, which resulted in a dramatic recovery and considerable expansion. By the early fourth century Taras was the richest and most powerful city in Magna Graecia, deriving enormous economic benefits from her splendid double harbour, her industry—which included the manufacture of woollen goods, dyed purple with the extract from the famous murex shellfish—her natural produce as listed above, all of which were exported, and advantageous trading opportunities. By the middle of the fourth century Taras enjoyed additional prestige from the enlightened leadership of Archytas, a democratic politician who appears to have combined all the talents: brilliant scientist and mathematician, Pythagorean philosopher, distinguished general who was never defeated, and wise ruler. He had the sense to keep on good terms with Dionysius of Syracuse, and was a friend of Plato, pleading successfully on his behalf when the philosopher's life was threatened during an ill-fated visit to the tyrant in Syracuse. During the time of Archytas the city of Taras reached a pinnacle of splendour, elegance and good living, and at that ime it has been estimated that 300,000 people resided within the ten-mile circuit of the city walls.

However, easy-living led to decadence and a lack of will to defend themselves, so they appealed to the King of Sparta to help them in their war against the Messapians, and after his death turned to Alexander of Epirus, who in turn was killed while fighting the Bruttians. When in 275 B.C. Pyrrhus was defeated by the Romans and returned to Greece, the city, weakened politically, fell into Roman hands. After a period when Hannibal was in control of the city, the Romans retook Tarentum, and ruthlessly pillaged its artistic treasures, which found their way into many public and private places in Rome and elsewhere. It is our great good fortune today that so many objects from the time of the city's golden age may be seen again in Taranto, in the finest archaeological museum south of Naples—most of which were disinterred from the cemeteries of Taras, uncovered during the building of the arsenal and other modern constructions at the eastern end of the town.

Part III

APULIA

15.   Taranto and its environs

Anyone approaching Taranto from the west by road will know by the time he reaches the Ponte di Porta Napoli, what to expect in the streets of the city. Having crossed the bridge we join the one-way flow of traffic circulating to the south of the Citta Vecchia. Perhaps 'flow' is an inappropriate word, since the traffic is largely static and only proceeds by fits and starts, leaving one ample time to enjoy the seascape on the right with the Ionian swell breaking against the rocks, or to peer down the narrow dark alleyways on the left that lead into the interior of the old city. For anyone pressed for time however this crawl towards the modern and major portion of the city beyond the swing-bridge, is something of a trial, and the temptation to dart out and make use of the exclusive bus and taxi-lane on the side nearest the sea often proves too great. Cunningly placed round the bend of a right-angled corner on the evening of my arrival, were traffic-police waiting for such trans-gressors, and it made up for the tedium of our funereal progress to watch the gesticulations and listen to the excuses volubly expressed by those who were caught red-handed.

For such an important industrial and commercial centre, (Italsider operates the largest integrated steel complex in Europe here) Taranto is not well-off for hotels, having only two of the first category and three of the second, so that pre-booking is most advisable. The position of the two first-category hotels, the Delfino (217 rooms) and the Jolly Mar Grande (97 rooms), are a considerable distance east along the Viale Virgili, overlooking the sea. From here, in order to reach the Citta Vecchia, it is a pleasant walk along the Lungomare Vittorio Emanuele under the shade of palms and flowering shrubs, with, on the left, the wide expanse of the Mare Grande reaching out to the Cheradi islands of S. Pietro and S. Paolo encircling the outer harbour, and the long line of hills behind Ginosa as a backdrop. On a clear day, the Lucanian Appenines are visible many kilometres to the west and the south.

Having crossed the swing-bridge into the Citta Vecchia one can either go straight ahead across Piazza Castello and along the narrow

Via del Duomo so as to reach the cathedral, or follow the traffic to the right, down the hill and round the corner into the Via G. Garibaldi, which leads to the quarter where the fishermen's families live in weather-beaten buildings and where one can find some good fish restaurants. I can testify to the excellence of at least two of the restaurants (the Tarantese *zuppa di pesce* is a gargantuan dish and a meal in itself) but I will admit to cowardice (or commonsense) when it came to sampling the 'fruits of the sea' on display at the highly popular sea-food stalls . . . an astonishing variety of edible crustacea. Incidentally as regards the eating of these shell-fish of Taranto—mussels, which are normally boiled, are one thing, and oysters usually eaten raw, quite another. In other words, one should take into account the risk of eating oysters which come from the far from pristine-pure sea-bed of the lagoon.

The Cathedral of Taranto can be found by taking one of the small streets southward from the Via Garibaldi, but it is best reached either from the Piazza Castello, as described, or from the south along the Piazza Arcivescovado. The latter approach gives one a good view of the interesting exterior architecture at the crossing, featuring a windowless drum with a shallow conical roof, possibly of Byzantine inspiration. Long slender columns divide the drum into many sections, breaking up the mass. The present building is basically Romanesque, keeping closely to the form of Belisarius' church at Monte Cassino. It was built by the Normans in 1071, but has since been much rebuilt or modified. The campanile, for instance, recently rebuilt, was originally constructed in 1413.

The interior of the Duomo, basilican in form, has very recently been completely restored. Six years ago, the whole of the inside was a forest of scaffolding, but now the simplicity and dignity of the original building has returned, and the unsightly baroque accretions in the main body of the church swept away. There are some fine details, and much variety in the individual carvings, especially the capitals. One of these is a most graceful Byzantine carving, showing foliage and birds in various postures: here two peacocks lean delicately inward and dip their beaks into a drinking vessel. Another capital looks to be a typical Lombard creation; we see fierce lions, and human faces that might well be in a state of shock from the sudden appearance of Antichrist himself.

The original church on this spot was dedicated to St. Cathal in the seventh century (Italianized to San Cataldo) and the dedication remains. He is the patron saint of Taranto, and it is rather surprising to find an Irish missionary from Munster so honoured. St. Cathal was one of a considerable number of holy men from Ireland who set out in the

Dark Ages, either on pilgrimage or as proselytizers. He was returning home from a visit to the Holy Land when he rested for a while at Taranto, and was invited by the town's clergy to remain as bishop. Finding every kind of vice and corruption in the city, he deemed it his duty to accept.

S. Cataldo's remains are preserved under the altar in the chapel named after him—a distinctly florid example in polychrome marble of the Baroque style. Doubtless there have been many opinions expressed about this chapel. The little local guide-book I had acquired calls it 'sumptuous', while to Norman Douglas it was 'a jovial nightmare in stone'. Above the altar the bronze statue of St. Cathal stands in his alcove with an arm outstretched. Here we see a really jolly Irish face, with a twinkle in his eye. There are generally a few worshippers to be found in this chapel, usually elderly women cocooned in voluminous black dresses and shawls regardless of the weather. I sometimes wonder what these folk make of the stripping of their beloved baroque cathedrals and churches in the interests of purity of style, and foreign visitors. Will they ever come to like the sombre northern beauty of the Norman and Lombard builders? They have been brought up, in a religious sense, among the warmth of the many-coloured marbles of these southern chapels and churches, and I find it difficult to believe that they will. But at least in front of their patron saint the worshippers of Taranto can find peace in familiar surroundings.

The Via del Duomo, which passes the northern side of the cathedral, eventually reaches a small straight narrow street on a north-south axis, which leads past the handsome exterior of S. Domenico Maggiore, an eleventh-century church reconstructed by Giovanni Taurisano in 1302. The main portal stands high above double steps of the baroque period. The façade is very elegant, with a beautiful rose window, and a Gothic doorway which is surmounted by a canopy similar in style to Romanesque models.

At the Oratorio della SS. Trinità also in the Citta Vecchia there are slight remains of a Doric temple in the courtyard. The church is situated at the Piazza Castello end of the Via del Duomo. In this street in recent years excavations have brought to light a deep tomb with a well-built arched support dividing it in an unusual fashion. Other recent discoveries include a flight of ancient steps leading to the old port near the hospital of the Marina Militare; substantial remains of an ancient street in Via Nitti; a mosaic pavement uncovered in Via Dante, and a furnace from Greek times in Via Cesare Battisti. However the bulk of Greek Taras lies inaccessible below the tenements, shops, churches, office buildings, banks and supermarkets of the old and new cities—and are unlikely to be disturbed unless in times to come it is ever decided to bulldoze a whole area of the decaying fabric of the largely medieval Citta Vecchia and commence large-scale operations in the area where the acropolis once was. But there would bound to be strong opposition to any wholesale destruction of the old town, by residents and conservationists alike.

The Museo Nazionale in Corso Umberto has a magnificent collection of antiquities—unrivalled in Southern Italy except by the Naples Museum. The collections illustrate, as well as the Greek and Roman periods, the early history of the native peoples—not only in the Taranto area where the Messapians were predominant, but also other Italic races, the Peucezi, the Daunians and the Bruttians who came from the areas around Bari, Foggia and Reggio. These regions are all represented by exhibits on the ground floor.

The first floor of the museum is entirely devoted to finds from the Taranto area—from the earliest prehistoric sites to the Greek period and later. The exhibits constitute an enormous variety of amphorae, craters, cups, vases, jewellery, fine fragments, superb carvings and excellent heads executed over a wide period of time—and such is their volume that it will not be possible to describe individual items here.

In the corridors numbered from XII–XV one can find the terracotta figurines for which Taranto was famous. Nearly all of these are of a sacred character, being ex-voto offerings for holy sanctuaries. They are quite small, and very numerous, and some have surprising grace and vitality, though in many the standard of artistry is not very high. They are fascinating for all that, and consist mainly of little statuettes of female figures, probably representing Aphrodite or the Muses, sometimes dancing or at times just reclining in graceful attitudes. There are some delightful poses; in one instance a female appears to be putting on a shoe. One can also see animals and animal heads among this very large collection. The earliest statuettes were made by hand, but later moulds were made, and after casting the figurines were retouched by hand before being painted in bright colours.

A number of interesting excursions may be made from Taranto. The dramatic hill-town of Castellaneta, 36 kilometres away, is on the main highway No. 7 from Taranto to Matera and stands at about 735 feet in a spectacular situation at the edge of a ravine which plunges to a depth of many hundreds of feet. This ravine or *gravina* is of grey rock and studded with clusters of the 'prickly pear' cacti. There is a marvellous view from the town towards the Gulf of Taranto and of the mountains of Basilicata and Calabria. The town possesses a cathedral containing a number of interesting paintings and other works of art.

Another town perched on the rocky hills which half-encircle Taranto is Massafra, at about half the height of Castellaneta. Again deep ravines dominate the scenery and the town is built around the Gravina di S. Marco. Here there are clusters of perfumed bushes, carobs and prickly pears, and the countryside is planted with centuries-old olives. Massafra is famous for its caves and cave-churches built into the sides of the ravines. These troglodite dwellings are often high up on the rock and difficult to reach. They came about as a direct result of the destruction of homes during the barbaric invasions that followed the breaking up of the Roman Empire in the West, so that for shelter and safety the wretched inhabitants resorted to these homes cut in the rock, taking with them a few animals. Basilican monks and hermits also came here in course of time, and it was because of their example and encouragement that the crypt-churches were hewn out of the tufa. More than 20 of these have now been excavated, and they all date from the period 800–1300. Their architecture is varied: some take the form of a Latin cross, and others are Greek in form. It is fortunate for us that several of the interesting frescoes are quite well preserved. Perhaps the finest of these churches is the Chiesa-Cripta di S. Marco (though moisture has destroyed all the frescoes except one), but there are many crypt-churches of great interest—notably that of S. Leonardo, and the Cappella-Cripta della Candelora.

Almost due East 23 kilometres from Taranto, is the prosperous small town of Grottaglie, a centre of the ceramics industry. For centuries the art of modelling clay has been handed down from father to son, and for outsiders there is an important art school that turns out trained artisans in ceramics for work-shops all over Italy. In the centre of the town the Chiesa Matrice was founded at the beginning of the twelfth century and possesses a beautiful doorway in the style of Apulian Romanesque, although the façade was rebuilt in 1379, probably by Domenico da Martina. The interior, much altered, contains some fine works of art.

The old part of the town is very picturesque. The balconies decorated with locally-made majolica, brighten up the houses with their white walls. There is a suggestion of the orient about the narrow streets with their low arches. In the narrow lanes are the potters' workshops, the products of which are often stylistically based on the models of ancient Greece.

16. The Salentine Peninsular: Lecce

There are two ways from Taranto of reaching (via Gallipoli) the very point of the heel of Italy, at Capo di Leuca—either by the coast road, taking in several small marinas or Lidos, or by the inland route along the straight roads through S. Giorgio Ionico and Manduria. The former route is certainly the more attractive scenically, but for the purpose of this chapter we will now travel along the ss 7 as far as Manduria. The countryside along this route, the dull rolling landscape of the Murge Tarantine is in great contrast to the rugged mountain scenery to the west of Taranto, but the towns in the Salentine peninsular make up for the monotony of the landscape.

Manduria is a good example, being an ancient and very interesting place: it was probably the most important Messapian centre in this area. The earliest of the three concentric circuits of megalithic walls that can be seen today, in fair condition, probably belong to the fifth century B.C. The Messapians, about whose origins there is no exact knowledge, were almost certainly non-Italic and may have originated from the Illyrian side of the Adriatic. On the whole the Greeks were successful in their bid for peaceful coexistence with the Messapians, but there are recorded instances of strife, and it is thought that the Spartan King Archidamus was killed beneath the surviving fourth-century walls, in the course of giving military aid to the Tarantines against the Messapians and Lucanians.

The town has a cathedral, originally Romanesque, but with additions and alterations through the ages, and a splendid palace—the Palazzo Imperiale built in 1709. Certainly worth a visit is the Biblioteca Marco Gatti in the Municipio, which contains some interesting early medical books (rare first editions) and a collection of Mandurian antiquities.

From Manduria the ss 174, the Via Salentina, proceeds with only gentle and infrequent undulations to Nardo, a wealthy commercial and market town of about 28,000 inhabitants. There are a number of palaces and churches in Nardo in a florid and exaggerated baroque style—of which the Palazzo della Pretura and the church of S.

Domenico (sixteenth century) are the most interesting and also the attractive Piazza A. Salandra, in the centre of which stands the extraordinary Guglia dell' Immacolata. There are no hotels at Nardo, and only two small *pensioni* at the nearby seaside resort of S. Maria al Bagno, but 14 kilometres to the north-west at the attractively positioned Porto Cesareo, there is the Club Azzuro with 121 rooms (Cat. III) and several small hotels and *pensioni*.

From Nardo it is a run of only about 16 kilometres to Gallipoli, in part one of the most attractive small towns in southern Italy—and clearly this was also the case in ancient times since the translation of the Greek *Kallipolis* means 'beautiful city'. It is thought that the town may originally have been founded by Taras, but this Greek colonial origin is far from certain. Its Greek character extended beyond ancient times since it became a centre of Byzantinism until it fell to the Normans in the same year that Bari was captured—1071. It succeeded in repelling the Turks in 1480, but was later for a short while held by the Venetians.

Old Gallipoli is beautifully situated on a long tongue of rock, now an island, and is joined to the promontory where the modern city, the Borgo, is situated by a stone bridge. There is still a distinctly Greek atmosphere about old Gallipoli—a combination of light and architecture. The buildings are flat-roofed and are mainly white-washed, though sometimes in pale shades of pink and blue.

The town owes its prosperity mainly to wine, grapes and oil. Before the Bolshevik Revolution large quantities of olive oil were shipped to Russia for the icon lamps, and in Ramage's time, in the early nineteenth century, there was a substantial trade in oil with England in English vessels. He wrote: 'As Gallipoli is one of the few cities in the Kingdom of Naples frequented by English merchantmen, the public *albergo* was somewhat more comfortable than usual; I waited on the English vice-consul and the *sottointendente* to both of whom I had letters . . .'. Well, travellers may still have expectations of comfort. The splendid sandy beaches and the unpolluted sea have attracted ever-increasing numbers of tourists, and Gallipoli now has a Category I hotel, the Grand Hotel Costa Brada—(64 rooms—rather absurdly, more expensive than any hotel in Lecce) and the second-category Joli Park Hotel (83 rooms) and Albergo Lido S. Giovanni (108 rooms).

One of the most attractive objects in Gallipoli is the charming fountain known as the Fontana Ellenistica made up in 1560 of various distinctly weathered Greek reliefs of Hellenistic times and assembled in its present form in the seventeenth century. It stands opposite the buildings of the Comando del Porto in the Borgo just before reaching the Città. On this side is the interesting castle of various epochs beginning with the Byzantine and including Angevin work. Places of interest include the Museo Cirico and the cathedral of S. Agata (1630–1696). At the extreme western end of the Città the church of S. Francesco, possesses some startlingly realistic carving, including that of the Two Thieves by the sixteenth century wood-carver Vespasiano Genuino, which so impressed C. T. Ramage: ' . . . the only curiosity that I saw was a carved figure of the Impenitent Thief on the Cross in wood, whose countenance exhibited more hardened wickedness than I imagined it possible for wood to express.'

The best road to the south from Gallipoli, No. 274, after passing through Ugento, slowly climbs the low bare limestone hills of the Murge Salentine, nowhere rising much above 400 feet. There are no regular valleys here, and a marked scarcity of water. At various points along the road between the village of Patu and the gradually descending road between Gagliano and the Cape, one has splendid views across the ocean, where on a very clear day, the mountains of Albania can be seen. The Convent and church of S. Francesco, just after the right-hand turn into ss 275, is interesting having been built by the Castriota Skanderbeg family in 1613 on the site of an earlier church destroyed by the Turks. Ramage makes some interesting comments about mirages in these parts: 'These optical deceptions take many varied shapes, and assume the most fantastic forms . . . In the middle of the fifteenth century, when the country was kept in a constant state of alarm by the Turks, the whole coast from Monte Garganus . . . to the Capo di Leuca was roused at the same hour by the appearance of a large fleet . . . approaching from the east.' As we shall see a little later on, the events which took place in Otranto in the year 1480 were no mirage.

There is a sanctuary at Leuca (named from the Greek *leukos* because of the white limestone cliffs) which is the Land's End, or *Finibus Terrae* of the heel of Italy. This sanctuary of S. Maria di Leuca has been visited by pilgrims for centuries, and still is, the popular legend being that a visit is a first step on the road to Paradise; it is also believed that St. Peter preached here. The church stands on a spot where a Temple to Minerva is thought to have once stood. Finibus Terrae is in the shape of a rocky bay which extends for about two kilometres between Capo di Leuca and Punta Ristola, the latter being just to the south. There are a number of caves here which are best visited by boat. The sea around these shores is marvellously clear.

The road north from Capo S. Maria di Leuca hugs the coast for the entire route to Otranto, and along these shores there are a great many caves, some of outstanding interest, and many, not so famous, open to exploration for anyone who has a boat or who is sure-footed. Indeed it is to this rocky shore that this area owes all its character; inland the bare outcrops of limestone often give a desolate aspect. The resort of Castro Marina, 26 kilometres from Capo di Leuca, is a good place to stop for visiting the Grotta Zinzulusa and the Grotta Romanelli, the two most famous caves on the littoral. For long this village was a fishing port for the attractive but devastated town of Castro, sitting picturesquely on the hill behind (which to this day has not recovered from the treatment it received from the Turks), and now the Marina has been developed as a tourist resort. Castro has a castle and a medieval cathedral.

The Grotta Zinzulusa was occupied in the Upper Palaeolithic and the Copper Ages, and is of special importance to biologists since it contains several species of tiny crustacea which are unique in Italy, suggesting that at one time there was no break between the continent at Albania and Apulia. The cave is very long and rich in stalactites of beautiful shape and colour, and the colouring of the rock surfaces under the water at the entrance is exquisite. The main points of interest in the Grotta Romanelli are the figures of animals engraved or painted on walls, and also engraved on loose blocks of stone, which have a certain stylistic resemblance to engravings found in France and Spain. Fossil remains include types of elephant, and rhinoceros, and it is certain that the cave was occupied by man in the Upper Palaeolithic period. These are the only palaeolithic paintings to have been discovered on the Italian mainland.

The beautiful coast road—the *litoranea*—continues northward past S. Cesarea Terme, then sweeps round Capo D'Otranto with its lighthouse, before turning inland and running into Otranto. S. Cesarea Terme is a small state-owned spa specializing, with its sulphur-bearing waters, in the treatment of rheumatic complaints. There is a choice of hotels. S. Cesarea is only about 5 kilometres from the two grottoes described above.

Otranto has been very little developed in the tourist sense since I first visited this attractive small town and port six years ago. Although there is now a Club Mediterrané, there is still only one hotel (Miramare, Cat. II, 66 rooms) and a small *pensione*. Otranto, then, remains little more than a fishing village and a small port for the ferry services to Corfu and Igoumenitsa in Greece, with a population of just under 4000. In 1910 M. S. Briggs was prophesying: 'Of this beautiful little fishing village it cannot be said that any future lies before it, or that it will ever become more than a relic of the past.'

Things were different in the days of Roman power. Then known as Hydruntum, and probably founded centuries earlier by Greeks from Taras, it aspired to rival in importance the neighbouring port of Brindisi—both being the embarkation points for Roman legions and administrators sailing for Illyria and Asia Minor. The city quickly rose in importance during the Empire and in the course of wars between the Goths and Byzantines became a key port. It was one of the last strongholds in Apulia to fall to the Normans, succumbing in 1068, three years before the fall of Bari. During the period of the Crusades it developed in military and commercial importance, like many other Apulian ports, and trade with the Levant and Venice flourished. So that by the time the most fateful blow in its history was struck—in July 1480—it was a thriving prosperous town of about 20,000 inhabitants.

The international situation at this time, already touched on briefly, cannot be gone into here. Suffice to say that Ferdinand of Naples was in alliance with the Pope, in an effort to stem the rapid advances of the victorious Turkish forces on the other side of the Adriatic; and for the unfortunate citizens of Otranto the sudden arrival of 10,000 vengeful Turks under their fierce commander Kedyk Ahmed meant certain defeat, destruction of their homes and misery. And for a large number of them, 800 prisoners, it also meant martyrdom—though only after having been offered a free pardon with restitution of their property if they would embrace the Muslim faith. In addition a huge number died in the siege which lasted for two weeks, the citizens having responded to the Turkish commander's call for surrender by throwing the keys of the city down a well. But the end was inevitable once the heavy Turkish cannon had breached the walls: the archbishop was cut down in the Church of St. Francis of Assisi, and both he and the commandant were sawn in half—a typical Ottoman practice in those times. Although relief came eventually, with Ferdinand's son Alfonso at the head of an army, and efforts were made to put the town on its feet again, it never recovered from the massacres, the destruction and the occupation by Turkish forces. Nearby marshes were allowed to go undrained and malaria became a scourge, thus adding to the human misery.

Fortunately throughout these disastrous times the town never lost its archiepiscopal status, so that we can visit today its beautiful cathedral with its unique artistic treasures. As one enters the small piazza in front of the main doors, the most striking feature is the lovely fifteenth-century rose window, put in place in the same year that the town was relieved by Alfonso's troops. The outstanding piece of decoration in the cathedral is a vast allegorical pavement mosaic which covers the entire floor of the nave and aisles. Since the Turkish cavalry had used the church as a stable it is extraordinary that this has survived in such good condition. The church was built by the Normans between 1080 and 1088, in all likelihood by Robert Guiscard's son Bohemund, and the mosaics were completed almost 80 years later in 1166 being, as the floor inscription states, in the reign of *domino nostro Willelm, rege magnifico*, (King William II of Sicily).

The mosaics were the inspiration of the priest Pantaleone, and are based on the Tree of Life. The roots of the tree start at the rear of the church where two elephants stand, and the trunk grows towards the High Altar, the branches spreading out left and right at regular intervals. Between these branches and hanging from or balancing on them, sometimes entwined in them, are an incredible collection of monsters and mythical beasts, as well as familiar characters from sacred and profane history—Alexander the Great, Cain and Abel, Abraham and Isaac, and rather surprisingly for those who think his fame was restricted to British shores, King Arthur of the Round Table. For inventiveness, inspiration and humour, this vast mosaic can have few if any equals today, though it would seem that several of the great churches in Apulia at one time possessed floor mosaics of comparable size. Of course they do not compare in execution and craftsmanship with the wall mosaics of approximately the same date in Sicily—for instance those at Monreale Cathedral; the latter are a product of Byzantine work-shops with centuries of tradition behind them. The human figures at Otranto in particular are rather crudely done. But whatever these mosaics lack in technical brilliance, they certainly make up for in exuberance and invention, so that the uninhibited style of their execution and the wonderful freedom of movement of men and animals make them a work of joy.

In the Chapel of the Martyrs you can ask the sacristan to show you the dry bones and skulls of 560 of the martyred citizens, stacked in tall mahogany cupboards—a curious sight certainly but not one that inspired me with any pious thoughts. We were also taken down to the vast crypt, consecrated in 1088, and here there is a wonderful variety of columns and capitals—smooth columns with Roman classical capitals, or fluted, with Byzantine Theodosian ones; some carvings are traceable to Asia Minor, and some are damask or pattern-carved columns capped with Lombard work . . . in fact a treasure-house of different styles and periods, assembled by the Normans.

The castle of Otranto was built only five years after the relief of the town, by Ferdinand of Aragon in 1485. It is an impressive building with cylindrical bastions placed at the corner angles of massive walls. There are additions by the Emperor Charles V.

Certainly worth a visit is the delightful small tenth-century Byzantine church of S. Pietro. The church is in the form of a Greek cross with triple semi-circular apses, with faded, but in some instances beautiful, frescoes of various periods, often with Greek inscriptions. It is an interesting example of the provincial Byzantine style.

To arrive in LECCE after weeks spent travelling in southern Italy is a truly surprising experience. The characteristic feature of the city, and its particular charm, is the Baroque style of architecture known as *barocco leccese*, so called because its exuberant style cannot be confused with any other. Here then, far down in the heel of the boot, is an oasis of Baroque churches and palaces in an area otherwise dominated by Byzantine and Norman Apulian-Romanesque influences, making Lecce one of the most delightful small cities in Italy.

A major factor contributing to the success of Lecce's architectural style has been the quality of the local limestone. This is very soft when first cut, allowing the masons and carvers full scope for their elaborate fancy, yet on exposure to air it quickly develops a hard patina, resulting in the excellent state of preservation of the buildings today. Combining well with the intricacy of the carvings is the texture of the stone which has a natural warmth and is a beautiful golden colour.

The best and most typical example of *barocco leccese* is the large church of S. Croce, situated alongside the very fine Palazzo della Prefettura, which, in part, now houses the Provincial Museum. The centre-piece of the façade of Santa Croce is the rose window, which for sheer exuberance can seldom have been matched. Yet there is a discipline in these marvellous circles of decorative carvings. Standing on its own this window would be an impossibly sumptuous showpiece, but balanced with the whole of the façade it finds its natural place in the highly ornate decoration of the rest. As a glorious fantasy in stone this façade takes one's breath away.

The interior of S. Croce is large with many side chapels, and the carvings and decoration extremely rich. This is true of all the baroque churches in Lecce, of which the best known in addition to S. Croce are, S. Matteo, S. Chiara, the Chiesa del Gesù, and S. Irene.

The origins of Lecce are obscure, but are probably Messapian. In Roman times the town, then called Lupiae, emerged from obscurity (there is a large surviving amphitheatre), but after a period of prosperity it got caught up in the wars between Goths, Lombards and Byzantines and its fortunes declined. The Norman conquest however, heralded a new age of prosperity, for the Terra d'Otranto seems to have escaped the worst of the civil wars and revolts of the powerful Barons. So we find that 100 years after the Norman conquest of the South, Lecce possessed one of the most brilliant courts in the Kingdom of Sicily. Robert, the Count of Lecce was rich, he was lavish with his entertainments, and he was able to attract the pick of Apulian chivalry to his court. It was here that Roger, son and heir of Roger King of Sicily, wooed, loved and had two illegitimate sons by Sibylla, the beautiful daughter of his host, a fact concealed from the King until his son returned to Palermo. Although he obtained his father's consent to marry Sibylla by proxy, Roger died before the event could be solemnized. A grief-stricken father then sent a strong force to besiege Robert, who fled to Greece with his daughter and the two babes. It was one of these, Tancred the Bastard, who later became a notable Count of Lecce, one of the greatest leaders of his time in a kingdom starstudded with brilliant men, and who himself was to be elected King of Sicily in 1189, after the sudden death of William the Good. Earlier he had had a distinguished military and administrative record, as Grand Constable and Master Justiciar of Apulia, and in command of the Norman fleet.

Tancred's church, that of SS. Nicolo e Cataldo, was built in 1180 and is the oldest surviving church in Lecce. The façade is largely baroque, but it includes a graceful rounded portal with beautiful Romanesque decoration. Henri Bertaux has described the building as 'a Burgundian church of Leccese stone in a shell of Greek-Apulian architecture' which, while a neat summary, does not give credit to the strong Saracenic influences of the soaring pointed arches of the interior. The building formed part of a Benedictine monastery founded by Tancred, the cloisters of which, rebuilt later, are now used as a hospital for the aged poor of the district.

In the early sixteenth century Lecce was undoubtedly a town of some importance, but of the architecture of this period only the small churches of S. Marco and S. Elisabetta, the chapel of S. Sebastiano (deconsecrated), the castle and the Triumphal Arch remain, together with some of the small *palazzi*. Then, as now, it was market for all the surrounding agricultural districts, and a commercial centre. The Venetians had a trading colony there; their church, S. Marco built in 1543, is attached to the Sedile.

A most important influence on the city was the arrival of several religious orders—the Oratorians in 1548, the Jesuits in 1574 and the Teatini in 1591. With these orders came great wealth, and the churches of the Gesù and the Teatini (S. Irene) are perhaps the best designed and the most sumptuous in Lecce. These years, between 1520 and 1590, mark the first great period of architectural activity when more than a dozen important buildings were either completed or put in hand. The list includes, as well as the Gesú and S. Irene, the church of S. Maria della Grazie, just off Piazza S. Oronzo, Santa Croce, and the Sedile, where the civic authorities used to meet.

The second great period of building activity opened in 1658 after a long gap caused by civil unrest, due to misgovernment by the Spanish viceroys. In this year Zimbalo a local architect, commenced work on the re-building of the cathedral, planned the magnificent campanile, started work on two new churches, and turned his hand to the completion of Santa Croce which had been in the process of being built for over a century.

From the middle of the seventeenth century to the end of the first decade of the eighteenth, was the golden period of Leccese architecture. A beautiful fountain was built in the main square (now destroyed) by Zimbalo, and work was begun by the master's outstanding pupil, Cino, on the Seminario, the Sacramento, and the Carmine; and to this period also belongs the churches of S. Chiara, S. Matteo, the façade of SS. Nicolo e Cataldo and the Porta di Rusee. It was the most prolific building era in the history of Lecce and a sure indication of the prosperity of the city.

In the very heart of the town is the main square, the Piazza S. Oronzo, its wide open spaces built in a more gracious age for lengthy evening promenades. High above the scene S. Oronzo, the patron saint of Lecce (he was an early martyr thought to have died during one of Nero's persecutions), stands with his arm outstretched in benediction on a classical column brought here from Brindisi—one of a pair that stood to mark the end of the Via Appia. The considerable remains of the Roman amphitheatre intrude into the area of the piazza (it is thought to have held 25,000 spectators) and quite close to it is the attractive sixteenth-century pavilion—the Palazzo del Seggio, or Sedile, now the tourist information office.

Lecce is comfortably off in terms of hotel accommodation, since rather surprisingly there are as many hotels in Category I (Jolly (66 rooms), Patria-Touring (60), President (150) and Risorgimento Palace(59)), as there are in Category II and Category III. Heavy industry has now arrived in the vicinity of Lecce, and an expansion in the number of hotel beds can be anticipated.

There can be few pleasanter places to stay in southern Italy than Lecce. In a city of distinctive churches and beautiful palaces—some large, some quite small—one is surrounded by elegance. The poise and distinction of this splendidly built town are communicated in a feeling of well-being as one admires the work of the superb masons, carvers and sculptors of Lecce, making it hard to leave this jewel of the south.

17. From Brindisi to Bari:
trulli country

One never seems to lose contact for long with the sea at Brindisi; the harbour opens up from a narrow entrance like two giant antlers and envelops the city on its promontory, allowing splendid views across the waters to the open sea. One of the best positions for this panorama is at the end of the Via Colonne at the top of the flight of steps, where the remaining column of a pair marking the end of the Via Appia Antica, now stands. It is a most handsome column of African *cipollino* with a magnificent white marble capital and figures of Jupiter, Mars, Neptune and Pallas, erected in the second century A.D.

This column is the only remaining monument of Roman times, which is surprising considering the importance of Brundisium, as it was called then, to the Romans, and the size of the ancient city. It was the chief link with Illyria and the Eastern Mediterranean. The harbour was probably in use in the time of the Messapians as early as the seventh century B.C. but it was only after the decline of Tarentum (sacked by the Romans in 209 B.C.) and the extension of the Via Appia Brundisium that the port expanded dramatically, becoming one of the most cosmopolitan cities in the Roman world. It was here in 49 B.C. that Julius Caesar tried unsuccessfully to block Pompey's fleet, and nine years later Mark Antony and Octavian signed a truce at Brundisium. It was here too that Virgil died in 19 B.C.

Walking along the streets of Brindisi today the atmosphere is still distinctly oriental, as it must have been in Roman times, and indeed many of the signs and notices in the shops or tourist agencies are in Greek as well as Italian. Brindisi is a port of departure for ferries leaving for Corfu, Igoumenitsa, Patras, Crete and Rhodes, run by a number of different shipping lines. Industrially the city has developed enormously since World War II; the colossal Montedison petro-chemical complex in Brindisi is one of the largest industrial sites in the whole of the *mezzogiorno,* and plans are well advanced to expand production still further.

Important though these plans are for the economy of the region, they do not feature in the brochures or leaflets of the official Tourist

Agency, which concentrate on the many beautiful and interesting buildings that can be seen in the town. These are outstandingly of that period of the Middle Ages which began after the city fell to Robert Guiscard in 1071, and especially during the time of Frederick II, who was quick to realise the strategic importance of the port. It was he who built the very impressive Castello right on the water's edge commanding the Seno di Ponente. (The castle is now the headquarters of the Comando Militare Marittimo and cannot be visited.) There are additions to Frederick's building by Ferdinand of Aragon and Charles V.

One of the most attractive parts of Brindisi is the area where the cathedral stands in Piazza Duomo. The exterior of the cathedral which extends the whole width of the piazza is handsome, in warm mellow stone, but the interior is very plain, though restoration has brought to light a mosaic pavement of animals and birds behind the high altar. The church was begun in 1140, but much of the fabric has been restored since the earthquake of 1743. To the left of the cathedral is the Portico of the Knights Templar, a striking relic from the days when the Knights were active in the city, consisting of three fourteenth-century arches raised on sturdy pillars and a single column. The continuation of the arcade is modern. Another building connected with the Knights Templar is the delightful small church of St. John at the Sepulchre (S. Giovanni al Sepolcro). It is an unusual building, basically round in shape with a double roof of warm red tiles. The extreme simplicity of the exterior walls is offset by a handsome Romanesque portal—the canopy carried by two columns supported by extremely weathered lions. Perhaps this building was once used as a baptistry by the Knights, by whom it was erected in the eleventh century, though later it passed into the hands of the Knights of the Holy Sepulchre.

The beautiful church of S. Benedetto, founded with its monastery in 1080, has been very well restored. The bell-tower is simple but well-proportioned and handsome. In the architecture of the south portal there is a powerful piece of low-relief carving showing men fighting animals. The cloisters are very fine, the small rounded arches grouped in sets of four on slim tapering columns supporting trapezoidal capitals and impost blocks. Some of the capitals are carved in formalized designs of Byzantine inspiration.

About two kilometres outside the town stands the interesting church of S. Maria del Casale founded in 1320 by Philip of Anjou, Prince of Taranto. The style of architecture is in the traditional stage between Romanesque and Gothic. A beautifully balanced canopy, combining a blind-arch motif with a trefoil opening is the outstanding feature of the exterior.

20   The owner of a shell-fish stall in Bari, and his fine selection of sea-food

21 The cathedral of
Bari, begun in 1170, a fine
example of Apulian-
Romanesque architecture

22 The interior of Bari
Cathedral, where in the
colonnade good use is
made of classical spoils

In the second half of this chapter we will take two routes between the cities of Brindisi and Bari—the first basically direct, through the towns of Ostuni, Fasano, Monopoli and Polignano—and the second a very roundabout way in order to give some account of the towns of Francavilla Fontana, Martina Franca, Alberobello, the Grotte Castellana and the town of Conversano. In a book covering such a wide area as this, it will not be possible unfortunately, in many cases, to give more than a passing reference to the great wealth of architecture that these Apulian towns possess, or to do more than hint at their individual character.

Taking, then, the ss 16 out of Brindisi, we pass through the small towns of S. Vito dei Normanni and Carovigno (with its odd-shaped castle) and arrive at Ostuni—a most attractive town, its narrow streets, steep outside steps, and chunky irregular-shaped white-washed houses, full of character. The thickness of the walls and general solidity of the buildings make it clear that the old parts of Ostuni are indeed very ancient, and the oriental flavour is enhanced by the flat roofs and dazzling whiteness of the buildings, which show up in marked contrast to the grey and brown stone of the cathedral and the majolica cupola of the baroque S. Maria Maddalena. The only distinctly *un*oriental thing about Ostuni is the cleanliness and freshness of the streets. In recent years many artists have arrived from other parts of Italy to live in the town, but efforts are being made to preserve the normal way of life and to prevent it becoming merely a show-piece.

The height of the town (just over 600 feet) is sufficient to allow a commanding view over the plain to the shore only six kilometres away. In recent years great efforts have been made to attract tourists to this part of the coast, with considerable success. The most important developments are the two large holiday villages of Rosa Marina, which can accommodate nearly 2,400 guests, and Villagio Valtur, about one-third of the size. The villas provided at these villages give self-contained accommodation for families or parties—with a choice of restaurants and an element of home-cooking—and the many facilities provided, both sporting and domestic, make them an attractive proposition for many people.

Ostuni is Messapian in origin, but it is not until the tenth century that it comes into historical focus as the seat of a Byzantine bishop. It was taken by the Normans in 1071 and later held in fief by the ruling houses of Lecce, Taranto, and Bari, later passing to the Zevallos family, who owned it until the beginning of last century.

The finest church in Ostuni is the cathedral—a Gothic building, rare in Apulia. It was begun in 1435, but not completed for another 60 years, thus covering a span between the rule of Angevins and Aragonese, reflected in the style of the architecture, which has a Spanish flavour. There is a rose-window over each of the three Gothic portals, the middle window being a magnificent example of its kind. The interior is distinctly on the heavy side, but where the organ has recently been removed one can see two beautifully carved capitals (one badly damaged) and also a large fresco and a fragment of another, making it seem certain that other exciting discoveries will be made in due course, since the eighteenth century decoration was heavy-handed and possibly unappreciative of medieval artistry.

Fasano, 22 kilometres from Ostuni, is a pleasant little town, once owned by the Knights of Malta, and nearby there is a very popular holiday resort in the hills—Selva di Fasano—situated at slightly over 1300 feet and considerably cooler than the plains in summer. A few years ago there were no hotels at this resort, but now there is the large Hotel Sierra Silvana (Cat II, 120 rooms) and two other hotels, plus two *pensioni*. There are lovely views from Selva di Fasano across the uplands of the Murge and towards the coast. The land here is intensively cultivated, with olives and fruit-trees predominant. We are now in what might be described as *trulli* country, *trulli* being the remarkable little buildings with conical roofs which are so characteristic of this part of Apulia. However I would like to reserve detailed comment on the *trulli* until we reach Alberobello, the 'capital' of the *trulli* country.

Not far up the coast from Torre Canne (about nine kilometres) important Roman remains have been excavated at Egnazia (ancient Gnathia). Egnazia was a Greco-Messapian town later Romanised, and it is now possible to see the early Roman walls, the Forum, and a considerable number of shops and houses, all in a very ruined state. Part of the Via Traiana can also be seen; it was this road, running through Benevento, Canosa, Bari and Egnazia to Brindisi—originally called the Via Egnatine—which was rebuilt in part by the Emperor Trajan and named after him. The modern ss 16 follows over a good part of it.

The next place on our coastal route to Bari is the town of Monopoli, a busy and prosperous industrial town with cement works and refineries for olive oil. It is also a major fishing and agricultural centre. The old town, which is mainly in the port area, has a natural beauty, quite devoid of any 'quaintness'. In order to reach the harbour one has to walk down fairly steep and very narrow streets, an area that includes a great many medieval houses. In the Via Amalfitana there is the delightful little church of S. Maria Amalfitana, built in the twelfth century, during a period when a colony from Amalfi lived in that part of the town.

At one time during the town's rich history it was controlled by Venice, and there is a palazzo overlooking the harbour at almost water level which is a beautiful example of Venetian-style architecture. I first visited Monopoli some years ago and I remember arriving on a very warm afternoon not ideal for sight-seeing. I walked along the whole length of the inner quays to inspect the great castle guarding the entrance, hoping to be refreshed by cool sea-breezes. But the light dazzled off the rippling water, and the sun, beating against the high solid walls, radiated and reflected waves of hot dry air. Children sitting on iron bollards played rather than fished with home-made rods, and their elders, some quite old with white hair and corrugated sun-blackened faces, sat cross-legged on the quayside patiently mending nets—quite absorbed, impervious to heat.

The castle dates from the time of Frederick II, but was largely rebuilt and much strengthened in the sixteenth century by the indefatigable Emperor Charles V. The importance of Monopoli as a port can be said to have begun during the years of the Crusades in Norman times.

A few kilometres beyond Monopoli one reaches Polignano a Mare, and here the height of the rocky shore has increased slightly, so that part of the old medieval town is perched over the sea a little dramatically at the very edge of limestone cliffs. The buildings have a marked Saracenic flavour, with starkly vertical walls, squared deeply recessed openings as windows—sometimes without shutters—and flat roofs. An occasional carved Gothic window-frame or decorated balcony stands out in striking contrast.

From Polignano we pass through the small towns or fishing villages of S. Vito, Cozze, Mola di Bari and Torre a Mare before entering the city of Bari by way of the Lungomare Nazario Sauro.

Leaving Brindisi on the ss 7 which follows the Via Appia Antica, we arrive after 33 kilometres at Francavilla Fontana, a medium-sized town notable for the number of its fine *palazzi*. The best of these is the Palazzo Imperiali begun in 1450 by G. A. Orsini, added to in 1536 by B. Bonifacio and completed by the Imperiali at the beginning of the eighteenth century. These palaces are a sign of the opulence and style in which the noble families of Apulia lived. In this part of the Region the most powerful of the feudal magnates were the Acquaviva Counts of Conversano and the Imperiali Princes of Francavilla.

Only a short distance from Francavilla Fontana is the town of Oria, famous for its tremendously impressive castle crowning the hill. It is one of the finest examples of Frederick II's military architecture, with three good towers commanding the angles of its mighty triangular plan. Oria (ancient Hyria) was an important town in Messapian and Roman times, and later in the Middle Ages it was the focal point in the many wars that followed the break-up of the Western Empire, involving Goths, Byzantines, Lombards, the Frankish Emperor Lewis II, and in 925 the Saracens. The castle of Oria stands just high enough at 550 feet to command splendid views over the flat plains of the Salento and the rolling Murge Tarentine to the Gulf of Taranto.

The road from Francavilla Fontana is dead-straight (like so many in Apulia) as far as Ceglie Messapico, and then curves over the Murge to Martina Franca, a substantial town at a height of about 1400 feet. Martina Franca is a charming and graceful town distinguished by its baroque and rococo town houses of the seventeenth and eighteenth centuries, and by its baroque churches and palaces. The Palazzo Ducale, now the Municipio, is the finest of the latter, erected in 1669 and attributed by some to G. L. Bernini, (though I haven't discovered a reference to it in the literature on Bernini). The church of S. Martino (1774–5) has a restrained and beautiful baroque façade rather spoilt by the over-elaborate representation above the portal of St. Martin and the beggar.

From the town one can quickly reach the astonishing Valley of Itria (Valle d'Itria)—a patch-work of rich red soil and green vegetation dotted with innumerable *trulli* dwellings, mostly farmhouses, standing out with their brilliantly white walls and grey conical roofs. An abundance of grapes are grown here, and the area is noted for its strong white wines (*bianco neutro di Martina*) which are sometimes used for fortifying other wines.

Of course when it comes to *trulli* one thinks automatically of Alberobello, a large part of which is composed of these delightful little dwellings. We will make then for this attractive small town—at 1410 feet very nearly the highest place on the Murge—proceeding along the ss 172 via Locorotondo (on the other side of the Valle d'Itria), and reaching Alberobello after 15 kilometres. Alberobello is the unofficial 'capital' of the *murge dei trulli* but in fact very few of its dwellings built in the *trulli* style are very old. The origin of genuine *trulli* is not known, but the buildings are certainly ancient, possibly dating from the Neolithic and Bronze Ages when this countryside was intensively occupied, and made by people who had migrated from the Levant; in Syria there are similar structures. What we see in Alberobello or the Valle d'Itria are of course much evolved versions of the original type, though faithfully copied in many respects.

A genuine *trullo* is a small round building, generally stepped towards the centre, and constructed of thin flat courses of local limestone (which is liberally scattered over the fields) and put together skilfully and neatly without mortar in the manner of Cotswold dry walling. These *trulli* are found over a wide area of Apulia (well north of Bari for instance) and by no means restricted to the *murge dei trulli*. Often to be seen in orchards, the genuine *trulli* are sometimes used by farmers to house their implements. It is however in the *trulli* country that we see the modern versions, consisting of *trulli* villas, *trulli* farmhouses and even a *trullo* hotel. The roofs of these buildings usually come to a point like a cone and are capped by a filial, looking not unlike the round 'bobble' of a pawn chess-piece. The conical roof is sometimes white-washed but often left the natural grey, in which case a cross in various forms is generally painted on the roof—or other signs, heathen or magical, depending on the beliefs or superstitions of the owner. The walls of the buildings are invariably white.

At Alberollo the view is made colourful by great splashes of green from the many trees in the main street—which bisects the more orthodox town from the *trulli* zone up to the hill on the other side—and also by the multi-coloured shawls, head scarves, rugs etc., produced locally, which are sold from stalls either in the main street or outside individual homes. The whole of the zone has been declared a national monument.

It is inevitable of course that a place which is so much out of the ordinary should attract a large number of tourists, and also that the locals should make capital out of the great interest in their *trulli* dwellings. My visit to the town coincided with siesta time, the streets were practically deserted, and the sole stall-holder in evidence made little effort to sell me her home-spun articles—the heat being too great for any kind of exertion. However she did ask me in to see the inside of her *trullo* house, (a small payment may be made—though not solicited—if articles are not bought) and showed me with much courtesy and politeness the snug living-rooms of her home. There were no windows in the bedroom; the fitted bed took up most of the space, and ventilation was through an opening in the roof.

To reach Conversano from Alberobello one leaves the ss 172 after a couple of kilometres to take a secondary road via Castellana Grotte, a small market-town kept scrupulously clean, as are the great majority of the hill-towns of the Murge. The *grotte* near Castellana are famous for being probably the most extensive and spectacular caves in all Italy.

From Castellana to Conversano is only a few minutes run by car (10 kilometres), the road steadily descending. Conversano is one of those towns, so common in Apulia, where there is almost an embarrasment of riches, architecturally and in the arts, which would take up a disproportionate amount of space in a general book such as this, if they were all to be fully described. The following account then amounts to little more than a synopsis.

It is clear from the number of palaces, churches and splendidly built town houses that Conversano was once an important and wealthy town. As for its origins, these go back far into antiquity; the remains of megalithic walls indicate that the town was an important centre between the fourth and third centuries B.C. the Normans won the town from the Lombards who had long disputed possession of it with the Byzantines. However it was during the Aragonese period that the town reached its height of prosperity. The owners of Conversano between 1508 and 1801 were the Acquaviva family of Aragona. The impressive and beautiful round tower of the castle (Norman foundation) was built in the fourteenth century.

I arrived at Conversano at a time when the town had not yet awoken from its communal siesta, a time which gives all Italian urban places between the hours of one and four p.m., the atmosphere of an English town on a Sunday morning before the pubs open. With the minimum of distraction therefore I was able to wander around this really delightful little town, its medieval streets beautifully paved and immaculately clean. The high standards of workmanship of the medieval masons can be seen in many *palazzi* and churches, giving to this quiet market town an air and style not quite in accord with its modern rôle.

The eleventh-century cathedral, much renovated after a disastrous fire in 1912, is a handsome building inside; the modern architects have paid much attention to proportion and scale and dispensed with lavish ornamentation.

One approaches the monastery of S. Benedetto down a narrow street and can see the baroque dome of the church framed between buildings. This first sighting is misleading, for the foundation of the monastery took place long before the ninth century (from which period there are documentary records), the traditional founder being S. Mauro, a disciple of S. Benedict. The cloisters at the side of the church have a charming intimacy. I wandered around for a few minutes quite undisturbed with the warm afternoon sun slanting in and adding a contrast of light and shade to the man-made subtleties of the carved stone.

18. Bari

The commercial and industrial significance of Bari has grown very rapidly in the past few years, and the population expansion has kept pace with it. It is now a town of over 350,000 inhabitants and growing all the time. It is the second largest city in the south of Italy, and, like Naples, an important port. The Levant Fair held at Bari annually in September is an important International exhibition.

Bari, like so many cities in Italy, has a chronic problem of traffic congestion. The Barese have long since become resigned to it, and sit with glum faces in their stationary cars until someone's frayed nerves give way in an outburst of hooting, no doubt easing the tension but having a minimal effect on progress.

The best way to get about the town, as I soon found out, is to walk. The lay-out of the 'new' town is compact in grid-iron fashion, and while there are two or three fine streets, on the whole modern Bari is not a place of beauty. It makes up for it by having a number of excellent shops, especially in the Via Sparano, some first-class restaurants, a number of good hotels of which three, the Delle Nazioni, the Jolly, and the Palace are in the first category—and a sufficient variety of eating-places to satisfy every mood and economic fluctuation. An attractive corner of the town is the area of the Porto Vecchio, close by the Old City where in days gone by stall-holders used to pitch their tents and stalls, and demonstrate their considerable persuasive powers in the course of selling octopus, squid, mussels, whelks, sea-urchins, spider-crabs, starfish and a number of denizens of the ocean whose names are unknown to me.

The old city of Bari forms a promontory dividing the Porto Vecchio from the main port. It is fortunate for us today that when, in 1808, King Murat decided that Bari should become the new provincial capital in place of Trani, he ordered that the inevitable large-scale development should not be at the expense of the old city. We can therefore have a pleasure of visiting at Citta Vecchia what is basically a medieval town. One gets an immediate impression of low, deep, rounded arches leading to small courtyards, of narrow passages between high walls, the paving stones polished smooth by countless feet. Looking at the various buildings it is difficult to judge their age, but some were probably built as long ago as the twelfth century.

One can enter the old town at several points, and a good way is from the Porto Vecchio which leads into Piazza Mercantile, humming with the extrovert way of life which is second nature to the people living here. But for us, as we follow the ancient narrow passages and coming straight from the modern streets with their endless apartment blocks and offices, it is a remarkable experience. Old Bari is another world. The cries and calls of itinerant salesmen, children, caged-birds and impatient mothers form a strident concerto of sound; the air is heavy with conflicting but usually delicious aromas . . . the smell of freshly baked bread; the whiff of hot olive oil or of roasting almonds; the fragrance of charcoal braziers grilling meat; the heavy scent of herbs as one passes a provisions shop . . . If it is fairly early in the morning one can expect to see housewives spreading out freshly cooked pasta in wire-bottomed trays to dry in the sun in the street outside their homes. Commonly they are shaped like little shells and are called *recchietelle*.

The first call for many people visiting the old town is the famous Basilica of San Nicola, and so it was for me. At first glance the west front seems a little disappointing. For a church of such renown—the prototype of all Apulian-Romanesque churches—the decoration lacks the grandeur one expects. But it is a very early church (the crypt was begun in 1087) and the treatment is restrained, which gives it dignity. There is only a very small round window high up, but exotic rose windows came considerably later. The portal too is less elaborate than later styles, for which it serves as a model, but it is a beautifully balanced piece of architecture. The style is early Apulian-Romanesque, the doorway surmounted by a richly carved rounded arch encased in a roughly triangular canopy, the whole supported on two slender columns. It would be usual, in the style of Romanesque, for these columns to rest on the backs of lions, but here at S. Nicola the animals are oxen—looking slightly odd without their horns, but clearly bovine.

The use of oxen must be an allusion to the incident that is supposed to have occurred on 9 May 1087 when the remains of St. Nicholas were being taken in triumphant procession from the port to the town. At a certain point en route the two oxen stopped dead, and no beating or cajoling would make them budge. This, it was at once assumed, was clearly the manifestation of the Divine Will, and at that very spot a site was cleared for the building of a basilica in the saint's honour.

It might be wondered how the bones of St. Nicholas, who was Bishop of Myra in Asia Minor in the sixth century, ever found their way to the streets of Bari, and the story is not altogether to the credit of the citizens. The bald facts are that the saint's relics were robbed by a party of Barese sailors from his tomb in Myra (the site of the town is in Southern Turkey) and ferried across the sea to their home port.

What possible justification could have been put forward by the perpetrators of that act of desecration? The usual excuse, that the holy relics had to be protected from the infidel, was hardly valid, since the territory had not at that time been overrun by the Seljuks. Nevertheless the Seljuks were exerting great pressure on the Byzantine outposts, and this no doubt was sufficient excuse for the sailors of Bari. In those days of religious zeal the acquisition of the relics of a saint as important as St. Nicholas was considered a unique triumph, and the returning sailors were accorded a hero's welcome. Not only was the presence of the saint's remains a great stimulus to the religious life of Bari, but it ensured a boost to the city's revenues from the stream of pilgrims who have continued over the centuries to visit his shrine. A great festival is held between the 7th and 9th of May in the course of which the statue of St. Nicholas is carried out to sea in a fishing-boat 'dressed overall', accompanied by boat-loads of devotees.

For a saint whose earthly record is so obscure, the popularity of St. Nicholas is remarkable. In the Middle Ages he was ranked high in the saintly charts and his popularity has never diminished. He was, and for some doubtless still is, the patron saint of Russia; he is claimed by sailors as their patron; and he is known to millions of children as Santa Claus, the American corruption by Dutch-German immigrants of San Nicolaas or Santa Niklaus.

The inside of the Basilica is impressive. Above the main rounded arches of the nave, carrying a considerable weight of masonry, there is set an arcade of much smaller arches—all of them, upper and lower, carried on ancient columns with finely worked capitals. The interior proportions are so good that there is no suggestion of heaviness, except from the intrusion of two great transverse arches which spring from alongside the first two columns of the colonnade. These were added in 1451 to give extra structural support.

The crypt, where the remains of St. Nicholas lie, is in normal times a quiet and dignified place, the many orange-coloured lights around the tomb and altar dimly illuminating the superbly carved capitals of the columns propping the low vaulted ceiling. While I was there there were a few pilgrims present, their curiosity almost getting the better of decorum, as they pushed to see through the railings that screen off the altar and tomb. Others remained quietly at prayer on the benches behind. During the three days of pageantry in May the trickle of pilgrims turns into a flood.

There is an outstanding *ciborium* in the church mounted on four fine columns of antique *breccia*, each with an unusual and splendidly carved capital. The Apulian ciborium is normally a two-tiered octagonal structure, each tier balanced on a multitude of miniature columns. This one at S. Nicola is an exceptionally refined and graceful example. It was made in 1150 and has many times been copied in Apulia.

Behind the altar stands an episcopal throne, originally the throne of Abbot Elia the founder, whose work on the crypt began in 1087. The weight at the front of the throne is borne on the shoulders of two crouching figures who have dropped to one knee; they are stripped to the waist and the strain they are undergoing is shown by the brilliantly realistic carving of their agonized features. Between them a figure with a long club in his hand looks up and with his free hand seems to be adjusting the alignment of the seat. He is the slave master, and the slaves either Saracens or negroes. The whole group is a marvel of imagination and movement in stone, for which art historians have given some credit to Byzantine influences, though this is probably shared by artists from the north.

Before visiting the Cathedral of Bari (S. Sabino) I decided to take a look at Bari Castle. It stands at the end of the street leading to the west front of the cathedral, and is separated by a deep moat from the road encircling the old city. The moat is now converted into a pleasing formal garden. Above it the massive bastions come to a knife-edge point at the east and west corners, these being the work of Sforza in the sixteenth century.

The history of Bari castle has some heroic and bizarre episodes. At the time of the great siege, which began on 5 August 1068 and lasted for nearly three years, the fortified town of Bari was the capital of Byzantine Langobardia, and also the military headquarters of the Greek army on the Italian mainland. Guiscard knew that the fall of the city would mean the end of Byzantine power in Italy. After nearly 30 months under siege conditons, having suffered great losses in defence of the walls and being almost at the point of starvation, the defenders only succumbed when the Greek relief force with men and supplies was routed by the Norman fleet.

The Cathedral of Bari was begun in 1170 as a replacement for the Byzantine *duomo* destroyed by the Norman King William I, when Bari was razed to the ground in 1156 (only the Basilica of S. Nicola was spared) as a punishment for rebellion. The new cathedral, which was completed in eight years was, like its predecessor, dedicated to S. Sabino, Bishop of Canosa, whose remains had been transferred to Bari in 872.

The exterior of S. Sabino is very fine, superior in my view to that of

Bitonto cathedral which is thought by many to be the most perfect example of Apulian-Romanesque style. There are two particularly striking features: a tall, elegant, subtly proportioned campanile, and an oriental-looking octagonal drum, domed and with a beautiful Byzantine inspired frieze that sits snugly at the crossing, making a splendid composition with the vertical lines of the campanile.

The fact that the cathedral was built about 80 years after the Basilica of S. Nicola explains the extra richness of the carvings which developed considerably in that span. There is an exterior dwarf gallery running along the south side of the building modelled very closely on S. Nicola's. High up at the end of the south transept is a beautiful rose window with a graceful semi-circular canopy resting on a beast on either side. It is, in my view, one of the finest windows in the region, where there is no lack of competition.

Beneath this masterpiece we find a very different style of decoration at the base of the lower windows. Here is a good illustration of Lombard imagination run riot. We see the tail of a snake being devoured by a reptile, who in turn is about to be chewed in half by a mythical winged beast with the head and beak of a giant parrot; in another group a lioness has pounced on a man who lies on his back vainly trying to keep the hungry jaws away with his hand . . . doubtless there was a symbolic meaning. C. A. Willemsen writes:

> All these capitals, porches, pediments and bosses originally had their established order and individual significance . . . As time went by, the original symbolism undoubtedly waned and the pleasure of inventing such fabulous creatures grew freer and bolder . . .

Inside, the church has a noble simplicity, all baroque accretions having been stripped. Now one can see the fine lines of the original work, the true harmony of scale. Its plan is that of a triple-apsed basilica, though unlike S. Nicola, it does not have a triforium gallery. There is an immediate impression of space due to the height of the nave with a plain open-timbered roof. A most satisfying harmony is achieved by an immaculate sense of scale in the arrangement of the double colonnade, the smaller above the main columns of the nave.

The ciborium stands out as a brightly coloured and quite effective piece, but it is modern, and hardly any of the original remains. The pulpit, which has a fine upstanding eagle with the lectern balanced on its head, is also reconstructed using fragments of the original, and the episcopal throne is likewise a reconstruction, done in 1954. On the left of the nave one can enter a twelve-sided building known as the *Trulla* which was begun in 1618. This is used as the sacristy, and one can ask to be shown the Archives which include an eleventh century *Exultet* roll on parchment in Beneventan script with beautiful Byzantine illumination.

The Archaeological Museum is housed in a wing of the grandiose Palazzo Ateneo, a building it shares with Bari University—the long promised modern museum having failed to materialize as yet. There is some very interesting material exhibited in these grand salons—figures, vases and jugs from ancient Peucezia (modern province of Bari), Dannia (Foggia) and Messapia. The work is often over-ornate, but there is no lack of imagination by the ceramic artists.

19. Castles and Cathedrals
of the interior

When making a selection of cathedrals to describe in Apulia, one is faced with a difficult choice, for the quantity of important monuments is almost embarrassing. In the following chapter we will look at the cathedrals that adorn like a string of pearls the shores of the Adriatic from Bari to the Gulf of Manfredonia—but here we will concentrate our attention on the hinterland with its pleasing contrasts of stern fortresses and magnificent Apulian-Romanesque cathedrals, and in the case of the southern town of Altamura, a rather later work—the inspiration of Frederick II.

But before describing these perhaps a few words on the historical background to the flowering of Romanesque arthitecture in Apulia may not be out of place. The term Apulian-Romanesque is a convenient way of describing a sophisticated blend of Byzantine, Saracenic, Lombard, Pisan and French influences in both architecture and decoration—but does less than justice to the dominant part played by the Norman rulers, who in nearly every case were the prime movers behind the foundation of these fine eleventh and twelfth-century churches in Apulia.

The Norman conquest of the south of Italy had small beginnings in about the year 1019 with infiltration of small bands of impoverished knights and mercenaries. But within a span of 50 years large Norman-led armies were achieving dramatic victories, and, as we have seen, by 1071 the Byzantines had been thrown out of Italy. Twenty years later the last Saracen stronghold in Sicily had fallen to the Normans. The triumphs of Robert Guiscard, Duke of Apulia and Calabria, and his brother Roger, Count of Sicily, came to fulfilment when Roger's son Count Roger II was crowned King of Sicily, Apulia and Calabria (the Kingdom of Sicily) in 1130.

The significance of these events is that with the arrival of the Normans the previous indecisive administration came to an end. The Normans were brilliant administrators, and their system as it gradually evolved in the course of the twelfth century was the envy of Western civilization. The Normans imposed their feudal system with rigid severity, and their courts of administration and justice governed with absolute power. The details of the extent to which they managed to establish control over their enormous territory makes fascinating reading. Suffice to say that because of Norman authority, both civil and ecclesiastical, every major building project in the territories of the Norman Kingdom must have had the authorization if not the direct involvement of the Norman rulers. Also it is not unreasonable to assume that in a significant number of cases the supervising master mason was a Norman.

The Norman Kings—especially Roger (1130–1154) and William II (1166–1189)—were strongly motivated by the desire to build great churches and monasteries to the glory of God. Both men were probably genuinely pious, and certainly each had a great respect for the Church (both Latin and Eastern persuasions), and its steadying influence on a volatile society of feudal lords. Even Robert Guiscard, the first of the great Norman conquerors—ex-freebooter, ex-brigand, ex-outlaw—was not slow to build churches once he had attained respectability and authority. His was the power of the mailed-fist, but like all Normans, he understood the unique place of the church in the order of things.

When it comes to looking at the actual achievements in the style of Apulian Romanesque, we find that the similarity in over-all plan between many of the Apulian cathedrals (Bari, Trani, Bitonto, Troia) and certain Norman cathedrals in France and England cannot be coincidental. The likelihood is that the masons and masters came either from Norman monasteries, or foundations with the mother-houses in Normandy or central France. As for the decoration this was nearly always the work of Lombards, Tuscans, Byzantines or Saracens whose exquisite craftsmanship the Normans sometimes tried to copy but never matched. (The Lombards also made a major contribution to the architectural style of these southern churches, and Pisan influence was important.)

There was a marked freedom of artistic, intellectual and religious practice in the Kingdom of Sicily. Mosques abounded in Palermo, and Jews had free access to their synagogues. Greek churches and Basilican monasteries flourished co-existing with Western foundations. This enlightened attitude (the Normans were pragmatists—they were only a tiny minority among the peoples they ruled) eased the passage of a flow of artists from the north, east and south, and explains the diversity of artistic skills which are evident in all the important churches.

It is a pity but inevitable, that (with a few exceptions) the castles and palaces that are liberally scattered over the Apulian countryside are in a poorer state of preservation than the churches. The latter have been maintained and restored over the centuries with loving care (the *Cassa per il Mezzogiorno* can take credit for much excellent work in the last decade or so) whereas some of the castles have been allowed to deteriorate or have been converted to more peaceful uses—a school at Otranto, a prison at Trani, a hall of residence at Conversano. At least one can say that these great castles and hunting lodges have been saved the indignity of serving as museum-pieces for those curious enough to tramp round their deserted corridors and ghostly dungeons.

The first visit on our tour of major inland cathedrals and castles is to Bitonto, a small town but an important agricultural centre about 17 kilometres west of Bari. The centre of the town is a maze of narrow medieval streets which lead one up stone steps or under low arches, and which twist between high walls. Occasionally one comes across a fine town house, and there are substantial remains of the ancient city defences, such as the Porta Baresana and its neighbouring round tower.

When one reaches the cathedral square the church seems so large and the piazza so small, that the one seems to dwarf the other. Seen from the south-west corner of the piazza, the façade and the south side of the cathedral make a magnificent composition. The building was begun in 1175 by the Normans and took only 25 years to complete, and it is considered by many to be the best example of the Apulian-Romanesque style.

The decoration of the exterior is very fine: every lightly carved piece of ornamentation is balanced by solid strength—as when the beautiful row of capitals in the dwarf gallery on the south side are offset by the deep boldly rounded arches of the blind arcade below, with their sturdy piers. (We have already seen this distinctive feature at S. Nicola, and at S. Sabino, in Bari.) Looking in more detail at the west front we can see how the architect has given harmony and balance to this very large area by dividing the façade into three parts. The rose window is a beautiful example of the Apulian-Romanesque style—very rich, with a carved hood supported by lions which stand on two slender columns. Two more lions, almost weathered beyond recognition guard the main portal.

This magnificent building certainly looks its age, for the cleaning of the stone was restricted to the interior, when the baroque trappings were removed, and the outside still shows the centuries of weathering which has stained and darkened the stone. This is not unpleasing and adds to its dignity, emphasising the impressive fact that after 800 years it is in such a marvellous state of preservation as a whole.

The inside of the cathedral has been beautifully restored, repaired and cleaned, and one is struck at once by the skill of the masons who built it. The carvings are of a very high standard, especially the capitals of the nave colonnade. The plan of the church is that of a Latin cross, with three semi-circular apses, and a typical basilican plan of a nave and two side aisles. Great rounded arches, as usual, support the triforium gallery above.

An object of exceptional interest is the ambone—the name given to the pulpit or reading desk in early Christian churches. This masterpiece is the work of Nicholas, priest and architect, who made it in 1229. He was one of the finest and most original artists of his time in Apulia. Here we see on the outside of the pulpit a puny man bending under the weight of a magnificent haughty eagle, on whose head rests the marble lectern—beautifully decorated—with the words Nicolaus Magister showing underneath.

If the capitals in the nave can be said to be unusual (one finds monkeys and birds among the carved foliage) those in the crypt have more than a touch of fantasy. A high degree of virtuosity is displayed in the 30 carved capitals and columns supporting the vaulting. Eagles or griffons—sometimes lions—can be seen squatting on the curved leaves of the foliage, the lions at times accompanied by little men with tasselled caps who appear to be keepers or trainers. There is much humour in these fantastic creations.

Ruvo di Puglia, with its 25,000 inhabitants, manages to maintain the unspoilt atmosphere of a small medieval town. It is a prosperous little place, being an important agricultural centre notable for its fine dessert grapes, and the quality of its olive oil. When I first visited the town a few years ago, in the autumn, an abundant crop of almonds had been gathered. Everywhere I went I found great heaps of nuts being spread out to dry in the sun on the pavement outside people's front doors. It was a major home industry. Along one stretch of road, with nuts several inches deep, an old man shuffled backwards and forwards airing them with his boots.

Ruvo has a known history that goes back to the times of the early Italiot peoples, when it was an important town of the Peucezi. In the fifth century B.C. it came into contact with the cities of Magna Graecia, and quickly assimilated certain aspects of Greek culture. In particular it became famous for its production of vases, at first almost certainly the work of Greek potters and vase painters. Also, many of the vases found at Ruvo were imported Corinthian and Attic products. However the workshops gradually developed their own style, and Ruvo vases became the most celebrated of all the local products of the region which came to be known as Apulian ware.

The Museo Jatta in Ruvo, founded by Giovanni Jatta at the begin-

23　Inside the old town, Bari

24　An ancient dwelling at Vieste, Apulia

25 The rich Apulian-Romanesque style of the portal of S. Leonardo di Siponto

26 S. Leonardo: detail of carving depicting Balaam and the Ass on one of the capitals

ning of the last century and carried on by his son, an archaeologist, until the end of the century, has a magnificent collection of these Greek and Apulian vases and ceramics numbering over 1700 in all. The museum is housed in the family palazzo and the collection is split up into four rooms for easier viewing.

The cathedral, when one comes across it suddenly from the west end of a narrow street, looks smaller than it is, perhaps because the ground of the piazza slopes towards the façade. It has as its main decoration on the west front a large rose window, and a very fine Romanesque portal with three bands of carvings.

The Cathedral of Ruvo is one of the major cathedrals of Apulia. It was a Norman foundation of the twelfth century, and has had at least three major restorations before the latest one which has removed the baroque features internally. Externally the building has many decorative features typical of the period, in particular a row of corbel masks along the frieze beneath the long line of the nave roof—beautifully carved. An unusual feature of the church is that the bell-tower is quite isolated from the main building. This is rare in Apulia, though at both Trani and Barletta the single towers stand close to the body of the church and are linked to it only by an arch.

The cathedrals of Palo and Bitetto, both within easy reach of Bari, are churches of great interest, basically Apulian-Romanesque in style, with important later additions.

CASTEL DEL MONTE, the first secular monument we will look at in this chapter, is almost equi-distant from Andria or Ruvo—about 18 kilometres from the lattter. For students of the life and habits of the Emperor Frederick II (1197–1250) the castle is a place of extraordinary interest. It was for Frederick a retreat, a hunting-lodge and a palace stronghold all in one, and as such was sited with exceptional care. It stands high over miles of gently undulating land, thick with olive groves, but otherwise featureless, and its position is commanding.

It is not known to what extent Frederick had a hand in the actual design of Castel del Monte, but there can be no doubt that he was the inspiration for the spirit and style of the building. It is designed with mathematical precision in the shape of an octagon, having at each of the eight corners an octagonal tower, so that the field of fire not only covers every angle but overlaps or crisscrosses. The openings in these towers are not more than slits, wholly for defence, but the walls between the towers do have fair-sized windows, in style more suited to a palace, and the general effect from the outside is of a very handsome building—beautifully symmetrical with clean vertical lines.

Frederick's extraordinarily liberal interests extended to almost everything known at the time of scientific matters (he was called by his

contemporaries *stupor mundi*—the wonder of the world) and this led
to a genuine scientific interest in animals. He collected a menagerie
which followed him all over Italy and even into Germany, and rich
assortment they were, including camels, elephants, leopards, panthers,
lions, white falcons, gerfalcons and dromedaries. They illustrate well
Frederick's love of the exotic and unusual. His great joy was hunting,
for which he used coursing leopards and panthers as well as hawks and
falcons. His knowledge of birds and falconry was profound; his own
treatise *De arte venandi cum avibus* was not only the first book on falconry, but is even today considered to be an authoritative work. He
devoted much of his leisure time over a period of 30 years to the preparation and writing of the book.

For Frederick the Castel del Monte was a retreat as much as a fortified royal palace which could be used for entertaining. He called it his
'place of Solace', for here he could retire and write, and keep his hand
in at his favourite sport. In all directions there was splendid hunting in
this part of Apulia in the Middle Ages, (especially on the Gargano
peninsular) with extensive forests, of which the Forest of Umbra is all
that now remains.

Inside the castle very little remains now of its former magnificence.
Walking through the rooms one needs to draw considerably on one's
imagination to visualize how the castle must have looked in imperial
times. But there are some good decorative details in the stonework of
this superbly constructed building, and one can admire some fine
vaulting—and from the windows, an extensive view.

The palatial aspect of the royal residence was a feature of Frederick's style, both here and at Lucera and Foggia. At Castel del
Monte the residential quarters contained many fine sculptures and
marbles, and the apartments were furnished with oriental rugs and
cushions, and silk draperies woven in Sicily by Saracen craftsmen. It is
unthinkable that the libraries would not have contained manuscripts
illuminated by the finest contemporary artists, among other riches.
Some of the floors were covered with mosaic, and the walls decorated
with sheets of red *breccia* or white marble.

One can only hope that when the restoration of the castle is complete the Italian authorities will furnish the residential quarters in a
style which will do justice to the setting, and so bring these fine rooms
to life again.

Altamura is the largest of the Murge towns, with a population of about
45,000 and it is an important communications centre with a fair
amount of light industry. A few years ago, when I first visited the town,
one was met at the railway station by an ancient bus and taken clat-

tering through the streets to the town centre, where there are gardens and a wide piazza, and, at 1600 feet, splendid views.

In olden times Altamura had the reputation of being one of the intellectual oases of Apulia, with its own university—founded in 1748—but this was lost when the town, a strong supporter of the Parthenopean Republic, fell into the hands of Cardinal Ruffo's army in 1799 and suffered appalling reprisals. In the ninth century the town must have endured similar suffering at the hands of the Saracens who destroyed it and scattered its inhabitants. The town owed its rebirth to Frederick II, who introduced a mixed population of Italians, Greeks and Jews, and set them up with promises of special municipal privileges. Then in 1228, having perhaps taken to heart the words of Thomas of Gaeta, he initiated the building of the cathedral. Thomas had cause to write to his Emperor because of his alarm, shared by others in the kingdom, at the vast scale of his building projects, at the hectic pace at which he tried to carry them out, and because they were restricted to fortresses and castles.

One approaches the cathedral from the Porta di Bari through the narrow streets of the old quarter. The great building is rather a baffling mixture of styles. The form is clearly Romanesque—in this case very late, but much of the detail is foreign to it. A glance at the official guide-book clears up the mystery—the building was severely damaged by an earthquake in 1316, and subsequently rebuilt; a major change was carried out in 1534 when the main portal and the rose window were removed from their original positions and placed in the west front—and the two towers added. The latter are faithfully modelled on earlier examples in the district, such as Acquaviva dei Fonti, except for the baroque 'cushion' domes and pinnacles which were added in 1729.

The finest external features of this great brown stone church are the rose window and the central portal, both fourteenth-century works. The Altamura window, later than most in Apulia gives nothing away in terms of richness. The same can be said of the portal, a masterly work, pure Romanesque in inspiration. An outer pair of four columns rest on the backs of lions and support a deep canopy, splendidly carved. The whole composition is thought to be the most richly decorated of all portals in Apulia.

Inside the cathedral is decorated on a grand scale. It is all very baroque and very sumptuous—but also impressive, for in this case it has been well done. Immense round, smooth grey or grey-pink columns of fine marble support a triforium gallery which is absolutely Romanesque in its form, though entirely faced with marble.

Like most towns in Apulia, LUCERA has a history reaching far back into antiquity. For many years it was a loyal ally of Rome and in Imperial times it flourished, enjoying special privileges, and those marks of a prosperous Roman community—baths and an amphitheatre—that can be seen today. The Normans took possession of the city in about 1070 and later Frederick II made Lucera into a fortress of such strength that it became known as 'the key of Apulia'.

It was primarily to see the castle that I went with some friends, a few years ago, to vist Lucera, but large though it is, it took us some time to find, for it is set well back from the town behind a large wooded park. It is an immensely impressive structure, the outer walls and towers, built by Charles II of Anjou, being over half a mile in circumference.

It is certain that many of the rumours that were spread about concerning Frederick's palace stronghold at Lucera were no more than idle gossip. It is not in the least surprising however that the Emperor was called 'the Sultan of Lucera', though it is unlikely that the walls of his castle embraced the royal harem, as many imagined. Outwardly uncompromisingly built for defence, inside there was a courtyard where fountains played, and around which there was a series of apartments with every refinement of luxury. The second of the 'baptized Sultans' (his grandfather King Roger of Sicily was the 'original') was no less enamoured of oriental influences than his illustrious grandparent. Unhappily when the palace building subsequently fell into decay, it was used by the local people as a quarry, so that little remains to be seen today.

Whether or not the stronghold of Lucera contained a large garrison of Saracen troops is a matter of dispute among historians. That there was a large population of Saracens (up to 16,000) at Luceria Saracenorum, as the town was called, is not in question. Their removal from Sicily by Frederick II was a direct result of their unruliness, obliging Frederick to fight a series of campaigns against them. It must have seemed a cruel and hard decision at the time to force alien conditions on the descendants of the Arab conquerors of Sicily, but it was not long before the hatred of the Saracens turned to respect, and respect to devotion. Mainly serfs from the central hill districts of Sicily, they were put to work to improve the barren land, and were given religious freedom and their own civic leaders. Frederick raised a bodyguard from among them that was fanatically loyal to him. It is believed that at Lucera the Muslims lived entirely among their own kind, and it must have been a strange sight for a northern traveller to come across, in the heart of Christendom the views of the mosques of Lucera with their minarets piercing the skyline over the hills of the Capitanata.

Today in the vast desolate spaces inside the castle walls there are few noteworthy sights. However one can climb up on to the top of the walls and enjoy a magnificent view of the surrounding countryside, with the foothills of the Appenines on one side and the high mass of the Gargano mountains on the other, with the great plain of the Capitanata stretching out between them like a vast orchard.

There are several other monuments and places in Lucera worth a visit. The Duomo, an impressive building in the French style, was begun in 1300 by Charles II of Anjou, and contains several interesting objects of religious art. The Museo Civico has a good collection of local terracottas, a fine bust of Proserpine, and the *Marine Venus* a copy of a first century statue. The Roman amphitheatre is thought to have been the earliest dedicated to the Emperor Augustus. It was erected by a magistrate, M. Vecilius Campus in honour of Caesar and the colony of Luceria.

20. Between Bari and Barletta

The coastal road, ss 16, running north-west from Bari passes through some featureless countryside, mainly olive groves, and is disfigured by the usual advertising hoardings, so it is a relief to pull off and visit the towns and ports that stud the coastline every ten kilometres or so.

The first of these, Giovinazzo, is typical of many Apulian towns in that it is part new—with modern apartment-buildings— and part ancient. Down at the harbour the small port gives one the impression that history has passed it by. The boats are painted in dashing hues of red, blue and green, adding colour to the ancient stones of the water-front buildings.

Set only a little way back from the sea is the twelfth-century Romanesque cathedral (consecreated in 1283). It is a rugged weather-beaten building, and at first glance the style appears to be almost primitive in its simple robustness. But a closer look reveals a number of fine exterior details—some beautifully carved capitals, the unusual treatment of the original southern tower, and some very handsome interlaced shallow blind arcading on the southern wall.

Molfetta, the next town along the coast, is a place of far greater importance; it has around 60,000 inhabitants, some local industry, and a large fishing fleet. Molfetta is a vigorous bustling place, especially compared with sleepy Giovinazzo. The old town is beautifully situated around the port, and the buildings of blanched limestone dazzle in the sun as if whitewashed. The setting of these ancient flat-topped buildings surrounding the calm blue water of the inner harbour is very oriental—one might be at an ancient port in the Levant, such as Jaffa or Acre.

The Duomo Vecchio, or old cathedral (the newer cathedral was begun in 1785), is best viewed from the quayside where the fishing boats are moored. It is a magnificent example of composite western and oriental styles, being a triple-domed building with twin Romanesque towers. It is a unique combination of Saracenic and Byzantine ideas blending with the new influences that had infiltrated from the north. The three domes rise from the mass of the building as a most

effective architectural composition; they are not circular but polygonal, and the roofs come to a point like pyramids. There is vitality in
this architecture which springs from lack of repetition. The eastern
towers are the only absolutely regular features.

It is interesting to speculate whether the Duomo of Molfetta was
achieved by design rather than just by chance. If one looks at the
ground plan one sees that the side walls are not so much irregular as
lopsided. Within, the four great central piers are by no means in a
square, and the central dome is thus more oval than circular. Only the
dome at the eastern end is a perfect circle. This may point to a lack of
supervision by a clerk of the works directing the master masons or
work-gangs.

On the outside the accomplishments of Lombard craftsmen is evident in several places, and the beautifully worked shallow interlaced
arcading is of Saracen inspiration. Within there is a wonderful blend of
oriental and western styles. One would imagine that there were multi-
racial teams of masons at work here—Saracenic, Byzantine, Tuscan,
Lombard, Norman and perhaps Burgundian. If there was a master
direction behind all this, the person responsible, like so many masters
of the early Middle Ages, has preferred to remain anonymous.

The town and small port of Bisceglie, ten kilometres from Molfetta,
is a prosperous centre for the fruit and vegetable trade of the surrounding districts. It was not founded until the early Middle Ages, but
it quickly grew in importance. Today the medieval quarter of the town
is fascinating with many interesting houses and streets. It is the sort of
place that would repay an overnight stay, and fortunately hotel
accommodation has improved in recent years; it now has the modern
Hotel Europa (23 rooms) and the Hotel Villa (45), both in the second
category.

Although the cathedral of Bisceglie is very ancient, founded just
over 900 years ago, the original rose window has been replaced by a
baroque one, and the interior has also been baroqued. More interesting then are two smaller churches—S. Adoneo, begun in 1074 and
S. Margherita, of the late twelfth century. The former has some good
exterior detail of its time, and the latter is a very well-preserved example of its period and style.

The port is in a beautiful setting enclosed by old medieval houses. It
is not large and not important, and shelters mainly small fishing boats,
though an occassional coastal barque probably finds its way here.
While I was there a slight sea from outside the harbour caused a gentle
swell that barely disturbed the reflection of the brightly coloured boats
drawn up on the shore. There is seldom anything to disturb the tran-
quility of the waterfront scene. I once passed through Bisceglie while a

horse-fair was in full swing which added a dash of excitement to the normal routine. It was interesting to mingle with the dark-skinned, tough, intense, humourless country people—in sharp contrast to the laughing crowd of children who were watching proceedings with intense interest from the flat top of the quayside wall. But for country folk horses and livestock are their livelihood and for them the fair was a serious matter.

The district of Bisceglie is noted for the survival of a number of dolmens. These are pre-historic stone structures very crudely constructed with large slabs forming the sides, and generally one great flat stone forming a top covering, or roof. These Bisceglie dolmens belong to the Bari group of gallery graves and probably date from as early as the second millenium B.C. They are thought to be of Western European origin. They are rather difficult to find, usually hidden among olive groves. It is in this rural setting that one often sees a *trullo*, quite small but well made and genuine. The people of Apulia have an affection for these little buildings, and fruit growers often use them to store their implements, and keep them in repair.

TRANI is perhaps the best known of the Apulian coastal towns north of Bari since some effort has been made to promote it as a tourist centre. It possesses some good hotels (Grand Hotel, (50 rooms) Miramar (26), Hotel Trani (51) all in the second category) and there is a fine stretch of sand at the Lido di Colonna. But compared with developments on the Adriatic coast further north, the scale of tourist activity is small. The old town is situated far away from the tourist scene on the other side of the harbour, and it is here that one of the most famous buildings in Apulia soars up so close to the shore that from a distance its foundations might almost be sunk into the sand . . . the cathedral of Trani.

The broad stone quayside of the port curves round almost a full circle, and is wide enough for several cars to pass abreast. Set back from the characteristic outline of flat-topped ancient stone buildings, bleached by centuries of sun, gives the old port a distinctive charm. The cathedral seen from this side of the harbour appears to be strangely out of proportion due to the great height of the apse, which will be explained a little later. At the corner of the quay where the road swings right, and fitting in snugly between old buildings, is one of the most attractive small churches in Apulia, called Ognissanti,—All Saints. This beautiful little triple-apse building dates from the twelfth century and once belonged to the Order of Knights Templar (it was in the courtyard of their hospital), until the Order's dissolution in 1312. It was undergoing restoration at the time of my visit.

Compared with the antiquity of some Apulian towns (Canosa, for instance) Trani is not of very ancient foundation, being known at first as Tirenum in the third or fourth centuries A.D. It wasn't until the destruction of Canosa by the Saracens in 872 that Trani developed into a town of some consequence, for it was then that the Byzantines recognised the strategic importance of the port for trade with Constantinople and with key ports in the Adriatic. The development was accelerated under the Normans, at which time with trade greatly boosted by the Crusades, the port rivalled Bari and Barletta in commercial importance. Colonies of Genoese and Florentines and traders from Amalfi and Ravello took up residence—always an indication of prosperous times. In ecclesiastical circles the influence of Trani grew significantly, and in judicial matters the town became increasingly important as a place for the itinerant royal justiciars, under Norman rule, to hear pleas and decide cases. It was in the Middle Ages, when Trani was enjoying self-administration that the *Ordinamenta Maris* was enacted—possibly the oldest maritime commercial code—though many would give credit for this to the Amalfitans with their more famous *Tavole Amalfitane*.

Under Frederick II the town reached a new peak of prosperity. The emperor made a point of establishing local trades—for instance he founded a silk industry in the town. It was Frederick, too, who built the castle—a magnificent building and one of the few fortresses in Apulia to have retained its original form, though much altered within. It is massive outside but contains a courtyard and apartments internally. It was begun in 1233, and is closely linked with the fortunes of Manfred.

It has been mentioned earlier that the height of Trani Cathedral seems to be quite out of proportion to its length, and this is especially noticeable when looking towards the triple apses. The explanation is that the Normans built their church over an already existing seventh-century Byzantine cathedral, with the result that at Trani we have a double church—the Byzantine S. Maria della Scala below, and the Norman S. Nicola Pellegrino above.

One of the best features of the cathedral externally is the campanile standing at a majestic height of 225 feet over a fine, lofty Saracenic-pointed archway. The balance and proportions are splendid, and there is much variety and subtlety in the detail. Work started on the crypt in 1094, but the cathedral was not finished until the middle of the thirteenth century, though in use by 1186. The church has in recent years been completely restored inside and out, and enormous care has been paid to detail. When for instance it was found that a slight subsidence was threatening the tower, it was taken down stone by stone and rebuilt with the original materials.

The bronze doors of Trani are justly famous. They stand out a weathered green against the white stone of the façade, and are the work of Barisanus, a native of Trani. He was a great master of the art of bronze casting, and other examples of his work can be seen at Ravello, and also in one of the two fine doors of Monreale Cathedral in Sicily. At Trani, Barisanus has broken away from Byzantine tradition in the sense that his reliefs on the 32 panels are much more realistic than scenes depicted on earlier pairs of doors. He cast the doors in 1175, considerably later that the doors of Troia by Oderisius (1119) which closely followed Byzantine models. The entire composition of the doorway benefits much from the presence of these beautiful doors with their aged green patina, baked in the afternoon sun for over 800 years, and it is sad that so few doors have survived of the many that must once have adorned the portals of Apulia's cathedrals.

The carvings on the jambs at the sides of the entrance and the archivolts above, are of exceptional quality. Here is a richness of detail and imagination which is breath-taking. Let us take a closer look at the archivolt: the motif is a long chain-like tendril in which flowers, animals, leaves, people, birds and mythical creatures are entangled—the artist showing a nicely developed sense of humour as well as a marvellous technique. The door posts and arch above appear to have been carved by another artist—the style indicates Lombard work—but the facing, more exposed to the elements is badly weathered in places. Inside the jambs however, there is some typically lively Lombard carving, which repays close inspection.

On entering, what immediately strikes the eye are the twin columns flanking the nave aisles, unique in Apulia, each pair tall and antique with very weathered capitals. So ancient are they that many have strengthening steel bands to keep them steady. Above the main arcades there are triforium galleries, with a group of three miniature arches above each main arch. Standing in the middle of the nave one is struck by the graceful soaring lines of the main apse, the purity of which is unspoilt by spurious ornamentation, as indeed is the whole of the interior which has a robust simplicity. There are many signs of careful restoration, and the plain stone, devoid of any frescoes now, is warmed by a soft light that passes through the selenite windows.

It is odd to find light from windows streaming into the crypt of S. Nicola, due to the unusual composition of the entire building. From here one can pass into the Byzantine church of S. Maria della Scala, which occupies the space under the nave of the cathedral. There are remains of important frescoes in the church, in particular a picture of the *Madonna between two saints* thought to be by Giovanni di Francia (1405–48). The church has a natural grace and simplicity. From here one can descend some steep steps to the *Lypogeum of S. Leucio,* built to house the saint's relics. Through the iron gate one can see the barrel-vaulted structure of this very early place of devotion—perhaps as early as the Roman Christian era—over which the Byzantines built their church. It is a relief however to exchange this dimly lit place for the airy lightness of the crypt. Here the vaulted ceiling is carried on high columns with splendid capitals.

The more modern parts of Trani are on the other side of the harbour, and here there are pleasant public gardens with pines and palm-trees and sub-tropical flowers that extend to a parapet overlooking the sea. There is a magnificent view from here of the Apulian coastline, with the Benedictine monastery of S. Maria Colonna on the peninsular to the right standing out against the skyline.

BARLETTA is one of those towns that grow on one. On my first visit I had found it uninspiring, but on a later visit I had more time and was able to do it justice. It is the port, which throughout its history has made Barletta an important centre for trade and communications. Under the Normans it was one of the main places of departure for the Holy Land. One can get an idea of the status of Barletta during past eras from the number of fine palazzi still surviving. The Palazzo Bonalli, for instance, is in much the same condition now as when it was built in the reign of Robert of Anjou in 1324. This part of the town is very interesting: space is confined, with streets narrowing, only to open out suddenly into small courtyards or piazzas . . . one might be walking through the town in the Middle Ages.

The cathedral of Barletta, S. Maria Maggiore, is built in three distinct styles, the earliest of which is Apulian-Romanesque, the middle—early Gothic, and the latest—the ambulatory and polygonal apse—in the French Gothic style of the early fifteenth century.

It is interesting to see how clearly defined are the different styles as seen from the outside. The apse is five-sided and strongly buttressed rising from the roof-line of the ambulatory. Round the corner from here a wide arch supports the splendid campanile, almost separate from the church as at Trani, and similar in style though quite different in detail. On the west front there is a very richly carved window in three receding steps, beautifully ornamented. The plainer rose window above has been renovated. Cut into the central stone above the rounded arch of the left-hand doorway is an interesting inscription. It is a eulogy in medieval Latin to Richard Coeur de Lion, benefactor of the cathedral and donor of the door. The carvings on this west front are Lombardo-Byzantine.

It is quite easy to become lost in the labyrinth of narrow streets and alleys while searching for the small twelfth-century church of

S. Andrea, but perseverance is rewarded when one comes upon this little gem. The entrance must be one of the most attractive of the Romanesque style in Apulia. The portal has had much praise lavished on it, understandably since the carvings are of an exceptionally high standard. The work is Byzantine: foliage and vine tendrils weave in curving, wavy lines around delicately carved birds. On the inside of the left-hand jamb (facing the door) there is a carving of the Madonna suckling the Child, and on the right Christ stands giving His benediction. These are works of great sensitivity and beauty of form, well illustrated by the flowing lines of the Madonna's garments, and the expressiveness of the faces of the two main figures convey a solemn almost sad note.

Probably the most prominent 'landmark' in Barletta is the colossal bronze statue of the Emperor Valentinian (fourth century work) that stands in the main thoroughfare outside the fine Gothic church of S. Sepolcro. The statue was salvaged in the thirteenth century from the wreck of a Venetian vessel which went down off the coast near Barletta; it is thought to be the largest bronze statue extant, and was looted from Constantinople.

The hostelry known as the Cantina della Disfada is famous throughout the district because of its association with the Challenge of Barletta, for it was in its cellars that the challenge was made. The dispute arose after a party of French knights were captured following an attack on Spanish positions at Barletta in 1503. On the night of their capture, whilst being entertained by the Spaniards and their Italian allies, and with the wine flowing freely, one of their number, Guy de la Motte, gave vent to certain personal views, casting doubt on the valour of Italian knighthood and accusing them of being traitors. Led by Ettore Fieramosca, the Italians immediately demanded satisfaction, and it was agreed that a contest between selected combatants would satisfy their honour. In the event the valour of the Italian knights won the day—the French, in their arrogance, not even having bothered to bring with them the ransom money which could have bought their freedom.

One enters the cantina down stone steps which lead from the road into the medieval building. Here one finds a large splendidly vaulted cellar where a good attempt has been made to reconstruct the original style and character of the hostelry. Drinks and refreshments are served, though the atmosphere is not especially commercial.

Canosa di Puglia lies 22 kilometres south-west of Barletta, along ss 93, and is noted for two monuments in particular, the mid-eleventh-century cathedral dedicated to S. Sabino (one of the earliest Romanesque churches in Apulia), and the tomb of Bohemond, which is constructed alongside the cathedral and is entered from it.

Bohemond was the eldest son of Robert Guiscard, but lost his inheritance after the Norman leader had put away his first wife Alberada (having conveniently discovered a prohibited degree of kinship) in order to marry Sichelgaita, the sister of Gisulf, ruler of the Lombard city-state of Salerno, a much more advantageous connection. Bohemond remained implacably opposed to the inheritance of his half-brother Roger Borsa, contested it at his father's death, and was bought off with a large slice of southern Apulia, where he remained a thorn in Roger Borsa's flesh until the First Crusade totally absorbed his energies. In Syria he built for himself an empire, becoming the first Prince of Antioch, and one of the great Norman leaders. But in the year 1111 he died in Apulia, broken by defeat and captivity by the Turks, and by the loss of most of his territory to the Emperor Alexius.

It was his mother Alberada who made arrangements for the building of his mausoleum. It is a small elegant building, square-planned, mounted by an octagonal drum with a rounded dome, which gives it a distinctly oriental look. The bronze doors leading into the tomb are very fine—the work of Roger of Melfi. There are a few lines of eulogistic inscription on the left-hand door. The interior is plain, and the bare tombstone in the centre of the floor has the single word

BOAMUNDUS

inscribed on it, so that by its very simplicity the effect is powerful.

The cathedral of S. Sabino is strongly influenced by Byzantine styles; it has five domes, and the interior has some remarkable features including a very high pulpit, more than likely the prototype of later examples in Apulian churches, built in about 1050 and remodelled in 1904. The church contains an episcopal throne of unusual interest: it is a sturdy piece, resting on two elephants with double eagles carved on the front. An inscription beneath one arm names Romualdus as the sculptor and Archbishop Urso as his patron, by which it is possible to date the work between 1078 and 1089.

The city of Andria is an important bustling agricultural centre with a population of over 70,000. It is in the cathedral of Andria in the gloomy depths of the crypt under rough stone vaults that there lie, if tradition is to be believed, the mortal remains of two of Frederick II's wives, Yolande and Isabella.

Yolande, Frederick's second wife, was only a child of fourteen at her betrothal, which took place at Acre in the church of the Holy Cross in Frederick's absence. Here a Sicilian Bishop placed the ring on her finger, and the Knights of Jerusalem arrived to pay homage to their Queen. Then with great ceremony she embarked on the imperial galley and sailed to meet her husband. Poor Yolande had little or no influence on her husband, she died giving birth to her son Conrad at the age of seventeen in 1228.

It was not until seven years after Yolande's death that Frederick took for himself another wife at the age of forty-one. She was Isabella, sister of Henry III of England, aged 21 at the time of her betrothal. Isabella greatly impressed the imperial envoys with her beauty and grace. Yet her brilliant reception was in marked contrast to the treatment she received at Frederick's court. Her fate was the same as that of her predecessor, and it was to wear out her spirit and her youth. Frederick's wives were treated as little more than breeders for his legitimate heirs; all of them died after a few years of marriage, and none of his mistresses survived him.

It is rather extraordinary that the English historical connection with Andria should be emphasised by another tradition, which is that the patron saint of the town, S. Riccardo arrived from England in the year 492. It is possible that Richard was a Celt or of Romano-British stock and might have come from that small part of Britain not overwhelmed by pagan Teutonic hordes. It is known that Celtic saints of Britain, like those from Ireland, were great travellers. My own view is that Richard was either a Celtic-Briton or a Welshman (the deeds of the early Welsh Christian churchmen are historical and authentic), or, if he was an Englishman as claimed, that he probably arrived 150 years or so after the traditional date.

On the left-hand transept of the cathedral there is a chapel—the Capella di S. Riccardo—where the 13 Italian knights involved in the challenge of Barletta are said to have prayed before the combat. In the treasury there is a statue of the saint in silver, and here also, in a reliquary, are kept his bones. The cathedral, dedicated to the Assumption has very early origins, dating from the ninth-century crypt and passing through many periods until the completion of the façade, with its atrium-portico, in 1844.

21.   Foggia and the Gargano promontory

Foggia does not have much to offer to those hungry for culture; an earthquake in 1731 and the bombing during the last world war saw to that. As a result of the first of these disasters, the cathedral begun by the Norman King William II is unrecognizable from the original, having been reconstructed in the eighteenth century in the baroque style. However, at the time of writing the cathedral is undergoing restoration, and some interesting early work is being revealed.

Though not a beautiful city Foggia has many advantages as a place to stay, with excellent communications with the surrounding places of interest—Lucera, Troia, Siponto, Manfredonia and the whole of the outstandingly beautiful Gargano promontory. Also it has some good hotels and restaurants, pleasant public gardens and a wide variety of shops. Foggia is a wealthy town, a market for the extremely rich agricultural and vinicultural produce of the great plain called the Tavoliere, which extends for a distance of 30 kilometres to the north, east and south. The amount of grapes gathered and the volume of wine produced in this area is enormous. The finest wine of the district comes from San Severo (another important commercial and market town 30 kilometres to the north-west), in particular the white and rosé varieties.

Twenty-two kilometres south-west of Foggia, just before the foothills rise to the Appenines proper, and at a height of about 1450 feet stands the small town of Troia. A visit to this little cathedral town is well rewarded since the cathedral is one of the best examples of the Apulian-Romanesque style in the Region.

The town itself is attractive—narrow paved streets and dressed-stone archways giving the place a characteristic medieval atmosphere. The outside of the cathedral has many fine features, but it is only when one reaches the wide street facing the west front that one gets the full effect of the beauty of this building. The whole of the lower storey is arcaded, six round arches on slim pilasters, three on each side of the door, with diamond and circular decoration under the arches, as at Pisa.

Above there is a glorious rose window of an open stonework pattern, its intricacy reflecting Saracenic influences. The whole of this upper storey is a remarkable creation. Lombard craftsmen seem to have been given a free hand, with lions and even two bulls projecting into space from the stone facing. Included in the semi-circle of carvings above the rose window is an astonishing collection of creatures. No doubt the oddness of these figures is due as much to weathering as to the imagination of the Lombard sculptor.

The building of the cathedral began in 1093, but the delays were such that over a century separated the beginning from the end of the work. The town fell to the Normans in 1066, and the speed at which a major church was planned fits the pattern of Norman behavior. The bronze doors of Troia, although striking and major examples of bronze-casting, do not for me compare in beauty with those by Barisanus at Trani. They are the work of Oderisius of Benevento, and he employs in part the *niello* technique of inlaid silver to outline the figures, and although freely borrowing from Byzantine tradition, his own creative ideas predominate.

There are still a few cathedrals in Apulia which inside are a great disappointment, due to inept renovations (usually at the height of baroque fashion)—though careful modern restorations have transformed the situation in the last decade or so—and it was with some trepidation that I entered past Oderisius' bronze doors. Great then was my delight to find the nave and aisles and apse restored to their original condition. At once one is struck by the solemn majesty of the vaults. Generally speaking, subtle proportion and dramatic spaces were more important to Norman architects than decoration. This, outside Sicily, was normally confined to exquisite carving, which can be seen at Troia in the capitals of the main colonnade—and also the really fine pulpit, which however was not originally part of the church, but probably came from the nearby earlier Romanesque church of S. Basilio. The date of the pulpit is 1169, and it stands high on four elegant columns with capitals of splendid craftsmanship.

The railway from Foggia to Manfredonia—it is one of many private lines in Italy—passes close by the small church of S. Maria di Siponto, and one catches a tantalizing glimpse of this gem of a little church just before the train reaches the station of Lido di Siponto.

A colony was settled by the Romans in Sipontum (the ancient port and town no longer exists) in 194 B.C., and under the Byzantines and Lombards it became an important town. It fell to the Normans in 1039, quite early in their long process of conquering the south. Disaster overtook the town when earthquakes shattered it in the thirteenth century, as a result of which the inhabitants were moved to a new town founded six kilometres away, also on the coast which bears the name of Frederick II's son and successor, Manfred. Of the ancient site all that remains above the ground now is the twelfth-century church of Santa Maria. The church of S. Leonardo with its ruined monastery is several kilometres nearer Foggia and was isolated from the old town.

In the course of the last five years the church of S. Maria has undergone a major restoration and for this we can thank the *Cassa per il Mezzogiorno* which has provided funds for a great deal of work of this nature in the south, and especially in Apulia. The church of S. Maria was, in the days before the earthquake, the cathedral of Siponto. One approaches it along a path with pines on either side, and this opens up to reveal the front of the church, and we can see how the decoration gives grace and charm to a building that would otherwise be rather box-like. It is really a question of balance and proportion; the two blind arcades on either side of the portal are of the same height, and the decorative work is just enough to catch the eye without detracting from the magnificent doorway.

As regards the church itself, there is a touch of the Byzantine in its general design, with its square plan and central cupola, and the abstract designs of the diamond-shaped ornamentation in the blind arcades suggests the orient. The arcading is repeated on three sides of the church, and wraps around the small apse in a particularly imaginative manner. The church was consecrated in 1117, but building probably began considerably earlier.

A few kilometres further along the road to Foggia one finds the church of S. Leonardo di Siponto standing a little back from the road.

I arrived to find the church and associated buildings deserted except for a profusion of grasshoppers that were sunning themselves in the courtyard.

I found the door to the church locked; outside a notice stated that Mass is celebrated once a week on Sunday mornings, so presumably that is the only occasion when the church is open to the public. Before describing the carvings, a word about the church in general: it is an exceptionally interesting building, rectangular in shape with hexagonal domes of eastern inspiration, of which the main dome has miniature arcading around the drum.

But the real glory of this church is restricted to quite a small area; central to the building and catching the eye immediately as one approaches down the short driveway, is a truly magnificent portal in rich Apulian-Romanesque style. The strong Byzantine tradition shows itself in the very delicate carving in the band above the lunette over the door, but the styles, western and eastern are so integrated that it is impossible to assert that either one or the other predominates. The motifs of both the tympanum and the door jambs are a complex inter-weaving of foliage and animals, sinuous stems and mythical beasts, and here and there a creature half man and half beast. The two lions at the portal steps, one in the process of devouring its prey, are very much in the Lombard tradition, as are the Sphinxes standing on the columns above them. Perhaps the most eye-catching of all the carvings are the two capitals on either side of the doorway—the one on the left side depicting the story of Balaam and the Ass, and the other on the right, the Adoration of the Three Magi. The detail here is exquisitely hand-led.

These carvings and the artistic refinement as a whole leaves little doubt that this is the work of a team of artists of a major workshop. Whether the inspiration is Tuscan, with a strong debt to Pisan influence as is the case in several churches in Apulia—or whether it comes from the Abruzzi where the Benedictine monastery of S. Clemente Casauria was to the forefront in architectural development, is not certain. But whoever the individuals were, whether Lombards, Pisans, Saracens, Greeks, or a composite team (as is most likely), the standard of their artistry is wonderfully high.

A brief history of S. Leonardo is that from 1127 to 1261 it was in the possession of the Canons Regular of St. Augustine, and was then transferred by Pope Alexander IV to the Teutonic Knights, who later built a hospital, the ruins of which can be seen today. The restoration of the church was completed in 1950, after being abandoned for over a century, and in the same year it was re-dedicated.

It is extraordinary to think that only a few years ago—less than a decade—the Gargano promontory was almost completely neglected by tourists, for it is a region of very considerable beauty, with a glorious coastline. Moreover the architecture of its small towns and villages is always interesting, and occasionally, as at Monte S. Angelo, of high quality. Indeed, the topography is surprisingly varied; the dry sun-burnt crags and rocky outcrops of the foothills around the coast (clev-erly terraced however, and liberally planted with superb olives and almonds) give way on climbing to the highlands in the east, to a thickly wooded table-land, reminding one of similar forests in the Sila. These fine woods, called the Foresta Umbra—the Forest of Shade—are composed of extensive beech woods and great areas of ash, oak and tall mountain pines, where a large number of wild deer roam. The woods make a refreshing change to the bleached sands and rocks of the sun-baked shore. The height of the forest is between 2500 and 2800 feet, and the trees thrive on water trapped in natural cisterns and springs in the limestone rock.

One of the reasons why tourists seldom found their way to these beautiful parts is that until recently there were hardly any facilities in the way of hotels or camps. With the construction of the Autostrada A14 linking Bologna, Ancona, Pescara, Vasto and Canosa, the situation has of course been transformed, and the Gargano has been opened up. In addition a fair number of hotels or hotel complexes and a variety of holiday villages or camping sites now provide visitors with a wide range of accommodation. But I should hasten to add that it should not be thought that because of these developments the Gargano has become just another tourist trap. To a large extent the area remains unspoilt, and the planners can be congratulated on their efforts to make the tourist sites as unobtrusive as possible. Fortunately the Gargano promontory is large—56 kilometres from east to west, and between 30 and 45 kilometres wide throughout the length of the peninsular—and at a rough estimate the coastline is at least 120 kilometres in length. It forms the spur of the natural boot of Italy.

As one approaches Manfredonia one can make out the outline of the flat roofs of the white building of Monte San Angelo. Manfredonia is a small market town, and also a port, with a sizeable fishing fleet. From here the boat for the Tremiti Islands leave twice or three times a week depending on the season, calling at Vieste, Peschici and Rodi Garganico (a delightful voyage of about four hours: times can be checked at hotels).

The climb up to Monte San Angelo is a slow business, but it does give one a chance to admire the scenery and the splendid views of the Adriatic. The promontory of Gargano has been famous for its shrines for centuries, and the most famous of them is the sanctuary of St. Michael the Archangel at Monte S. Angelo. Its fame dates from the fifth century A.D. when, accoding to legend, the archangel appeared three times to St. Laurence Bishop of Siponto, who was investigating a bizarre incident at a cave on top of the hills. At the last of these visitations, in 493, the Bishop was instructed by St. Michael to convert the cave into a church—whereupon water in a well in the grotto took on miraculous healing properties.

Whatever one might think about this legend, there are no doubts in the minds of the pilgrims who pour into this little town every year—following in the footsteps of the countless numbers who have preceded them during the past one and a half thousand years. The greatest days are the feasts of St. Michael on May 8th and September 29th, when they arrive from all the surrounding villages, often turned out in their traditional dress.

Monte S. Angelo is traditionally held to be the meeting place in 1019 of the Norman knights (returning from a pilgrimage to the Holy Land)

and the Lombard leader Melus, who it is said, implored their help in their struggle with the Byzantines; this meeting led to the large-scale movement south of impoverished knights, adventurers and mercenaries from Normandy, with consequences that these early Norman warriors could not have imagined. At the time, the Norman knights must have mingled with very much the same sort of pilgrims as one sees today—peasants from far-away villages speaking their local dialects, priests, monks and novices in small bands, nuns and holy women herding parties of children.

After the long descent of 86 steps to the grotto, the excitement changes to a hush of devout respect (or curiosity) on entering the dim and dripping cave. To reach the sanctuary one has to pass through a Romanesque doorway, the doors of which, exquisitely worked, were the gift of Pantaleone of Amalfi, and were made in Constantinople in about 1075. They are made of bronze and consist of 24 panels depicting various Biblical and holy scenes, and the outline of the figures are inlaid with silver—the *niello* technique. On reaching the doors the pilgrims invariably follow a delightful custom, raising one of the bronze rings which hang from the mouths of small lions' heads, and giving a tap before entering. The cavern itself—the Grotta dell' Arcangelo is damp and gloomy, the light provided only by the mass of guttering candles. The alabaster statue of St. Michael, despite the splendid gold wings is a disappointment, but the original statue was lost, probably looted by the Saracens on one of the two occasions they sacked the town—either in 869 or 920.

The small church of Sta. Maria Maggiore, to the right of the ruins of S. Pietro, has a façade of blind arcading—so typical of Apulia—and a doorway of great beauty. In the lunette there is a delightful low-relief of the Madonna and Child flanked by angels. The rounded arch over the door is enwrapped by tiers of semi-circular bands, on which carvings composed of spiralled foliage and outer rings of acanthus leaves are exceptionally fine.

Inside, the church is a disappointment, having been semi-baroqued, but traces of some early frescoes have been uncovered, and the layers of plaster almost certainly conceal many more.

There can be few stretches of coastline in southern Italy that match in beauty the coast of the Gargano promontory, between Punta Rossa on the southern side and Bellariva on the northern, a distance of 80–90 kilometres. The topography is a mixture of green tree-clad headlands plunging steeply into the sea, or precipitous cliffs—the rock the colour of clotted cream—and in between really fine stretches of sandy shore, some of the beaches quite small and others curving round in wide expansive arcs. In addition the relatively unexplored southern coast conceals in the rocky sections several beautifully coloured caves, one of the most surprising being the Bell Cave—a huge dome of reddish, purple, white and grey rock. At the extremity of some of the headlands are perched small towns, two of which, the fishing-ports of Vieste and Peschici are places of much character, as indeed is the small port of Rodi Garganico at the western end of a flat stretch of the northern coast, where the main road sweeps inland round the large Lake of Varano.

Before describing in a little more detail these coastal towns, I would like to add to what I have said about the hotel and other tourist accommodation in the Gargano. Very popular in Apulia these days are the hotel complexes and tourist villages, which are to a large extent self-sufficient in entertainment and sporting facilities, and other amenities such as hair-dressers, shops and so forth. On the south-eastern coast of the Gargano there are two hotel complexes in this category—the larger of the two at Pugnochiuso, and the other set back a little from a fine stretch of beach at Pizzomunno just south of Vieste. In each case there are two hotels, one of which caters for those, generally with families, who are prepared to accept a slightly lower standard of comfort, and the other for those happy to pay a little more and have a correspondingly higher standard of accommodation. The hotels at Pugnochiuso are called Del Faro, and Degli Ulivi—the two quite separate and connected by private hotel mini-buses—and those of the Pizzomunno combine the Pizzomunno Residence and the Vieste Palace Hotel. In each there is a comprehensive range of amenities with conference halls, a cinema, a night-club, excellent public rooms, tennis courts, large and small swimming-pools and a private stretch of beach. I was fortunate enough to stay several days at Pugnochiuso and can vouch for the efficiency, comfort and friendly management of this extremely well-run establishment. It is pleasing that every effort has been made to site the large complex with due regard to the landscape, though naturally buildings with nearly 200 bedrooms apiece cannot fail to stand out. Both these large hotels are in the second category, as also are the hotels Degli Aranci (76 rooms) Gargano (locality Portonuovo, 38 rooms) and the Merinum (locality Scialara 51 rooms). There are in addition three hotels in the third category at Vieste.

Along the entire extent of the Gargano coastline look-out towers are sited on the headlands, mainly built or renovated in the sixteenth century, as a guard against Barbary pirates, who were very active off this coast. There are about 30 towers, some now in ruins and one at least made use of as a restaurant. The names of these towers have a fine ring to them: Torre Preposti, Torre Portagreco, Torre Porticello and Torre Calalunga. Near the last-named is sited the Campeggio

Manacore, an attractive tourist village with a restaurant and other amenities—about four kilometres from Peschici. Here also is the only first-category hotel to date in the Gargano—the Hotel Gusmay, with 61 rooms. Other hotels at Peschici are the Morcavallo (30 rooms) and the Paglianza (50) both in the second category—and there are no less than six hotels in the fourth category.

Peschici is characteristic of the small fishing ports of the Gargano, the town huddled on its rocky promontory with a wide sweeping beach to the west of it. It is as yet undeveloped to any extent, and has plenty of charater. Its buildings, some flat-topped and others with low-domed roofs are Moorish in aspect. From a vantage point near the medieval castle one has a splendid view towards the Tremiti Islands (Peschici is a port of call for the passenger boat).

The Tremiti group of islands consisting of S. Domino, S. Nicola and Capraia (only the first two are inhabited), were known to the ancients as the *Insulae Diomedae*, being the resting place of Diomedes after the hero had founded all the cities of Dannia, as Apulia was then called. It was on the bare rocky island of S. Nicola that Benedictines from Montecassino founded an abbey in the eighth century which later passed to the Cistercians, and then the Lateran Canons, and shortly after its suppression in 1783 was in use as a prison. It was Bertaux who described the abbey as a 'Montecassino set in the middle of the sea' and today one can see for oneself how formidable was this monastic fortress and the fortified town of which it was a part. The interesting church of S. Maria a Mare was founded by the Benedictines in 1045. The larger island of San Domino to the south is in marked contrast to S. Nicola, being very fertile and covered with pines, and rises to a height of 280 feet at the Hill of the Hermit. Tourism has come to S. Domino in the shape of the Hotel Eden (Cat. II 103 rooms) and there is also a small *pensione* with nine rooms, but considering the natural beauty of these islands and the superb bathing and underwater fishing that their pure waters offer, they still remain remarkably unspoilt. They are quite tiny in size, S. Domino being only slightly over two kilometres in length.

Vieste, the largest of the Gargano towns (excluding Manfredonia) and the furthest east, is a place of considerable character. It has a narrow paved streets and chunky irregular architecture which is often interesting. It is undoubtedly ancient, for there are remains of megalithic walls, and Greco-Apulian vases have been found here. The castle high above the town was built by Frederick II, but has been restored in subsequent centuries. It is now in the control of the Italian Navy. Vieste suffered terribly at the hands of the corsairs: it is thought that when Dragut landed in 1554 he took away with him about 7000 captives, having concluded the customary massacre. The cathedral is a building of considerable interest. Although it has been 'renovated' over the centuries, many of the beautiful old columns, some round and some octagonal, have now been laid bare, exposing at the capitals some most attractive Romanesque carvings of horses, bulls and other animals. These capitals look to be too good for local work. However the very unusual painted wooden ceiling, nearly all in brown, was almost certainly executed by local artists.

Select Bibliography

Acton, Harold, *The Bourbons of Naples*, London, 1956.
Boethius, A. & Ward-Perkins, J. B., *Etruscan and Roman Architecture*, Harmondsworth, 1970.
Briggs, M. S., *The Heel of Italy*, London, 1910
Bulwer-Lytton, E., *The Last Days of Pompeii*, abridged edn., 1976.
Carrington, R. C., *Pompeii*, Oxford, 1936.
Douglas, Norman, *Materials for a description of Capri*, London, 1930.
Douglas, Norman, *Old Calabria*, London, 1955 edn.
Douglas, Norman, *Siren Land*, London, 1923.
Encyclopaedia Britannica, 1974
Gissing, George, *By the Ionian Sea*, London, 1956 edn.
Goethe, J. W., *Italian Journey*, trans. W. H. Auden, London, 1962.
Grant, M., *Cities of Vesuvius: Pompeii and Herculaneum*, London 1971.
Guida d'Italia del T.C.I., *Campania*, 3rd. edn., Milan, 1963
Guida d'Italia del T.C.I., *Lucania e Calabria*, 3rd edn., Milan, 1965.
Guida d'Italia del T.C.I., *Napoli e dintorni*, 4th edn., Milan, 1960.
Guida d'Italia del T.C.I., *Puglia*, Milan 1962.
Guido, Margaret, *S. Italy: an archaeological guide*, London, 1972.
Gunn, Peter, *Naples, a palimpsest*, London, 1961.
Haskins, C. H., *The Normans in European History*, New York, 1916.
Haskins, C. H., *Norman Institutions*, London, 1960.
Herodotus, *Histories*, Everyman Library, London, 1964.
Hutton, Edward, *Naples and Campania Revisited*, London, 1958.
Kantorowicz, E. H., *Frederick the Second, 1194–1250*, New York, 1958.
Lear, Edward, *Edward Lear in South Italy*, London, 1964.
Lenormant, F., *La Grand-Grèce*, Cosenza, 1961.
Lukas, Jan, *Pompeii & Herculaneum*, London, 1966.
Maiuri, A., *Pompeii*, Rome, 1953.
Maiuri, A., *Pompeian Wall Paintings*, Rome, 1960.
MacIver, David R., *Greek Cities in Italy & Sicily*, London, 1931.
Masson, Georgina, *Frederick II of Hohenstaufen*, London, 1957.

Morton, H. V., *A Traveller in Southern Italy*, London, 1969.

Murray's Guides, *Southern Italy*, (ed. Octavian Blewvitt), London, 1853.

Norwich, John J., *The Normans in the South*, London, 1967.

Pallottino, M., *The Art of the Etruscans*, London, 1955.

Ramage, C. T., *Ramage in South Italy*, (ed. E. Clay), London, 1965.

Seltman, C., *Greek Coins*, London, 1960.

Strutt, A. J., *A Pedestrian Tour in Calabria & Sicily*, 1842.

Swinburne, Henry, *Travels in the Two Sicilies*, London, 1777–80.

Trevelyan, Raleigh, *The Shadow of Vesuvius: Pompeii A.D. 79*, London, 1976.

Willemsen, C. A. & Odenthal, D., *Apulia*, 1958.

Whelpton, Eric & Barbara, *Calabria & the Aeolian Isles*, London, 1957.

Woodhead, A. G., *The Greeks in the West*, London, 1962.

Index